When the Kremlin

announces that the next generation of Americans will live under communist rule, *they mean it.*

This book tells you what the communist bosses are doing *now* to bring America to its knees. It shows the operation of the gigantic and powerful communist network. It tells you what *you* can do to combat it.

If you value your freedom, and your children's freedom, read this book. *It is a warning of the clear and present danger to your way of life.*

√ "Indispensable . . . the most authoritative book ever written on communism in America."
—The New York Times

√ "This is the most important—indeed the most imperative—book of the decade . . . powerful and informative and up-to-date." *—Christian Herald*

√ "Every thinking, patriotic American should give heed." *—Philadelphia Inquirer*

MASTERS OF DECEIT was originally published by Henry Holt and Company, Inc., at $5.00.

J. EDGAR HOOVER

Director, Federal Bureau of Investigation

MASTERS OF DECEIT

The Story of Communism in America
and How to Fight It

POCKET BOOKS, INC. • NEW YORK

Masters of Deceit

Henry Holt edition published March, 1958

Book-of-the-Month Club edition published June, 1958

Giant Cardinal edition published October, 1959
7th printing...April, 1961

Foreword

EVERY CITIZEN has a duty to learn more about the menace that threatens his future, his home, his children, the peace of the world—and that is why I have written this book.

If you will take the time to inform yourself, you will find that communism holds no mysteries. Its leaders have blueprinted their objectives. The time is far too late not to recognize this "ism" for what it is: a threat to humanity and to each of us.

Moreover, there is the sobering fact that since the end of World War II we have spent billions of dollars to defend ourselves from communist aggression. This burden will continue to mount until the world is free from the communist menace.

This book is an attempt to explain communism—what it is, how it works, what its aims are, and, most important of all, what we need to know to combat it.

In writing this book I have been guided by many years of study and observation of the communist conspiracy in action in the United States.

As a Special Assistant to the Attorney General of the United States in 1919, I was assigned to prepare a legal brief on the newly formed Communist Party and Communist Labor Party. This necessitated an extensive and penetrating study.

The amount of material was voluminous: Party statements, resolutions, platforms, news accounts, manifestoes, the very first documents of American communism. I studied also the writings of Marx, Engels, and Lenin as well as the activities of the Third International.

In this brief, which was submitted to the Attorney General, I concluded:

> These doctrines threaten the happiness of the community, the safety of every individual, and the continuance of every home and fireside. They would destroy the peace of the country and thrust it into a condition of anarchy and lawlessness and immorality that passes imagination.

Today, as I write these words, my conclusions of 1919 remain the same. Communism is the major menace of our time. Today, it threatens the very existence of our Western civilization.

In November, 1917, the Bolsheviks seized control in Russia, gaining state power for the first time. That breach has today widened into a vast communist empire. The attack is still being pressed. International communism will never rest until the whole world, including the United States, is under the hammer and sickle. This is what has happened to the Russian people, now held in bondage, who would be free if they could. (I wish to distinguish here and elsewhere in this book between these unfortunate millions and the small clique of communist rulers of Soviet Russia.)

Communism is more than an economic, political, social, or philosophical doctrine. It is a way of life; a false, materialistic "religion." It would strip man of his belief in God, his heritage of freedom, his trust in love, justice, and mercy. Under communism, all would become, as so many already have, twentieth-century slaves.

Ever since 1917, I have observed the rise of international communism with great concern, particularly communist efforts to infiltrate and infect our American way of life. The Communist Party, USA, started in 1919 as a small, disorganized group of fanatics. Today, it is a dedicated, conspiratorial group operating under modern conditions as an arm of revolution. There is no doubt that America is now the prime target of international communism.

Obviously, this book does not pretend to disclose a body of material known exclusively to the FBI. What it does express is the hope that all of us may develop a shared body of rudimentary knowledge about communism: a body of knowledge that we *dare not* be without. It attempts, in almost primer form, to set down certain fundamentals of the day-to-day operations of the Communist Party, USA: how a communist meeting is conducted; how a top Party official lives; what goes on in the underground; how discipline is enforced; how Party members collect money, attend indoctrination schools, hand out propaganda leaflets. Party members are shown organizing agitation campaigns, infiltrating noncommunist organizations, and manipulating communist fronts. The best way to appreciate the nature and objectives of an enemy is to observe him in action.

The Communist Party, never forget, is a state within a state. It has its own system of "courts," legislative assemblies, schools, and press. It enforces its own laws, has its own standards of conduct, and offers its own road to Utopia. The Party member may physically reside in the United States, but he "lives" in a communist "world."

The Party, moreover, serves as a "transmission belt" whereby the Soviet mentality is being imposed, both directly and indirectly, on thousands of Americans. The Party's objective is to produce a "politically mature" comrade—"communist man" —who will work ceaselessly for the revolution that would make our United States part of the Soviet system.

I have deep faith in the American people and in our American way of life. But I know what communism could do to us. Not because it is stronger than we are; it is not. Not because it has something better to offer; it has not. But we may not learn until it is too late to recognize who the communists are, what they are doing, and what we ourselves, therefore, must do to defeat them.

It is my sincere hope that members of the Communist Party will take the time to read this book—to see how, right before their eyes, the Party is deceiving them. As we know, many members, once awakened to the true nature of communism, have renounced the Party. By casting aside the communist spell, these men and women can do much to aid the cause of freedom.

I have sought to avoid sensationalism, even though much of the FBI's work in keeping abreast of day-to-day activities of American communists makes us ask in wonderment, "Can this be possible?" To recount the sensational activities of communists would defeat my objective. My purpose has been to assemble, organize, and present basic, everyday facts of communism which will be of maximum help to the people of our country in recognizing and fighting the enemy in our midst. Consequently, where illustrative incidents seemed advisable, I have selected those that have occurred most frequently and are most typical of the communism that is seeking daily to undermine our liberties. I have also deliberately avoided identifying many names and places.

I owe deep thanks to many for help in the preparation of this book. On the technical side, I am grateful to William I. Nichols, editor and publisher of *This Week* magazine, for much editorial guidance and advice. In a wider sense, I owe much to the courageous and self-sacrificing men and women of the FBI who have contributed so greatly to America's fight against communism.

But most of all, I have been guided by the thought of millions of loyal Americans everywhere and in all walks of life. Never has there been a time when we have so much need for one another. And we must never forget that if our government is to remain free, it needs the help of every patriotic man, woman, and child.

J. Edgar Hoover

Washington, D. C.
December, 1957

Contents

Part I

WHO IS YOUR ENEMY?

MANY AMERICANS have not stopped to realize what a "Soviet America" would mean. The communists, however, have no doubts. Their blueprints are already made. So, at the very outset, let us look at their dream and see what it would mean to you and me and all the people we know.

In June, 1957, Nikita Khrushchev, Soviet Communist Party boss, was interviewed before a nation-wide American television audience. With calm assurance he stated:

> . . . I can prophesy that your grandchildren in America will live under socialism. And please do not be afraid of that. Your grandchildren will . . . not understand how their grandparents did not understand the progressive nature of a socialist society.

William Z. Foster, former National Chairman of the Communist Party of the United States (now Chairman Emeritus of the Party's National Committee), also predicted that this nation will one day become communist when he stated in 1949, in dedicating his book, *The Twilight of World Capitalism*:

> To My Great-Grandson Joseph Manley Kolko Who Will Live in a Communist United States.

These words of Russia's top Party boss and one of the highest-ranking communists in the United States reveal the nature of the enemy we face. To make the United States a communist nation is the ambition of every Party member, regardless of position or rank. He works constantly to make this dream a reality, to steal your rights, liberties, and property. Even though he lives in the United States, he is a supporter of a foreign power, espousing an alien line of thought. He is a conspirator against his country.

The communist is thinking in terms of *now*, in your lifetime. Remember that within four decades communism, as a state power, has spread through roughly 40 per cent of the world's population and 25 per cent of the earth's surface. Some years ago communists were complaining that their "fatherland," Soviet Russia, was encircled, a communist island in a "capitalist" sea. Today the situation is changed. The world communist movement is on the march, into Germany, the Balkans, the Middle East, stretching across the plains of Asia into China, Korea, and Indochina. Communists have never won over an entire country by a free election and have never hesitated to shed blood if this would best serve their purposes. Moreover, in noncommunist countries thousands of Party members are working for Moscow. Communists firmly believe they are destined to conquer the world.

This belief is held in the United States too. A disciplined Party of hard-core fanatical members is now at work, with their fellow travelers, sympathizers, opportunists, and dupes. Communists in our country, though small in numbers, do not feel lonely. They have faith in the "big Red brother" who will come to their help. William Z. Foster's hope, a Red America, is today inspiring thousands of Party members and sympathizers to determined effort. They want to add America to Soviet Russia's list of conquests.

In recent years there has been a tendency to discount the menace of domestic communists solely because of a decline in Party membership. In fact, some have gone so far as to say, ". . . the party . . . is almost over." Let's examine that statement:

In 1922, when Communist Party membership reached 12,400, William Z. Foster said, ". . . we no longer measure the importance of revolutionary organizations by size. In some places where there are only one or two men, more results are obtained than where they have larger organizations. . . ."

This has been the communist line down through the years. Foster in 1951 stated, "Communist strength . . . cannot be measured even approximately by statistics. . . . The Communist parties' strength runs far beyond all formal measurements. . . ."

The Party's membership in this country reached a low in 1930 when it had 7500 members, and a peak of 80,000 in 1944; its membership at five-year intervals since 1930 has been as follows: 1935—30,000; 1940—55,000 (a drop of 15,000 from 1939); 1945—64,600 (a drop of 15,400 from 1944); 1950—43,200; 1955—22,600; and by the summer of 1957 membership had further declined. However, over the years it has been estimated by the communist leaders themselves that for every Party member ten others are ready, willing, and able to do the Party's work.

Fluctuations in the American Party parallel those in foreign countries. The record clearly establishes that Communist Parties have the power of swift and solid growth when the opportunity arises. The following figures reflect how Party membership can dwindle and then spurt:

In Italy, Party membership went from 6000 in 1943 to 2,500,000 in 1951; in France, from 20,000 in 1929 to 400,000 in 1956; in Syria, from 250 in 1931 to 10,000 in 1956; in Brazil, from 25,000 in late 1947 to 100,000 in 1956; and in Indonesia, from 30,000 in 1953 to 500,000 in 1956.

When the Communist Party was at its peak in the United States it was stronger in numbers than the Soviet Party was at the time it seized power in Russia.

The size of the Party in the various Soviet satellites at the time each came under Soviet control discloses how a well-organized band of revolutionaries can impose its rule over the majority population:

	Date of Communist Take-over	CP Membership on That Date	Population on That Date
BULGARIA	September, 1945	20,000	7,020,000
ROUMANIA	March, 1945	800,000	16,409,000
POLAND	January, 1949	1,000,000	25,225,000
CZECHOSLOVAKIA	May, 1948	1,329,000	12,338,000
HUNGARY	August, 1947	750,000	9,383,000
ALBANIA	December, 1945	12,000	1,120,000
YUGOSLAVIA	Mid-1945	141,000	14,500,000

Under communism, a tiny minority, perhaps ten to twenty men, would rule the United States. An open dictatorship called the "dictatorship of the proletariat" would be established. (For a definition of "dictatorship of the proletariat," see the Glossary, page 323.) Communists, in all their teachings, make this point clear. The capital city, as one communist leader pointed out, would be moved from Washington, D.C., to a large industrial center, probably Chicago. National as well as state and local governments would be eliminated. "Soviets" (meaning councils) would be formed throughout the nation. These would consist of local Communist Party henchmen who would depose and probably liquidate your mayor, chief of police, clergymen, and leading citizens.

The Constitution, and all our laws, would be abolished. If you owned productive property you would be arrested as an "exploiter," hauled before a revolutionary court, and sentenced to a concentration camp—that is, if you convinced the "judge" you were worth saving at all. All property used in production would be confiscated, thus leading ultimately to total communization, meaning state ownership. This confiscation would include your home, business, bank deposits, and related personal possessions. These would "belong to everybody." You have no "right" to own them under the communist scheme.

The revolution would affect every man, woman, and child in America. Communists do not propose to remodel our government or retain any part of it. They would tear it to the ground, destroy all opposition, and then create a new government, an American province in the Soviet world empire. Their recipe for action? The 1917 Soviet revolution, tailored to modern conditions. The communists themselves have made the claim:

> The principles upon which a Soviet America would be organized would be the same, in every respect, as those which guided the Soviet Union.

William Z. Foster, long-time head of the communist movement in our country, has boasted that the communist revolution, after the actual seizure of power, would "develop even more swiftly" than the Russian.

All industry would be nationalized and farms taken away from their owners. A small businessman is just as guilty as a large businessman; both must be liquidated. Rents, profits, and insurance would be abolished. Countless occupations, termed by the communists as "useless and parasitic," would be ended. Here is a part of their list: wholesalers, jobbers, real estate men and stockbrokers, advertising specialists, traveling salesmen, lawyers, "whole rafts of government bureaucrats, police, clericals, and sundry capitalist quacks, fakers, and grafters." The communists have a special disdain for lawyers. Perhaps it is because there will be no need for lawyers when there are no rights to defend. At any rate, Foster has said, "The pest of lawyers will be abolished."

Action would be drastic, immediate, and without appeal. An armed "Red Guard" would enforce the orders of Party henchmen. Hotels, country clubs, and swimming pools would be used for the benefit of "workers," meaning, in most cases, Party bosses. The workingman in the mines, factories, and mills would be told to work certain hours for certain wages. Labor unions, as we know them, would be obliterated. All such organizations would be owned and operated by the communist government, and no laborer would be permitted to organize a union or to strike against his "government."

The press would be muzzled, free speech forbidden, and

complete conformity demanded. If you expressed an opinion contrary to the Party line, you should have known better and your "disappearance" would serve as a lesson for others. Fear becomes an enforcement technique. Movies, radio, and television would be taken over by the government as agencies for government propaganda. Churches would probably not be closed immediately, but they would be heavily taxed, their property seized by the state, and religious schools liquidated. Clergymen would be required to accept the Party line. "God does not exist. Why worship Him?" say the communists. Children would be placed in nurseries and special indoctrination schools. Women, boast the communists, would be relieved of housework. How? Huge factory and apartment-house kitchens would be set up, so that women would be "free" to work in factories and mines along with the men.

This picture of a communist America is not overdrawn. Here are the words of William Z. Foster:

> Under the dictatorship all the capitalist parties—Republican, Democratic, Progressive, Socialist, etc.—will be liquidated, the Communist party functioning alone as the Party of the toiling masses. Likewise, will be dissolved all other organizations that are political props of the bourgeois rule, including chambers of commerce, employers' associations, rotary clubs, American Legion, Y.M.C.A. and such fraternal orders as the Masons, Odd Fellows, Elks, Knights of Columbus, etc.

Under this schedule many Americans are eligible for liquidation not once but several times, depending on their present freely chosen affiliations and social interests.

Communism is many things: an economic system, a philosophy, a political creed, a psychological conditioning, an educational indoctrination, a directed way of life. Communists want to control everything: where you live, where you work, what you are paid, what you think, what streetcars you ride (or whether you walk), how your children are educated, what you may not and must read and write. The most minute details, even the time your alarm clock goes off in the morning or the amount of cream in your coffee, are subjects for state supervision. They want to make a "communist man," a mechanical puppet, whom they can train to do as the Party desires. This is the ultimate, and tragic, aim of communism.

These statements are confirmed, day after day, by documented reports from areas where communists have already taken over: Hungary, East Germany, Bulgaria, Poland, Roumania, Czechoslovakia, Red China, and other areas.

When you read such reports, do not think of them as something happening in a far-off land. Remember, always, that "it could happen here" and that there are thousands of people *in this country* now working in secret to make it happen here.

But also, thank God, there are millions of Americans who oppose them. If we open our eyes, inform ourselves, and work together, we can keep our country free.

Part II

HOW COMMUNISM
BEGAN

1.

Marx—And the "Science" of Communism

THE PRINCIPLE of communism is not new. Some primitive societies practiced a limited brand of communism in that the whole tribe lived in common and shared property, food, and housing. But modern-day communism, known as the "science of Marxism-Leninism," is just a little over a century old.

This kind of communism is also known as "scientific socialism" to distinguish it from "Utopian socialism," which, according to the Marxists, is unplanned and does not operate on "laws" of society. "Utopian," or early, socialism predated Marx; and its exponents, such as Robert Owen, believed in making society socialist by peaceful means. Many of these men were visionaries, hence the word "Utopian."

A few years before the American Civil War "scientific socialism" stemmed from the mind of an egotistical, crabby, stubborn man who from student days showed no interest in productive labor to support his family and who used to pawn his overcoat in the middle of winter to buy a few loaves of bread. This man was born in Germany, became an exile in France and Belgium, later lived and wrote in England. From his extensive writings he is known as the "originator" of communism and is today regarded with the greatest respect by communists everywhere. His name was Karl Marx.

Marx was born in Trier, Germany, in May, 1818, the son of a prosperous German lawyer. He was an intelligent child, but temperamental. At school his marks were superior, and his capacity for work, a trait that was to continue all through life, tremendous. But he did not make friends easily, perhaps because of self-pride. He made arrogant remarks and wrote satirical verse. He was a "smart" young man, but already vain, bitter, and rebellious.

Strangely, his heart held an inner love for a home-town girl, Jenny von Westphalen, a devotion to remain bright despite the utter squalor, poverty, and despair that lay ahead. Jenny, four years older than Karl, was the daughter of a government official in Trier. She was beautiful, charming, and of a socially high rank, much higher than that of the Marx family. She, too, was desperately in love, but she feared to tell her parents. What would they think—the daughter of Privy Councillor Ludwig von Westphalen marrying Karl Marx?

Young Karl was obsessed. He wrote feverish love letters and poetry. ". . . a new world has opened for me," he wrote his father in 1837, "the world of love . . . art is not as beautiful as Jenny."

The time for marriage, however, was still distant. Karl was away at school. Then, after graduation, he did not have a job and did not seem to care to find one—another lifelong trait. He preferred to dabble in atheism, socialism, and polemics. After seven long years Jenny was still waiting, but finally, on June 12, 1843, they were married.

Marx had hoped to teach but drifted into journalism. He wrote acidly, pouring ridicule on everything and everybody with whom he disagreed. Strongly influenced by the teachings of Ludwig Feuerbach, a German philosopher who preached materialism, Marx had become an atheist and called for war against religion, a war that was to become the cornerstone of communist philosophy. In 1842 he became editor of a new left-wing paper, the Cologne *Rheinische Zeitung*, and immediately launched into bitter tirades against the Prussian government. As expected, the authorities took action, the paper was suppressed, and Marx, a short time later, went to France. Finally, in 1849, with his family, he went to England, where he was destined to remain until his death in 1883.

Marx was a man with few friends. But one friend, Friedrich Engels, a fellow German whom he first met in 1842, was to become his intellectual comrade, his financial support, his faithful champion. Engels, a vivid contrast to the morose and crotchety Marx, was gay, mannerly, from a wealthy family, and interested in having a good time. He too was an atheist and a revolutionary, a fact that deeply offended his father, a leading textile manufacturer and churchman. He would provide money for school, the elder Engels said, but none for revolutionary activities. Conflict was inevitable. "If it were not for my mother . . . whom I really love," young Engels wrote, "it would never occur to me to make even the smallest concession to my fanatical and despotic father."

Marx and Engels were close friends for some forty years. Engels, most appropriately, can be called the "collaborator" of Marx. He had an encyclopedic memory and his far-flung interests and knowledge of industrial techniques supplied Marx with important information. He also wrote independently and, in some instances, under Marx's name. (For a list of writings by Marx, Engels, Lenin, and Stalin, see pages 333-337.) Together they conceived and formulated the doctrine of communism. They were the parents of "scientific socialism."

Engels spent much of his time in Manchester, England, tending to his father's business, while Marx lived in London. Engels was tall and thin, blue-eyed, two years younger than Marx, and a lover of horses and women. He lived for years with one girl without marriage and then, upon her death, with her sister. He finally consented to marry the latter on her deathbed.

Marx, in contrast, lived in squalor. He was often sick; he suffered from boils, headaches, and rheumatism. Jenny's health began to give way. Her seventh child was born dead. She became wretchedly nervous, irritable, and upset. "Daily, my wife tells me she wishes she were lying in the grave with the children," Marx wrote in 1862. "And truly I cannot blame her. . . ."

Marx did not have a regular job but depended on pittances, especially from Engels. He lived from pawnshop to pawnshop. It is a bitter irony of history, indeed, that the founder of

communism should be literally kept alive by a wealthy indus-
trialist, and that a "capitalist's" son, turned communist, should
become the second "father" of this revolutionary movement.

The great classics of communism, such as *Das Kapital (Capital)*, were "hacked out" amid the most trying conditions. For
a period the Marx family lived in two furnished rooms on
Dean Street, Soho (London). Listen to this description translated from an article by Gustav Mayer:

> In private life Marx is a highly disorderly, cynical person . . .
> Washing himself, combing his hair, changing his underwear
> and shirts are a rarity with him . . . He is often lazy for days,
> but if he has a great deal of work, he works day and night
> with untiring endurance. Very often he stays up the entire
> night and then lies down on the couch fully dressed at noon
> and sleeps through until evening, undisturbed by the hustle
> and bustle of family life . . . The room overlooking the street
> is the parlor and the bedroom is to the rear. In the entire
> apartment there is not a single piece of clean and good furni-
> ture. Everything is broken, tattered and ragged; everything
> is covered with finger-thick dust, everywhere there is the
> greatest disorder. In the center of the parlor stands a large
> table covered by an overhanging oilcloth. It is cluttered with
> his manuscripts, books, newspapers, the children's toys, scraps
> of cloth from his wife's sewing as well as some tea-cups with
> chipped rims, dirty spoons, knives, forks, a lamp, an inkwell,
> drinking glasses, a Dutch claypipe, and ashes. In short, all
> this conglomeration is piled high and on one table. A junk-
> shop would have to cede honors to this extraordinary ensemble.
> When stepping into Marx's room the coal and tobacco smog
> makes one grope around the room as in a cave until one's
> eyes gradually develop a tolerance to these fumes and one is
> able to make out, as if in a fog, a few objects in the room.
> Everything is dirty; everything is full of dust. As for sitting
> down, that is a really dangerous matter. Here is a chair with
> only three legs; over there the children are playing at cooking
> on another chair which happens to be still unbroken. Sure
> enough, that is the one which is offered to the visitor, but
> without any effort to clean off the food. You sit down at the

risk of ruining a pair of trousers . . . Such is a faithful picture
of the family life of the Communist chief, Marx. . . .

Money was always short. Little Franziska died before her
first birthday. There was no money for the funeral. A pittance
was obtained from a neighbor which, as Jenny says, ". . . paid
for the small coffin in which my poor child now sleeps in
peace." Marx sometimes couldn't go out of the house: his
overcoats were pawned. His wife was sick, but he couldn't call
a doctor. There was no money for medicine. "For a week or
more I have kept my family alive feeding them bread and
potatoes, and it is questionable whether or not I will be able
to scare any up today." Another time he complained, ". . . the
children are without clothes or shoes in which they can leave
the house."

But Marx was stubborn. He kept plugging away, writing,
reading, denouncing "capitalist" poverty, and letting his family
starve. No wonder a remark, attributed to his mother, was
made that instead of writing about capital it would have been
better if Karl had made some. The main source of help was
money from Engels, from a relative, or from writings. The
"only piece of good news we have," Marx wrote to Engels on
February 27, 1852, "is from my ministerial sister-in-law [wife
of the Minister of Westphalia], namely, the news about the
illness of my wife's indestructible uncle. If the brute dies now,
I will be out of this mess." Marx, in scornfully referring to his
wife's uncle as "indestructible," meant the fellow simply would
not die. On March 2, 1852, Engels replied, "My congratula-
tions on the news of the old . . . inheritance-obstructor's illness
and I hope that the catastrophe will finally take place."

If the mind of Marx was perverted and biased, it was at the
same time sharp and keen. He was a deep student of history,
philosophy, and economics. Sitting in his dingy apartment or
in the British Museum, this German-born social theorist surveyed the world. In his arrogant pride he thought he could
recast it on his own terms; through his writings and his revolutionary organizations he undertook to do so.

"The Moor," as his children called him because of his coal-black hair and eyes, developed as his first line of attack an atheistic view of the world. He joined two very old ideas: (1) That everything in the universe, whether a blade of grass, a human being, or society itself, is constantly changing and at the same time is in conflict. This is called *dialectics.* (2) That God doesn't exist and the world is composed only of "living" matter. Hence, man is walking dust, without spark or image of his divine Creator. This idea is called *materialism;* hence, *dialectical materialism.* (For a fuller definition of this and other communist terms, see the Glossary.)

This concept was to undergird the whole communist "world outlook." Human society, as well as the physical universe, Marx said, is affected by this outlook. The principles have universal application. Noncommunist thinkers, as well as human experience, have punctured many holes in the thesis; but to communists it applies with the same certainty as does the law of gravity.

Constant and bitter struggle is not bad, Marx said, because it achieves progress. In fact, he viewed the whole recorded history of the world as a story of class struggle. Mankind, he said, has always been divided into *classes:* groups of people who have special interests, ideals, and ways of doing things. These classes, he added, have been struggling from the very beginning of time, and still are.

Marx explained this struggle by means of a special formula, commonly called the *thesis-antithesis-synthesis* dialectic, which he distorted from the philosophy of the famous German philosopher, G. W. F. Hegel. Here is how it works for communists:

Start, for example, Marx said, with a certain economic class (a *thesis*). This class is the dominant power in society, controlling the means of production, the way houses are built, the kind of clothes worn, and so forth. Soon an opposing class arises (an *antithesis*) which seeks to overthrow the first class. It has different ideals, motives, and ambitions. What happens? A fight occurs and soon a new class *(synthesis)* emerges which, according to Marx, incorporates only the best of both old classes. (Why some of the bad does not seep in, too, Marx does not explain.)

Then the process starts all over again. This is history, for as Marx held, historical materialism was nothing more than applying the concept of dialectical materialism to society. The new class (*synthesis*) is now dominant and thus becomes, in turn, a new *thesis*. It directs how to build houses, who gains wealth, etc., but, following Marx's ideas, another opposition class arises (a new *antithesis*). They struggle, a new *synthesis* is obtained, and again the world is off on a new cycle.

These ideas obviously are distorted and theoretical. But to understand modern-day communism, it is essential to grasp the underlying theory. False as it is, this theory is the spark that kindles the communist flame.

This class struggle, in Marx's reasoning, always produced a higher stage of civilization. First, years ago, came slavery. The slave-owning class, as expected, developed its own "antithesis" (meaning its rivals, who wanted to abolish slavery). A struggle ensued and feudalism developed, representing the best of both opponents. But feudal society, then the dominant class, was attacked by its own "antithesis," forces within its body which opposed its ideas. For hundreds of years this struggle continued, issuing forth finally in a new "synthesis" (capitalism), again representing the best features of both rivals.

When Marx wrote, history was still in the capitalist stage, but he said it could not remain there. It must (there was no alternative) move on to communism. The capitalist class had already developed its own "antithesis," which Marx identified as the "proletariat" (the working class), which was striving to overthrow the old system.

Communism, Marx proclaimed, represented the new "synthesis" of the capitalist-proletariat struggle and the apex of all history. At this point, said Marx, conflict would now cease, although, again, he does not say why. This new world would be the "perfect" and "final" society: stateless, classless, godless, where all property used in production would be held in common, and human activities would conform to the principle "from each according to his abilities, to each according to his needs."

Marx, with shrewd cunning, applied these concepts to the society of his day. He aimed this appeal to catch everyone who was greedy, ambitious, discontented, or downtrodden. Also, since the Industrial Revolution had led to some very real social abuses, the doctrines of Marx appealed to many sincere idealists and reformers who were impatient with slower and more gradual methods of improvement. The class struggle, Marx said, was now in progress between the "capitalists," who owned the tools of production, such as factories, railroads, mines, and the "proletariat," or people employed by the capitalists—the wage earners, the "propertyless," the "exploited."

When Marx wrote, capitalists were the dominant class. According to his interpretation, they set economic levels, what wages could be paid, what standards of living the workers could have, what social customs would prevail. They were the greedy "exploiters," wanting more and more profits. But, said Marx, according to his "law," capitalists were digging their own graves. The very rise of capitalism, Marx emphasized, called into existence its conqueror, the proletariat. The higher the state of capitalism, as then rising in France and England, the greater the number of workers required to tend the mills, mines, and shops; hence, the larger the proletariat would become. Wealth would accumulate in the hands of fewer and fewer people, the masses would become increasingly poor. Thus, conflict between the two classes was inevitable.

Already, Marx said, this conflict was in progress, as witnessed by European strikes, lockouts, and revolutions. The proletariat was striking against its oppressors, and the result of the struggle would be communism. The working class was destined to win. That was the "law." This was the way Marx viewed history and how he distorted events and situations to support his thesis, which followers were later to call a "science." This "science" has long since been disproved by man's experience and the record of events and situations in the free world.

In this struggle between the capitalist class and the proletariat, what is the role of the Communist Party? The Party, said Marx, was to be the vanguard of the proletariat. Most workers are stupid, uneducated in Marxism, and duped by capitalists. They could never start a revolution by themselves. They need guidance, the job of the Communist Party. Communists are wide awake, intelligent, and, most important of all, "learned" in Marxism. They know the "laws" of revolution, the "mysteries" of the development of society. Their task: to be the "general staff" of the revolution.

What about force and violence? Must they be used? Marx emphasized that capitalist society, most naturally, would not voluntarily turn over its factories, banks, and money to the workers. Moreover, it would probably organize a "counter-revolution"—which means defending itself. Hence, under the leadership of the Communist Party, the workers must, if necessary, be prepared to use force, that is, violent revolution. If the capitalists submit peacefully, good; if they resist, slaughter them.

But this is not all. After power is seized, opposition will remain which must be stamped out, utterly, completely, mercilessly. Again, this is a job that cannot be left to an untrained, untaught proletariat. It is a job, according to Marxist thought, for the *dictatorship of the proletariat*, conceived as a transitional stage between actual revolution and the arrival of the highest and final form of communism.

Who would direct the dictatorship? The Communist Party, of course. And what would it do? It would serve as a steamroller, liquidating through sheer force all "capitalist" elements. Then, and only then, could new "socialist" construction begin. The dictatorships in Russia and the satellite countries with their secret police, slave labor camps, and mass regimentation are living examples of the "dictatorship of the proletariat" in action.

These were, and are, vicious principles, destined to shake civilization to its roots. In 1848, Marx, in collaboration with Engels, prepared the platform of the Communist League, a revolutionary organization which included a large number of German exiles. This was the famous *Communist Manifesto*, the first sweeping blueprint of communist aims. The language is violent, the threats dire. "A spectre is haunting Europe—the spectre of Communism," it starts off, and ends by calling for a violent overthrow of existing society. "The Communists disdain to conceal their views and aims . . . Let the ruling classes tremble at a Communist revolution. The proletarians have nothing to lose but their chains. They have a world to win. Workingmen of all countries, unite!"

Well-intentioned and goodhearted men, Marx said, cannot be depended on to improve society. They are dabblers and botchers who make things worse. Mere social reforms strengthen capitalism, prolong "exploitation," and keep the corpse alive. Tear capitalism down, completely. Use force and violence. Set up a communist government!

To the very end of his life Marx remained a ruthless fighter. Invective, anger, and abuse were his weapons. He defiantly defended his position against all comers. He bitterly denounced all who dared disagree with him, such as Ferdinand Lassalle, the German Socialist leader, and Mikhail Bakunin, the Russian anarchist. He fought wordy battles that lasted for years. Always, by skill or skulduggery, he tried to impose his point of view. If he found that impossible, he worked furiously to destroy his opponent.

In 1864 Marx was involved in founding the First International, a motley group of "radicals," "have-nots," "socialists," and "anarchists." A number of congresses were held, but little was accomplished. Finally, in 1872, after many feuds and quarrels in which Marx was deeply involved, he succeeded in having the group's headquarters transferred from London to New York, then considered a remote outpost. This was a move made out of spite, Marx preferring to see the organization die rather than fall into the hands of his enemies. In 1876, at a congress in Philadelphia, it was dissolved. The First International's chief legacy to the cause of world communism lay in giving international structure, for the first time, to communist ideas.

Here is another irony of communism. This man who attacked the domination of the capitalists showed his own dominating nature again and again. In theory, he was "for" the common man and wanted to correct the ills of society. In practice, his fanatical intolerance and overbearing ego made him a tyrant, an autocrat, a dictator.

Marx's character helped shape the whole philosophy of communism and, as we shall see, forged a hideous instrument of power for those who were to follow him.

2.

Lenin—And the Russian Revolution

MARX AND ENGELS formulated the basic doctrines of modern communism. However, they supplied few guides to everyday revolutionary activity.

Remaining in the Marx-Engels stage, communism might well have been drowned in an ocean of angry words, manifestoes, quarrels, and personal feuds. If so, the world today would be a much different place for all of us.

But there was another man, whom Marx and Engels never knew, Vladimir Ilyich Ulyanov, later known as Lenin. It was Lenin's destiny to lead the first successful communist revolution, about which Marx and Engels had dreamed so long. He was the man who took communist *theory* and galvanized it into communist *organization* and *action*. Lenin's activation of communist theory resulted in the seizing of power in Russia. Lenin stands today, just after Marx and Engels, as the movement's third force. More than any other man he is the "developer" of modern-day communism and the father of Party structure and dictatorship. His importance is reflected in the communist description of its way of life as the "science of Marxism-Leninism."

Today Lenin's prestige has been inflated even more as a result of the "downgrading" of Stalin. He is looked upon as the "ideal" communist leader and, in the words of N. A. Bulganin, Chairman of the U.S.S.R. Council of Ministers, "the great founder of our party and the Soviet State."

Lenin was born April 22, 1870, in Simbirsk, now Ulyanovsk (changed after Lenin's death in 1924), a town on the Volga River, deep in Russia. His father was a school inspector and a devout member of the Russian Orthodox Church. Vladimir, one of six children, was a model student. He had a great capacity for concentration and could quickly answer his father's questions about schoolwork.

Youth, however, was short-lived; Lenin soon was on the way to becoming a "revolutionary." It is interesting and important to note here, as with Marx and Engels, that atheism was the first step toward communism. At the age of sixteen, as he later said, Lenin ceased to believe in God. It is reported that he tore the cross from his neck, threw this sacred relic to the ground, and spat upon it.

Soon after, in 1887, when Lenin was seventeen, Alexander Ulyanov, his elder brother and boyhood hero, was hanged in the courtyard of Schlusselburg Fortress in Saint Petersburg, later known as Petrograd and Leningrad, along with four companions, charged with conspiracy to assassinate the Czar of Russia. Alexander was a member of People's Will, a revolutionary organization. This event deeply affected young Lenin.

In the fall of 1887 Vladimir entered Kazan University and soon became involved in student disorders. He was arrested and lived for a while under police surveillance. A short time later, at the age of eighteen, he started reading Karl Marx and soon was expounding Marxist principles to his sister Anna and organizing Marxist discussion groups. In 1891, in Saint Petersburg, he passed his law examination with honors and was admitted to the bar. Although young in years, he was "old" in disposition. At the age of twenty-four, a companion remarked, Lenin already had a tired-looking face. His head was entirely bald, except for fringes of hair at the temples. "The most striking thing about him," went another description, "was his large head, with its large white forehead. His rather small eyes seemed perpetually narrowed, his glance was serious. . . ."

Within a few short years Lenin was to dominate the Russian Marxist movement. This man who loved to play with children, who, after he became dictator of all Russia, occasionally liked to sleep in a hayloft rather than in a bed, was utterly cynical and ruthless. In one instance an associate in Stockholm complained that couriers were not delivering newspapers on schedule. "Please send me their names," Lenin curtly ordered. "These saboteurs shall be shot."

Another time a companion complained about his work. Shut up, were Lenin's orders. "I will turn you over to the party court; we will shoot you." Without tenderness, with not a muscle responsive to mercy, he had one goal—revolution. For twenty years, whether as an exile in Siberia or as a wandering conspirator in Europe, he kept working, dreaming, and thinking about revolution. Guided by his "evil genius," he never deviated from that goal.

Russia, by the 1880's, was seething with discontent. A strong revolutionary movement, dating from the 1820's, was in rebellion against the despotic Czarist regime. Many of the suggested revolutionary programs were impractical. Some demanded greater voice for the peasants or industrial workers; some espoused violent revolution; others, democratic reform. But on one point they all agreed: there must be a change. The more radical groups believed in political terrorism. Their violent escapades, however, such as assassinations, led only to greater oppression.

Marxist writings had early found their way into Russia. The first language into which Marx's *Das Kapital* (originally written in German) had been translated was Russian. Many revolutionaries were attracted by these new communist ideas. In 1883 a Marxist group was founded. Ten years later, when Lenin joined an underground group in Saint Petersburg, the movement was strong.

These early Russian Marxists, however, were deeply divided. They were babblers of theory, not apostles of action. Lenin immediately undertook to change the situation. But in

December, 1895, he was arrested, imprisoned, and later exiled to Siberia.

In 1900 he was released and fled from Russia, more ardent than ever for revolution. With fiendish devotion and intensity he set about the task of creating a revolutionary organization that could seize power in Russia.

For most of the time after 1900 Lenin and his wife, Nadezhda, lived as exiles in Western Europe, going from city to city, often under aliases. Nadezhda in writing about Lenin gave a vivid account of their life in cheap boardinghouses. In Switzerland, on one occasion, they stayed in a room where the windows could be opened only at night because of the "intolerable stench" of a nearby sausage factory. Another time they took their meals at a house where, in the words of Lenin's wife, "the very 'lower depths' of Zurich" congregated.

Lenin was happiest when he could talk revolution. Nadezhda was constantly on guard to protect his health. Many times Lenin, engrossed in revolutionary activities, would work himself into a highly nervous state. One time, Nadezhda writes, he "came home after a heated debate . . . I could hardly recognize him, his face was so drawn and he could barely speak." She encouraged him to take a vacation. In London, Lenin "developed a nervous illness called 'holy fire.' " Nadezhda, after consulting a medical student, painted him with iodine. She, however, couldn't prevent her husband, lost in thought while pedaling a bicycle, from running into the back of a tram and "very nearly" knocking out an eye.

Borrowing from the autocratic character of Marx himself, Lenin made Marxism a highly disciplined, organized, and ruthless creed. How can revolution be achieved? Not by democratic reforms, ballots, or good will but by naked, bloody violence. The sword is the weapon. Everything must be dedicated to this aim: one's time, talents, one's very life. Revolutions do not just happen. They are made.

Lenin conceived of the Party as a vehicle of revolution. Marx, in his philosophical abstractions, had never thought out the day-to-day composition of the Party. Lenin did. The Party must be a small, tightly controlled, deeply loyal group.

Fanaticism, not members, was the key. Members must live, eat, breathe, and dream revolution. They must lie, cheat, and murder if the Party was to be served. Discipline must be rigid. No deviations could be permitted. If an individual falters, he must be ousted. Revolutions cannot be won by clean hands or in white shirts; only by blood, sweat, and the burning torch. These ideas were all inherent in Marxist thought, but they waited for Lenin to translate them into organized action.

In 1903 the Russian Social Democratic Labor Party (which was the Russian Marxist Party) met in convention in Brussels. The proceedings were later transferred to London, after Belgian authorities had warned several of the delegates to leave the city. One session of the congress was routed by an army of vermin.

A dispute arose. Should Party membership be restricted or open to anybody? Lenin fought for restricted membership and won. His group was called the Bolsheviks (the majority); the losers became the Mensheviks (minority). The Party, Lenin said, must be composed only of trained revolutionaries. To allow anybody, curiosity seekers, the halfhearted, weaklings, to join would reduce the Party's discipline, striking power, and fanaticism. The masses couldn't be trusted to make a revolution. They would run at the first sound of gunfire. What were needed were men willing to die because the Party told them to die. This principle of Party organization remains in full effect today throughout the communist world.

Lenin was an able propagandist and agitator. He thought chiefly in terms of battle plans, tactics, and strategy rather than of theories or philosophical abstractions. In 1900, from his exile in Europe, he helped found a revolutionary paper, *Iskra* (the *Spark*), printed in Germany but smuggled into Russia. (A young ex-seminary student in southern Russia, Joseph Vissarionovich Djugashvili, later known as Stalin, was a reader of *Iskra*.) This paper offered directions to the secret revolutionaries in Russia, told them the "line" to follow, urged better Party organization. In addition, Lenin pounded out his "rules of revolution" in articles and pamphlets that were widely circulated in the Russian underground.

Though militant himself, Marx was never able, in his detached atmosphere, to instill the spirit of militant action into communist policy as did Lenin. The crafty Russian, brought up in an atmosphere of revolutionary agitation, did not shrink from any crime. He held that there could be no hesitation or vacillation. Use any weapon—knife, hatchet, or gun—to achieve your aim, he urged. A man was either your friend or your foe. Find out quickly. If a friend, clasp his hand; that is, as long as he served a purpose. If a foe, take drastic action.

All during his lengthy exile Lenin was constantly studying, writing, debating, and expounding revolutionary principles. Like Marx, he used the facilities of Western democracy, such as the great library of the British Museum, to undermine the very freedom that gave him this opportunity. Nadezhda tells of his studies in the Geneva library:

> He would again take out the books left unfinished the day before. They would be about barricade-fighting or the technique of offensives. He would go to his customary place at the little table by the window, smooth down the thin hair on his bald head with a customary gesture, and bury his nose deep in the books. Only rarely would he get up, and then in order to take down a dictionary from a shelf and search for the explanation of some unfamiliar term. He would then stride up and down for a while, resume his seat, and in a tense manner rapidly scrawl something in minute handwriting on little squares of paper.

These studies, as later events were to prove, helped produce practical and concrete ways of making revolutions:

> [Lenin, says Nadezhda] not only read through, thoroughly studied, and thought over everything that Marx and Engels had written on revolution and insurrection. He also perused numerous works on the art of warfare, considering the technique and the organisation of the armed insurrection from all standpoints. He was occupied with this work much more than

people realised, and his talk about "shock" groups during the civil war and "groups of five and ten" was not the chatter of a layman, but a well-thought-out proposition.

Lenin labored day and night for seventeen years in perfecting his plans for the revolution. His opportunity was to come in November, 1917.

In March, 1917, revolution erupted in Russia. The German army had defeated Russian troops. The Czar's government was tottering, and a liberal regime, later headed by Alexander Kerensky, assumed control. The Czar was forced to abdicate. This was the signal for Russian revolutionaries of all types to return to Petrograd: Lenin from Switzerland, aided by the German High Command; Leon Trotsky, later to become a high official in the Bolshevik regime, from New York City; Stalin from Siberian exile.

Lenin plotted against Kerensky, eagerly awaiting the moment he could overthrow the new government. He created dissension in the armed forces. He refused to cooperate with the government except on his own terms. All the time he was desperately building up and training his Bolshevik Party. Lenin had a "sixth sense" in diagnosing revolutionary situations. He knew when to act and when not. Like a crafty tiger, he was circling his prey. Lenin was the true leader of the Russian revolution. Stalin, fresh from Siberia, was relatively unknown, but he was learning the skills of deceit and murder that were soon to catapult him to power.

In the fall of 1917, the Bolsheviks seized power in the October Revolution. Lenin became the dictator of all Russia. Communism had made its first breach in the wall of capitalism. (The revolution occurred on October 25, 1917, according to the Eastern calendar then in use in Russia. Hence, the term "October Revolution." Under the Western calendar, later adopted by the Soviets, the date is November 7, 1917.)

The Bolsheviks immediately instituted a terroristic "dictatorship of the proletariat." Marx had conceived the dictatorship of the proletariat as a transitory period for the establishment of a communist society. Lenin, however, dipped it in blood and gave it a prominence and ruthlessness that shocked the entire world. The secret police, then known as the Cheka, instituted a reign of terror; capital punishment was meted out widely. A search for enemies rocked the country. *Pravda*, the Party newspaper, urged drastic measures.

The Czar and members of his family were executed by the Bolsheviks and their bodies destroyed. Here is an eyewitness account by Leonid Krassin, a member of the early Bolshevik government, as related by his wife, Lubov Krassin:

> . . . we went through a period of so-called "Terror" . . . About six hundred to seven hundred persons were shot in Moscow and Petrograd, nine-tenths of them having been arrested quite at random or merely as suspect of belonging to the Right Wing of the S. R.'s [Socialist Revolutionaries, a Russian revolutionary party], or else of being counter-revolutionaries. In the provinces this developed into a series of revolting incidents such as arrests, executions en masse, and wholesale eviction of bourgeois and educated people from their houses, leaving them homeless.

The test of loyalty was often to what class the individual belonged, the extent of his education, how he was dressed, how much food he had in his house. If his pantry was too well stocked or his clothes too new, he might be accused of being an exploiter and sent before an execution squad.

This was an example of the dictatorship of the proletariat in action. This was a first step toward what Marx proclaimed as the "final" and "perfect" state of society, which is as visionary now as it was then. Millions of Russians found themselves gripped by a tyranny incomparably worse than that of the Czar.

Oddly, despite the predictions of Marx, communism seized power in a country where Marx would least have expected it. Marx had prophesied that the revolution was destined to occur in a highly industrialized nation. Russia was industrially backward.

During the years 1917-20 the Bolsheviks were forced to

fight for survival, first against the German army, then in a war with Poland. Also, the White Russians, a vigorous anti-Bolshevik group, assembled powerful military forces. A bitter White-Red civil war raged.

Lenin's answer was a policy of "war communism." Most industry was nationalized. Trade and commerce were officially abolished. The government undertook to distribute manufactured articles to the people. In agricultural regions food supplies were openly confiscated. Poor peasants were assembled in committees to spy on their richer neighbors who might be hiding grain. The setting of class against class was an established tactic of communism.

By 1921, when the last "enemies" had been driven from Russia, the nation was a shambles. The Bolsheviks, trying to adapt Marxist theory to a nation predominantly rural, had compounded confusion. Industrial production was down, peasants were in open revolt. Private incentive had been ruined. By 1922 famine raged, with tens of millions of people starving or on a semistarvation diet. Some estimates place the loss of life at five million. This was Russia's introduction to communism.

Fanatical Lenin, after years of working for the revolution, purging would not let it slip away from him now. He struck back furiously. Slave labor camps were increased; dreaded secret police compelled conformity; churches were closed. "Enemies of the people," those who opposed the Bolsheviks, were ruthlessly executed, Uprisings were cruelly suppressed.

However, terror was not the answer. In March, 1921, sailors of the Red navy in Kronstadt, formerly strong Bolshevik supporters, rebelled. Lenin, with his keen sense of timing, realized that a change had to be made.

The result was the NEP—New Economic Policy. Capitalist practices, so denounced by the Bolsheviks, were temporarily introduced to save the Russian government. Peasants were now allowed to keep surpluses of grain after taxation, instead of having them confiscated. They could even dispose of their surplus products as they chose, and private trade was allowed to develop. In the industrial field many businesses were returned to private owners, although the government retained control over larger concerns.

To the surprise of Bolshevik leaders the NEP proved a relative success. It gave them the breathing spell they so desperately needed to consolidate their gains. Both agricultural and industrial production jumped. Lenin never lived to see the final results of the temporary NEP, but the revolution was no longer in immediate danger.

Lenin's scheming mind was laying the groundwork for extending the communist conspiracy throughout the world. In March, 1919, Lenin founded the Third International (better known as the Communist International or Comintern). The Third International was a keystone of Soviet policy, whereby Moscow, through Bolshevik discipline, could guide the activities of communists around the world, including those in the United States. To the communists, victory in Russia was only the first step. The whole world, they said, must go communist. ". . . victory is ours," Lenin proclaimed at the First Congress of the Comintern in 1919; "the victory of the world Communist revolution is assured." In early days the regime confidently expected communist revolutions in Western Europe. A communist regime sprang briefly into power in Hungary, another flickered in Germany. Although no permanent communist successes were achieved outside Russia, an effective agency of conspiracy now existed to undermine noncommunist governments.

The skill of Lenin simply cannot be overestimated. He introduced into human relations a new dimension of evil and depravity not surpassed by Genghis Khan or Attila. His concept of Party supremacy, girded by ruthless and ironclad discipline, gave communism a fanaticism and an immorality that shocked Western civilization. Countless individuals, some in high places, simply did not believe that men could behave as did the Bolsheviks; that brutality, terror, and the utter meaninglessness of human dignity could be a policy of state. But that was the contention, and the legacy, of Lenin.

Underlying all of Lenin's thoughts and actions was the use of naked force to achieve Party ends. He held that there could be no permanent coexistence between communists and non-communists. The latter must be liquidated, by force if necessary. "Marxists have never forgotten that violence will be an inevitable accompaniment of the collapse of capitalism on its full scale and of the birth of a socialist society."

> Dictatorship is power based directly upon force and unrestricted by any laws.

* * * *

> The dictatorship of the proletariat is necessary, and victory over the bourgeoisie is impossible without a long, stubborn and desperate war of life and death. . . .

* * * *

> As long as capitalism and socialism exist, we cannot live in peace: in the end, one or the other will triumph—a funeral dirge will be sung either over the Soviet Republic or over world capitalism.

Lenin liked to use the word "ruthless," which is a clue to his thinking:

> There is still too little of that ruthlessness which is indispensable for the success of socialism. . . .

* * * *

> . . . capitalism cannot be defeated and eradicated without the ruthless suppression of the resistance of the exploiters. . . .

* * * *

> Contempt for death must spread among the masses and thus secure victory . . . the ruthless extermination of the enemy will be their task. . . .

This is the Lenin who has always been hailed by the Moscow ruling hierarchy as the guiding genius of communism in Russia and in this country. In fact, with the downgrading of Stalin, Lenin became increasingly extolled in Russia as the "guide to communist action." Nikita Khrushchev, speaking before the Twentieth Congress of the Russian Communist Party in February, 1956, stated categorically:

> The central committee has always and undeviatingly been guided by Lenin's teachings on the party.

> *   *   *   *

> Lenin taught us that a line based on principle is the only correct line. Never to deviate a single step in anything from the interests of the party. . . .

> *   *   *   *

> We must be guided by these wise injunctions of Lenin in all our activity.

In April, 1956, a Moscow journal, *International Affairs,* also made clear the pre-eminence of Leninism in Russia:

> Using the brilliant plan left by Lenin . . . All the complex questions of home and foreign policy are decided by the Party, basing itself on the teaching of the immortal Lenin. That is why the Soviet people recall the words of Vladimir Maya- kovsky [Soviet poet]:

> > "Lenin
> > is now
> > the most live of all living,
> > Our weapon,
> > our knowledge,
> > our power."

These sentiments have been echoed by communists in the United States. In January, 1957, for example, Eugene Dennis, former General Secretary of the Communist Party, USA, wrote, ". . . it is essential at all costs to consolidate and build the CPUSA as a strong Marxist-Leninist political party of the working class."

Another American Party leader, Hyman Lumer, stated in February, 1957:

> . . . he [Lenin] showed . . . the need for a vanguard type of party, armed with the Marxist theory of scientific socialism and possessing a high degree of unity and discipline . . . In its essential features, this is no less true today than it was when Lenin first formulated it.

Lenin could not have anticipated the lofty pedestal on which he was to stand in Moscow a generation after his death. However, his nation and the Party were to pass under the control of an ambitious, scowling, mustached revolutionary from the province of Georgia in south Russia, Joseph Stalin, who until recently was regarded as the fourth great personality of communism.

3.

Stalin—A Fallen Idol

In January, 1924, after a long illness, Lenin died, leaving open a struggle for power that was to last until the 1930's.

The Russian dictator sensed, some time before his death, the evil influence of the man who had squirmed his way to the position of the Party's General Secretary. Joseph Stalin, a cobbler's son, had been an old-time Bolshevik. Born in 1879, he had attended a seminary at Tiflis, in the Caucasus, but in 1899 had been expelled. Already he was involved in revolutionary activities. From 1902 until 1913, according to the communists, he was arrested seven times, exiled six times, and escaped five times from exile.

Plodding by nature, Stalin lacked the brilliance of his chief rival, Leon Trotsky. However, his grasp of the Russian mentality was tremendous. Years as an agitator, prison inmate, and political schemer gave him an insight into communist intrigue that other Party leaders seemed to lack. Working silently but meticulously, he was quick to exploit any opportunity to increase his personal power.

Stalin liked to represent himself as the heir of Lenin, the man predestined to carry on the Bolshevik revolution. This claim is not borne out, however, by a "testament" prepared by Lenin shortly before his death. "Comrade Stalin," wrote Lenin, on Christmas Day, 1922, "having become General Secretary, has concentrated an enormous power in his hands; and I am not sure that he always knows how to use that power with sufficient caution."

Then Lenin added a postscript dated January 4, 1923, a full year before he died:

> Stalin is too rude, and this fault, entirely supportable in relations among us Communists, becomes insupportable in the office of General Secretary. Therefore, I propose to the comrades to find a way to remove Stalin from that position. . . .

However, the time for action had passed. Lenin was too sick to implement his testament. The result: a terrific struggle between Stalin and Trotsky for power.

Trotsky (real name Bronstein) was born in 1879 (two months earlier than Stalin). Early a revolutionary, he spent many years as an exile from Russia. After the Bolshevik revolution he served as Lenin's Commissar of Foreign Affairs and later did much to organize the Red army.

Many differences separated Stalin and Trotsky, the chief one being Stalin's idea that Russia should concentrate on making itself powerful *first*, before undertaking extensive revolutionary action abroad. Trotsky, on the other hand, believed that the Russian revolution could survive only if communist revolutions were promoted in other countries. Both desired world conquest. Their dispute, clouded by a personal hunger for power, centered on how to achieve it. Stalin was the winner. Trotsky was exiled by Stalin in 1929, eventually finding refuge in Mexico. He was assassinated in 1940, reportedly by a secret communist agent.

Joseph Stalin was the fourth "top leader" of communism, claiming "divine" ancestry from Marx, Engels, and Lenin. Until his death in 1953, Stalin played a major role in the history of Russian and world communism, as a "continuer" of the work of Lenin. It was Stalin who, through murder, deceit, and brutality, gave communism *power*, firmly establishing Bolshevik control in Russia and spreading communism to other countries. However, he also was to become the first of the "Big Four" to be denounced by the communists and to have his name blackened by successors.

In carrying on the revolution Stalin became the interpreter of Marxism-Leninism. Under his rule the state, which Marx had visualized as "withering away," became even stronger, an agent of sheer oppression. The army, navy, secret police, and all political structures of the state grew ever more powerful and permanent. Slave labor camps multiplied. Soviet society became ironclad, more rigid than under the most autocratic Czar. Army officials, Party henchmen, industrial managers, all emerged as classes, each jealous of the other. The "workingman," whom Marx had extolled, was now an inferior class, exploited and downtrodden.

Stalin carried to the extreme Lenin's concepts of the Party as a fanatical, disciplined group. To Stalin the Party was not only a tool to seize and maintain power but also a method of liquidating all personal opposition and a means of educating the masses in the communist way of life.

The Party, for this reason, was kept "pure," meaning completely loyal, disciplined, and blindly obedient. Party schools, cadre training, and regimented discipline were needed to saturate the members in communism. Weaklings were purged, expelled and exiled to Siberia, or executed. In Soviet Russia, and all her satellites, the Party was constantly "Bolshevized"—made "more perfect in communism."

One result of this insistent demand for discipline under Stalin was the increasing crystallization of Marxism-Leninism

—already a harsh and regimented code—into an even more rigid, static, and often sterile body of doctrine. Like a shrinking garment, communist doctrine pressed ever more tightly on communists everywhere. Every action now had to be "justified" by theory. If the theory didn't fit, then it had to be reinterpreted. To deviate was to court disaster. Stalin, though not so good a theorist as Lenin, liked to pose as Marxism-Leninism's "expert" interpreter.

This ossification of communist doctrine, under which the individual was afraid to take any initiative, contributed largely to the violent reaction against Stalin after his death. His successors realized that *some* breathing room was absolutely essential, although during Stalin's reign they were content to serve, without protest so far as the record shows, as the executors of his policies.

Stalin also identified communism with nationalism and imperialism: *Russian* nationalism and *Russian* imperialism. To him, communism seemed an ideal vehicle for Russian world conquest, and so, once communism was firmly entrenched in Russia, he embarked on a policy curiously similar to that of Czarist imperialists like Peter the Great and Catherine the Great.

Aided by disturbed world conditions between 1939 and 1953, Stalin started the Soviet chariot of conquest. He directly annexed a number of areas, such as eastern Poland, Estonia, Latvia, Lithuania, part of Finland, eastern Czechoslovakia, part of Roumania. Then, using communism as an ideological adhesive, Stalin created a Soviet orbit: Yugoslavia, China, Poland, Hungary, Bulgaria, North Korea, Czechoslovakia, Roumania, East Germany, Albania, Tibet, Outer Mongolia, and North Indochina (where bloody fighting was in progress at the time of his death). No wonder William Z. Foster in February, 1956, could boast that seventeen countries were "actually building Socialism or are definitely orientating in that direction," having a total population of 900,000,000! He adds: "They constitute the beginning of the new Socialist world." Note the use of the word "beginning."

Native communist parties, aided by Moscow, were often

the instruments of subjugation, Trojan horses of the twentieth century. At other times Russian military power paved the way. Peoples with long traditions of freedom were betrayed into slavery. Significantly, no entire country has ever gone communist and become a satellite by the free choice of election.

This grandiose conquest was abetted by Stalin's inheritance of the tools of Marxism-Leninism, a way of life that is imperialistic, overbearing, and dictatorial. Some individuals may accuse Stalin, alone of the communist "Big Four," of being responsible for the terror of modern-day communism. Marx, Engels, and Lenin, however, are also fully accountable, and so are Stalin's henchmen, who still rule in the Soviet Union. Stalin may have been the active agent of conquest in our generation, but his knives were sharpened on the diabolical teachings of his communist predecessors.

Even in Stalin's time cracks had begun to appear in the communist empire. In 1948 a terrific fissure, the break with Tito's Yugoslavia, rocked Moscow. Currents of discontent, leading to national communism, spread through the European satellite nations. (National communism holds that nations can find their own way to communism and need not slavishly copy Moscow, yet also implies full confidence in the aims and doctrines of Marxism-Leninism, whose application will result in world communism.) "Treason trials" sprouted in many places: Vladimir Clementis and Rudolf Slansky in Czechoslovakia; Laszlo Rajk in Hungary; Traicho Kostov in Bulgaria. These high Party officials, all old-time communists, along with others, were executed. In Poland, Wladyslaw Gomulka, a deputy premier, was expelled from the Party and imprisoned. Stalin's tyranny became even more strongly entrenched.

Few observers, even in Russia, however, could have guessed the intensity of hatred that lay under Russian tyranny. Less than four years after Stalin's death the power of freedom was to erupt in Hungary. Poland swayed on the verge of revolt; unrest swept other satellites. Ironically, Gomulka, expelled as a traitor, now became Party boss of Poland; Rajk, along with others, was "rehabilitated." The "sorrowing" communists even dug up his body, staged a giant funeral, and buried him again, this time with honors. Stalin left a precarious legacy for his successors.

But in barely a generation Russia had moved swiftly forward in its campaign of world conquest. In the name of Karl Marx (who, in his day, had roundly denounced the imperialism of the Czars) and by the application of his doctrines, Stalin had created a dictatorial empire far beyond the dreams of any Czar. Such a dictatorial empire grows out of the very nature of Marxist thought and is inevitable wherever it is applied. In the Kremlin the dream of world conquest still persists. It threatens free peoples everywhere.

This Russian conquest was made possible, in large measure, by the tremendous strengthening of the Soviet state. In 1928 the first of a series of Five Year Plans, designed to strengthen heavy industry and collectivize agriculture, was launched. Step by step the New Economic Policy, adopted by Lenin in 1921, disappeared.

The government now undertook to control everything. Production quotas, which had to be met, were set. Compulsory labor increased. Private trade disappeared. A system of rationing was introduced. Consumer goods virtually disappeared.

In rural areas small farms were abolished. Peasants were compelled to live in giant cooperatives. Many of the more well-to-do farmers, called kulaks, were dispossessed and shipped to Siberia. Entire families were liquidated. The secret police became more active.

As under Lenin's "war communism," the Five Year Plan brought untold human misery. The forced collectivization of agriculture caused a shortage of food. Transportation broke down in many areas. In the Ukraine, the food basket of Russia, famine reappeared. Millions of people died. Disease stalked the land.

But Stalin held firm. Heavy industry must be expanded—steel mills, automobile and tractor factories, railroads. Coal mines must be operated. Armaments must be expedited. Stalin was preparing the base for world conquest. The price in human suffering and privation was incalculable, and unimportant.

At the same time Stalin was furthering a communist society. Art, literature, education, and the press were harnessed to the struggle. A new generation dedicated to following Stalin's will was being created. No opposition was tolerated. In 1936 Stalin brought forth a Soviet constitution, a document glittering with supposed "rights" for the people but actually a mask for ever-increasing tyranny.

From 1934 to 1938 was a period of great purges. The world witnessed the spectacle of gigantic public trials of old Bolsheviks such as Grigori Zinoviev and Nikolai Bukharin, both former presidents of the Communist International, and A. I. Rykov, a former Premier, all accused of treason. Even Yagoda, former head of the secret police, was brought to court. Many, as comrades of Lenin, had fought to create the Bolshevik revolution. Now they were denounced as arch traitors. Nobody knows how many thousands were killed in these blood purges. But one thing was obvious: Stalin was liquidating all possible opposition.

Inevitably Stalin became, in communist eyes, a virtual god on earth. He was pictured as the world's greatest military genius, scientist, author, critic, statesman, popular hero, thinker and engineer.

Here are some of the accolades:

> Long live the wise leader of our Party and people, the inspirer and organizer of all our victories, Comrade Stalin! (N. S. Khrushchev, October, 1952)
>
> . . . Stalin's work will live through the ages, and grateful posterity will, like us, glorify his name. (G. M. Malenkov, March, 1953, who in 1957 was junked like Stalin)
>
> . . . During those hard and grim days for our Motherland, the greatness of our leader and teacher, Comrade Stalin, was revealed in all its magnificence. (N. A. Bulganin, December, 1949)

On March 5, 1953, Stalin died. The communist world went

into mourning. His funeral was a state spectacle. His body, like Lenin's, was entombed in Moscow. Speeches extolled his "greatness."

The whole world wondered, What next? First a triumvirate, Malenkov, Molotov, and Beria, assumed control. Less than a year later Beria, head of the secret police, was executed as a "traitor." Then Malenkov, generally regarded as the Number One leader, was deposed as Premier. Later, Molotov, the old-time Bolshevik, was ousted from the Foreign Ministry, as was his successor, Dmitri T. Shepilov, former editor of *Pravda*. All three were denounced in 1957 as "enemies" of the Party. (Still later, Marshal Georgi Zhukov, Red Army hero, was ousted as Soviet Defense Minister.)

Gradually new faces began to appear, especially that of Nikita S. Khrushchev, a Politburo member, who became First Secretary of the Central Committee of the Communist Party, a powerful position. N. A. Bulganin, one of Stalin's "political" generals, assumed the job of Premier. These two, referred to as "B and K," became the most prominently known leaders.

Significant changes, both in foreign and domestic policies, appeared. But underneath, as the suppression of the Hungarian revolt was to prove, lay the ruthless policies of Stalin. Under Malenkov, attempts were made to encourage the production of consumer items, but with his fall, stress reverted to the old Stalinist emphasis on heavy industry. In the foreign field, "B and K" made a widely heralded trip to Yugoslavia, there to woo Tito back into the Moscow camp. The "Big Smile" was radiant at the Geneva Conference of July, 1955, attended by heads of state of France, England, the United States, and Russia, and during highly publicized visits of "B and K" to India and Great Britain.

The cult of Stalin, which had reached nauseating proportions, was toned down. Emphasis was laid on collective leadership. Then, on the night of February 24-25, 1956, came the bombshell that shook and shocked communists around the world—the bitter denunciation of Stalin by Khrushchev at the Twentieth Congress of the Russian Communist Party. It was as devastating a speech as was ever delivered by one man against another. Copies of the speech, not made public in Russia, found their way to the West and in June, 1956, were released by our own Department of State.

Khrushchev denounced Stalin, the "great Stalin" who had been idolized by all communists as a man who could do no wrong, as a murderer, pathological liar, and perverter of Marxism-Leninism. In fiery language and with specific names and dates, Khrushchev accused Stalin of mass terror, deporting whole populations, forging false evidence against alleged enemies, being a coward during World War II, and possessing a vanity that led him to believe he was a god. Khrushchev in his systematic destruction of Stalin dealt with such matters as:

1. *Mass terror:*

> Stalin acted not through persuasion, explanation, and patient cooperation with people, but by imposing his concepts and demanding absolute submission to his opinion. Whoever opposed this concept or tried to prove his viewpoint, and the correctness of his position—was doomed to . . . subsequent moral and physical annihilation.

❊   ❊   ❊   ❊

> Stalin put the Party and the NKVD [secret police] up to the use of mass terror. . . .

❊   ❊   ❊   ❊

> Mass arrests of Party, Soviet, economic and military workers caused tremendous harm to our country and to the cause of Socialist advancement.

2. *Suspicion and distrust:*

> Stalin was a very distrustful man, sickly suspicious; we knew this from our work with him. He could look at a man and say: "Why are your eyes so shifty today," or "Why are you turning so much today and avoiding to look me directly in the eyes?" The sickly suspicion created in him a general

distrust even toward eminent Party workers whom he had known for years. Everywhere and in everything he saw "enemies," "two-facers" and "spies."

* * * *

"It has happened sometimes that a man goes to Stalin on his invitation as a friend. And when he sits with Stalin, he does not know where he will be sent next, home or to jail."

* * * *

. . . after the war . . . Stalin became even more capricious, irritable and brutal; in particular his suspicion grew. His persecution mania reached unbelievable dimensions. Many workers were becoming enemies before his very eyes. After the war Stalin separated himself from the collective even more. Everything was decided by him alone without any consideration for anyone or anything.

3. *Illegal arrests:*

[In one case, Stalin curtly told an official:] "If you do not obtain confessions from the doctors we will shorten you by a head."

* * * *

When Stalin said that one or another should be arrested, it was necessary to accept on faith that he was an "enemy of the people" . . . And how is it possible that a person confesses to crimes which he has not committed? Only in one way—because of application of physical methods of pressuring him, tortures, bringing him to a state of unconsciousness, deprivation of his judgment, taking away of his human dignity. In this manner were "confessions" acquired.

4. *Abuse of power:*

It is clear that here Stalin showed in a whole series of cases his intolerance, his brutality and his abuse of power. Instead of proving his political correctness and mobilizing the masses, he often chose the path of repression and physical annihilation, not only against actual enemies, but also against individuals who had not committed any crimes against the Party and the Soviet government.

5. *Isolation from people:*

Stalin separated himself from the people and never went anywhere. This lasted tens of years. The last time he visited a village was in January 1928 when he visited Siberia in connection with grain deliveries. How then could he have known the situation in the provinces?

6. *Love of self:*

You should have seen Stalin's fury! How could it be admitted that he, Stalin, had not been right! He is after all a "genius," and a genius cannot help but be right! Everyone can err, but Stalin considered that he never erred, that he was always right. He never acknowledged to anyone that he made any mistake, large or small, despite the fact that he made not a few mistakes in the matter of theory and in his practical activity.

❖   ❖   ❖   ❖

The cult of the individual acquired such monstrous size chiefly because Stalin himself, using all conceivable methods, supported the glorification of his own person. . . .

Khrushchev, telling how Stalin, in his own hand, wrote flattering statements about himself for his own biography, said: "This book is an expression of the most dissolute flattery, an example of making a man into a godhead, of transforming him into an infallible sage, 'the greatest leader,' 'sublime strategist of all times and nations.' Finally no other words could be found with which to lift Stalin up to the heavens."

And then Khrushchev says, Stalin even had the audacity to add, again with his own pen, ". . . Stalin never allowed his work to be marred by the slightest hint of vanity, conceit or self-adulation."

No mention was made by Khrushchev of any anti-Semitic crimes committed by Stalin. However, on April 4, 1956, an article entitled "Our Pain and Our Solace" appeared in the Warsaw Yiddish-language newspaper *Folks-Shtimme,* which charged that Jewish culture had been largely liquidated under Stalin and many Jewish leaders executed. To date these allegations have never been denied by the Kremlin and American communists have reluctantly accepted them as true. On April 13, 1956, the East Coast communist paper, the *Daily Worker,* in an editorial entitled "Grievous Deeds," made mention of the earlier Polish "disclosures . . . that a large number of Jewish writers and other Jewish leaders were framed up and executed and that Jewish culture was virtually wiped out" in the Soviet Union. These monstrous deeds of anti-Semitism in Russia have had profound repercussions among communists in the United States.

No single event in Party history so unnerved communists abroad—and inside Russia too—as did the Khrushchev attack. Where did it leave communist leaders who year after year had fawned upon Stalin as the greatest of all leaders? Weren't they also responsible for such terrible perversions? What was this system called communism, represented as noble, when its chief exponent was a murderer, falsifier, and bigot?

History alone can tell the reasons for, and the ultimate effects of, this violent denunciation. We know about the growing unrest within Russia and the eagerness of the government to appease demands for a higher standard of living. We know how communists like to find scapegoats on whom they can place the people's hate and distrust, especially if the scapegoat is dead. We know of the jealous jockeying for power that is inevitable in any communist hierarchy.

Moreover, there also appeared to be an effort to rid communism of the growing "dead hand" of Stalin who, in his old age, had become capriciously tyrannical and personally maniacal. His successors saw how this crust of sludge, through fear, terror, and ossification of communist doctrine, was crushing initiative.

But the essential elements of Stalinism, brutality, illegality, ruthlessness, remain. In October, 1956, the Hungarians revolted against their puppet government, only to be violently attacked by Soviet tanks and troops. Nothing could illustrate better the unrepentant Soviet heart. Moscow still firmly controls her satellite empire. Nowhere in a communist country have truly free elections been held. Communist subversion against the free world continues. Atheism remains a dominant doctrine. Unremitting support for Moscow is still demanded of communists everywhere. Speaking before the East German Parliament, Khrushchev made this point clear by stressing the "holy duty" of every communist to help strengthen the communist world.

Apparently realizing he had gone too far in criticizing Stalin, Khrushchev backed up and started to praise the late dictator, showing that in actual fact Khrushchevism was actually Stalinism in a different dress. At a diplomatic reception in Moscow in early 1957, Khrushchev commented boldly:

> As a Communist fighting for the interest of the working class, Stalin was a model Communist . . . We have criticized Stalin, we still criticize him, and if necessary we will do it again. But we do not criticize Stalin as a bad Communist as far as the interests of the working classes are concerned. . . . God grant that every Communist should fight for the interest of the working class as Stalin did.

What can we expect in the future? Let Khrushchev himself answer: "Those who expect us to abandon communism will have to wait until a shrimp learns to whistle."

"What will the [Soviet] policy be like? . . . We will do the same, but with more emphasis."

This is the enemy we face today.

4.

How U. S. Communism Began, 1919-21

THE WORLD-WIDE DANGERS of the communist conspiracy started with the Russian revolution in 1917. There and then, for the first time, a communist party seized control of a nation. Almost immediately this conspiracy spread to the United States, seeking to take root by undermining our institutions and traditions.

The Communist Party, USA, first emerged in Chicago, Illinois, in 1919. In the beginning it seemed little more than a freak. Yet in the intervening years that freak has grown into a powerful monster endangering us all. Here is the story:

An emergency convention of the Socialist Party was scheduled to begin in Machinists' Hall, 113 South Ashland Boulevard, Chicago, on August 30, 1919. The air was charged with tension. The socialists were badly split. The left wing, thrilled by the Russian October Revolution, wanted to establish a Communist Party. The rightists opposed.

The procommunist left-wingers, however, could not agree on a program of action. One group wanted to use the emergency convention to take over the Socialist Party. Another group objected, wanting to set up a Communist Party right away.

A battle quickly developed. Men famous in the history of American communism—Benjamin Gitlow, John Reed, Charles Ruthenberg, Alfred Wagenknecht—were present. Each was trying to assemble followers for his point of view.

One group, the Reed-Gitlow group, refused entrance to the

Socialist Convention, retired to another room in Machinists' Hall (later to the IWW Hall, 129 Throop Street), and on August 31, 1919, founded the *Communist Labor Party of America* (CLP). Wagenknecht was named Executive Secretary. (John Reed, incidentally, was to become the Party's first "martyr." An American, well-educated, a poet, writer and newspaperman, Reed was in Russia during the October Revolution. Completely captivated, he wrote a book, *Ten Days That Shook the World.* He later returned to Moscow, participated in Comintern meetings, and died there in 1920. Reed was buried in the Kremlin.)

A rival group, together with a number of foreign-language federations, met at Smolny Hall, headquarters of the Russian Federation, 1221 Blue Island Avenue, Chicago. Its members criticized the Communist Labor Party as not being truly communistic. The CLP returned the retort, and all attempts at reconciliation failed. On September 1, 1919, this rival group formed the *Communist Party of America* (CP). Split off was a group from Michigan that was later to form the Proletarian Party. Ruthenberg was chosen as Executive Secretary of the CP.

Not one but two Parties, the CLP and the CP, each claiming to be the true representative of communism and bitterly maligning the other, came out of the Chicago turmoil. The CLP set up headquarters in Cleveland, the CP in Chicago. The Communist Party was born in America amid confusion, bickering, and partisanship, a condition that was to haunt it for years.

The communists of 1919 were a motley lot, vastly different from the highly disciplined, efficiently operating Party of recent years. Though not lacking zeal or fanaticism, they had little Party training or discipline. They varied in extremes from bitter die-hards, who were ready to do anything for the "cause," even throw a bomb or lead a riot, to comical show-offs, attracted by violent language and subversive possibilities. Many believed revolution in the United States was imminent.

The great majority were foreign-born. Many had difficulty speaking English. *The Communist* (June 12, 1920) states:

"The Communist Party, from the very beginning of its existence, found its work hampered because it had in its ranks only a few men capable of expressing Communist principles in the English language." The comrades lacked a practical understanding of American affairs, especially in the trade union field. Soon all kinds of wild-eyed plans arose. Each leader became his own interpreter of Marx and Lenin. Cliques, quarrels, and personal rivalries were rife.

The Russians (those who had been born in the "home of the revolution") thought they should play the predominant role. They argued: Wasn't Lenin a Russian? Didn't the revolution start in Russia? Hence they, the Russian-born, obviously had an "insight" denied all the others. They should be the leaders.

On one point, however, all agreed: obedience to Soviet Russia. Every communist considered Lenin a god and the Russian Bolsheviks models of perfection. These were the men who had made the October Revolution. They were the teachers; the Americans, the learners. Soviet Russia, at this time, was assuming an authority over communists in this nation that it has never relinquished. This control was to become ever more pronounced, inescapable, and dangerous.

The history of the Communist Party in the United States since 1919 is characterized by two main trends: (1) the development of a disciplined Party structure or, in the words of William Z. Foster, "the building of a Leninist Party of a new type," and (2) the complete and unquestioning subservience of the Party to Soviet Russia. Every word and deed, hope and aspiration, of American communists over the years has promoted these two objectives.

The conventions of the CLP and CP were over, but "civil war" continued. Communists roamed the country, denouncing each other.

Just a few weeks after the Chicago conventions Charles Ruthenberg, Executive Secretary of the Communist Party (the "American Lenin," who died in 1927 and whose ashes lie buried in the Kremlin), mounted a platform in Minneapolis, Minnesota.

He began his address. The Communist Party was the heir of the revolutionary spirit and its rival, the Communist Labor Party, was wrong. The CLP, he charged, was "centrist," a vile word to communists, just like the Party in Germany where the communists had failed. But *his* group, the Communist Party, was without sin. It represented the thoughts of the victorious Bolshevik Party of Soviet Russia.

When would the revolution come? Ruthenberg did not know; tomorrow or next week. But he was optimistic. The communists, he said, had better hurry to learn how to run the government.

Communist Labor Party orators replied in kind. They denounced their opponents. They alone held the sacred communist truth. Splinter factions, and they were many, raised their voices. They attacked everybody but themselves. American communism in these early days was bedlam.

There were other complications. Just a few weeks after the founding conventions, in the fall of 1919, the federal government and local authorities initiated prosecutive action against the communists.

As a consequence the communist movement went underground. Comrades met in secret hide-outs, maintained underground headquarters, and sent messages by couriers. Hidden printing presses poured out propaganda.

Underground or not, the "civil war" continued. The cramped quarters did not hinder the oratorical artillery. The inter-Party strife became fantastically bitter.

Moscow did not like either this bickering or the enforced underground work. The Kremlin wanted a single, unified Party, able to operate legally (above ground) as well as illegally (underground). Communism simply could not thrive on factional fights or in stuffy undercover cellars.

Moscow intervened through the Third International, an organization designed by the Soviets to control Communist Parties in other nations and to serve as an instrument of world revolution. The founding Congress of the Comintern, which opened March 2, 1919, in the Kremlin, was a bizarre affair.

The "delegates" were chiefly make-believe, picked from prisoners of war, visitors in Moscow, or "rubber-stamp" friends. The main problem was to find as many nationalities as possible. This was an "international" organization. That these individuals were not truly representative of their "home" groups did not matter. England was "represented" by a Russian emigré; Hungary by a prisoner of war.

The proceedings were impromptu. It is related that Lenin, during one session, sent Angelica Balabanoff (later to become General Secretary of the Comintern) a note on a scrap of paper instructing her to take the floor and announce the affiliation of the Italian Socialist Party with the International. She replied that she could not. She had not been in contact with Italian Socialists. They were "loyal." There was no doubt of that, but she could not speak for them.

Lenin's answer was prompt, scribbled in another note: "You read *Avanti* [their newspaper] and you know what is going on in Italy."

The Comintern soon became a powerful weapon of communist control. The Second World Congress of the Communist International, held in Russia during July-August, 1920, adopted the notorious twenty-one points of admission for Comintern membership. These were basic rules that every Communist Party must accept before being admitted. The twenty-one points established an ironclad discipline, a single type of Party structure from which there could be no dissent. Here are some of the conditions:

—All party publications must have communist editors.
—If communists cannot carry out their work legally, "a combination of legal and illegal work is absolutely necessary."
—Vigorous and systematic communist propaganda must be carried on in the army. If forbidden by law, it must be pursued illegally.
—Each Communist Party must develop communist agitation in rural areas, within trade unions, workers' councils, and other mass organizations.
—"Parties belonging to the Communist International must be

built upon the principle of democratic centralism," that is, "organized in the most centralized manner," controlled by "iron discipline," and with a leadership possessing power and authority.

—Parties operating legally must "make periodical cleanings" of the membership to weed out dissenters.

—"Every party that desires to belong to the Communist International must give every possible support to the Soviet Republics in their struggle against all counter-revolutionary forces."

—"All decisions of the Congresses of the Communist International, as well as the decisions of its Executive Committee, are binding on all parties affiliated to the Communist International."

Here is the final, clinching point:

—"Members of the Party who reject the conditions and theses of the Communist International, on principle, must be expelled from the party."

The Comintern made its position clear: either join on its terms, involving complete surrender, or become a renegade. Later congresses elaborated on this communist discipline. In July, 1921, for example, an order was issued by the Comintern Executive Committee that national congresses were to be held after the Comintern congresses so that they could ratify decisions. The Fourth Congress (1922) ruled that all Comintern delegates should arrive in Moscow uninstructed. Lenin was determined to make the Comintern the iron fist that controlled communism throughout the world.

The Third International exercised supervision not only by instructing American communists who flocked to Moscow but by sending representatives, or "reps" as they were called, to this country. These individuals would openly sit in communist meetings, participate in decisions, and issue orders. The "reps" represented Moscow, and that fact alone was proof of their communist "divinity."

The Comintern "reps" contributed to a picturesque period

in the history of American communism. Many were riffraff European Bolsheviks, of various nationalities, themselves knowing little about communism, who were hurriedly dispatched to the United States. Often, by their inept actions, they made American leaders more confused than ever. To gain admittance to the United States, they often used fake names, false passports, and special "covers."

This sounds like a crude system, and, in the light of present-day communist "diplomacy," it was. Nobody would imagine an official Soviet representative so identified in today's communist meetings or American communists openly going to Moscow to receive instructions. This "crudity" has been polished. The same channels of communication are still open, but more "professional" ways of supervision have been perfected.

Soon after the 1919 founding conventions, the Executive Committee of the Communist International sent a letter to the two underground Parties, the CP and CLP. The split, said the Comintern, had harmed the communist cause in the United States. Unity must be established "in the shortest possible time." The letter recommended the calling of a joint convention. The condition for unity was acceptance of the program of the Comintern.

This meant that personalities must be submerged, cliques ousted, and a uniform, standardized structure instituted. The concepts of a small, tightly knit Party (as taught by Lenin) must be put into practice. The Russian mentality must be imposed on *every* Party member. The Comintern was emphatic:

> . . . unity is not only possible, but absolutely necessary. The Executive Committee categorically insists on its immediate realization.

In May, 1920, a "unity" convention of the Communist Labor Party and a faction (led by Ruthenberg) of the Communist Party was secretly held at Bridgman, Michigan, resulting in the formation of the United Communist Party of America (UCP). The delegates, as a security measure, used assumed names. *The Communist,* in a special convention issue, was secretive: "Sometime recently, somewhere between the Atlantic and Pacific, between the Gulf and the Great Lakes, two groups of elected delegates assembled as the Unity Conference of the Communist Party and the Communist Labor Party." A Comintern "rep" was present.

Many elements of the Communist Party, however, refused to go along and boycotted the new UCP. A chief point of dispute between the CP and CLP was the position of the foreign-language federations: should they be autonomous within the Party, having the right, if they desired, to withdraw, or be completely subject to the will of the Party? This issue touched the very heart of communist doctrine. No Communist Party could ever allow a member the "right" to withdraw. The misguided members seeking to retain some of these "rights" were swimming upstream, destined to failure.

Finally in May, 1921, after another year of bickering, the UCP and the remainder of the CP formed the Communist Party of America, Section of the Communist International, at a secret two-week convention at Woodstock, New York. The group's program, among other things, provided that the Communist Party would work for violent revolution, preparing "the workers for armed insurrection as the only means of overthrowing the capitalist state." The convention officially accepted the twenty-one points for admission to the Comintern. The CP was now a complete prisoner of Moscow.

By early 1921 an "outward" unity was achieved in the communist movement, but the second problem still remained: bringing the Party into the open. The Third Congress of the Comintern (June-July, 1921) defined the problem:

> The Communist International draws the attention of the Communist Party of America (unified) to the fact that the illegalized organization must not only serve as the ground for collecting and crystallizing the active Communist forces, but that it is the Party's duty to try all ways and means to get out of the illegalized condition into the open, among the wide masses.

The outline of the Party of today was beginning to take shape, the true Party conceived by Lenin, having both a legal and illegal apparatus. The legal aspect would be necessary to conduct communist propaganda among the noncommunist masses, to infiltrate organizations and operate communist fronts. But the underground must exist, for the revolution, the final aim of the Party, could never be anything but illegal. The underground apparatus would handle espionage, super-secret Party work, and would always be ready to expand if the legal Party, because of "capitalist" opposition, could not operate fully. The Communist Party at all times has desired both an upper and a lower level.

In December, 1921, the Workers Party of America was formed, a "legal" outlet for the underground Communist Party. The founding convention, held in New York City, was organized, controlled, and directed by Party leaders. Acting as a front for the underground communists, the Workers Party set up "open" headquarters, issued a "public" paper, and operated in full view. The communist movement now had a dual setup: the underground Communist Party, affiliated with the Third International in Moscow, commonly known among members as *Number One*, and the Workers Party, not so affiliated, known as *Number Two*. They were, however, the two faces of the same communist coin.

Those were turbulent days in the American communist movement. Party leaders were grotesque characters, making speeches in underground meetings, sitting in secret conventions (sometimes in the middle of woods), or traveling to Moscow. They usually had several aliases for use on fake passports and in Party correspondence or to be given to the police if arrested.

Their obsessive love was Soviet Russia. Communists of all varieties streamed to Moscow. William Z. Foster, Earl Browder, Jay Lovestone, Benjamin Gitlow, John Reed, "Mother" Bloor visited there. Many had business: to attend Comintern meetings, to serve as "representatives" of the American Party, to enroll in a communist school. Others went as plain sight-seers, to view at first hand this land of "para-

dise." Sometimes whole groups would go, as for example
a delegation that sailed in 1927 to celebrate the tenth anni-
versary of the revolution.

The visitors were received cordially and treated well unless reason existed to the contrary. Some actually got to see
the great Lenin. William Z. Foster, telling of seeing Lenin
for the first time in 1921, commented that "It was one of
the most inspiring moments" of his life. They attended Comintern Congresses, talked to high Party officials, looked
around the town. They were being primed for their roles,
puppets to fight the communist battle in America.

Then back they came to tell their comrades of the marvels
of this new land. In speeches all over the country they
shouted communist propaganda:

> Russia is the only "real democracy" on earth; the working
> people are better off in Russia than in America.

Never has the American communist movement expressed
itself in more revolutionary, violent, and bitter terms than in
the early 1920's. Party leaders shunned the cautious, evasive
double talk of today's communists. They believed in violent
revolution and said so. The underground communist press
was filled with revolutionary statements. One journal tried to
outdo the other in the use of violent language.
The Party was controlled, just as it is today, by a very few.
Moreover, policy, at all times, was subject to the approval of
the Kremlin, acting through the Comintern. Loyal Americans
should always remember that the Communist Party, USA,
has never existed as an independent organization. Soviet
control was instituted at the very beginning. Acceptance of
the twenty-one points confirmed the imprisonment.

Party business of the underground apparatus and the above-
ground Workers Party was supervised by the Secretariat, a
group usually consisting of three of the most trusted leaders.
A larger group, the Political Committee of some seven to
ten comrades, handled many of the Party's day-to-day affairs, such as manipulating a strike, designating a new Party

official, planning infiltration tactics. The Secretariat, elected by the Political Committee, however, handled the most confidential matters, items not even brought to the attention of the Political Committee: the safeguarding of records, receipt of subsidies from abroad, maintaining contact with Russian espionage agents. These activities were too confidential even to be mentioned in minutes.

Relations between the Comintern in Moscow and American communists were almost like those between feudal lord and serf. Moscow wanted to know everything: the background of Party leaders, how a certain strike was getting along, the strength of the Party in various localities. The "reps" did not hesitate to criticize. In one Political Committee meeting a letter from the Comintern "rep" was read. It contained the following criticisms:

—Lack of information received relative to the Party convention;

—The Party's campaign on a certain issue, though going well, was not strong enough. The "rep" recommended a pamphlet be written;

—Editorials in the *Daily Worker* [the Party's newspaper] were politically incorrect;

—The Party had not taken a correct position against certain enemies of Russia.

The minutes of the meeting indicate that a motion made to accept the letter was "carried unanimously." The Comintern's influence was felt in practically every communist meeting. Every move of the American Party was watched from Moscow. No wonder a joke making Party rounds went as follows: Why is the Party like the Brooklyn Bridge? Because it is suspended on cables!

Besides controlling its over-all policy, the Comintern used the Communist Party in a variety of ways, especially to help the new Soviet government in its work. In one instance the Comintern sent over a "rep" known as Comrade Loaf. He sent a statement, which was read at the meeting of the Po-

litical Committee in New York City presided over by Max
Bedacht, as Acting General Secretary, outlining his need for
assistance in collecting information on the American labor
movement for the Communist International. The Political
Committee agreed to help.

In another instance, Moscow referred a request for a visa
by an official of the New York *Jewish Daily Forward* to United
States comrades. Moscow in these years often used the Communist Party in the United States as a consular clearinghouse,
seeking its advice as to whether visas should be granted or
denied. In answering this request, the already inherent anti-
Semitism of communism dictated the decision. The Soviets
were advised that the visit of the *Jewish Daily Forward* representative would be detrimental to the Soviet Union and the
communist movement.

On occasions, also, the Comintern helped the Party by
arranging to receive cordially American visitors sponsored
by the Party, thereby hoping to create a favorable impression of communism. A prominent author, for example, desired to visit Russia for *The Modern Quarterly*. The Political
Committee instructed that a letter be written to Moscow re-
questing that he be given a royal welcome. The Party wanted
him to be favorably impressed. Then, it hoped, he would
"paint a glowing picture" of the Soviet Union.

Russian control, moreover, was implemented through the
operation of another institution, the Lenin School in Moscow.
This training center was an adjunct to the Marxist-Leninist
Institute. Founded in the 1920's, the Lenin School had for
its purpose the training of an international corps of communist leaders. These graduates, regardless of the country
in which they operated, acted in accordance with the discipline and policies of the Communist Party of the Soviet
Union.

Each Communist Party was assigned a quota of students.
To be eligible, students had to have a working-class background with experience in a trade, shop, or union. They had
to be under thirty-five years of age, either a charter member
or a member with at least five years' experience in Party

work, and possess a "clean" Party record. The Comintern studied the students' background and approved those selected by the Party to attend. As a general rule, students traveled to Moscow under assumed names and with fraudulently obtained passports.

The original Lenin School was located in an old Czarist palace. Students and faculty lived under strict security conditions. The curriculum included not only Marxist-Leninist tactics but the theory and practice of organization, underground and conspiratorial operations, and the tactics of revolution and civil war. The students were taught how to erect stout barricades, conduct guerrilla warfare, and handle firearms. The Soviets wanted rough-and-ready revolutionists, men who would kill, murder, blow up trains, and start revolutions.

Many of the top leaders in Communist Parties around the world are graduates of the Lenin School. The National Committee of the Communist Party in the United States today includes such graduates of the Lenin School as Eugene Dennis, Claude Lightfoot, Carl Winter, Simon W. Gerson, William Weinstone, Nat Ganley, Steve Nelson, and others. Former Lenin School graduates also include such well-known communists as Betty Gannett, Gus Hall, Albert Lannon, Phil Bart, Rose Wortis, Loretta Stack, Henry Winston, and numerous others. The Lenin School became so notorious that it, like the Comintern, was discontinued. After all, it had turned out thousands of graduates, and the communists probably thought it had fulfilled its usefulness.

The American Communist Party began to grow up. From an infant, mostly mouth and little body, it gradually began to take on shape and form. It was soon to increase its participation in American life.

5.

The Party Grows Up

PRIOR TO 1921 communists in the United States had been so concerned with their own private squabbles and organizational problems that they had little time for external activities.

After the 1921 "unification," however, the Party, although still weak, emerged with greater stability. It was now being equipped with two striking arms: (1) the underground Party apparatus and (2) the above-ground, or "false-face," apparatus of the Workers Party.

The time was ripe for communists to move in on American life and American institutions. The first objective was organized labor. Later the battlefront was to be extended to include all aspects of American life up to and including activities of the federal government in Washington.

Prior to 1921, by their own admission, communists had not been particularly effective among trade unions. True, William Z. Foster had helped found the Trade Union Educational League in 1920, but this communist-dominated group had made little headway. The Party at that time had lacked the discipline and training to exploit strikes. Its aims were usually visionary and, above all, too openly revolutionary. During the 1919 steel strike, for example, the Communist Party had issued this proclamation:

THE WORKERS MUST CAPTURE THE POWER OF THE STATE. THEY MUST WREST FROM THE CAPITALISTS THE MEANS THROUGH WHICH THE CAPITALIST RULE IS MAINTAINED.

The answer to the Dictatorship of the Capitalists is the Dictatorship of the Workers.

No wonder the Party was left in complete isolation. Such impractical statements were but noise and scared away normal trade-union people.

But the communists soon learned. Gradually they worked their way into trade unions, and under the name of the Workers Party propagated their program. Little by little they became more active above ground. In 1924 the Workers Party nominated, as candidates in the presidential elections, William Z. Foster as President; Benjamin Gitlow, Vice-President. In 1925, becoming still more bold, the Workers Party changed its name to the Workers (Communist) Party. The underground Party in the sense of being a separate organization was discontinued, although, as in all Communist Parties, a small underground was maintained. In 1928 communist candidates in the presidential elections polled almost 50,000 votes. Finally, in 1929, by discarding the word "Workers," the camouflage was dropped, and the Party became known as the Communist Party of the United States of America.

During these years the communists multiplied labor troubles and participated in a number of strikes, such as the textile strikes in Passaic, New Jersey (1926); New Bedford, Massachusetts (1928); and Gastonia, North Carolina (1929); as well as the coal strike of 1922, the railroad shopmen's strike of 1922, and the New York furriers' strike of 1926. Moreover, they were becoming more active in other agitational fields, such as economic problems, race relations, and nationality groups. The Party, now becoming stronger, was testing its wings in mass agitational work.

Meanwhile the Comintern was developing the type of Party it wanted in America. Gradually many contradictory policies and personality conflicts were eliminated. But important differences still existed. Many communists, for example, thought the Party should remain underground. They opposed founding the Workers Party. In one phase of this fight the communists were divided into three groups, known as the Geese, the Liquidators, and the Conciliators. Another dispute involved the proper method of infiltrating labor unions, with some members being uncertain how far the Party should go to the "left" or to the "right." In 1923 a bitter struggle developed between factions headed by Charles Ruthenberg and William Z. Foster.

In 1928 and 1929, acting under Comintern instructions, the Communist Party conducted its first big "purges," the mass expulsion of large groups of members. In 1928 James P. Cannon, an old-time communist leader, was expelled from the Party for possessing Trotskyite tendencies, a reflection of the Stalin-Trotsky fight in Russia. The Cannonites later formed a new party, the Socialist Workers Party, loyal to Trotsky. In 1929 the purge was even more severe. Jay Lovestone, Executive Secretary of the Party, and Benjamin Gitlow, a high-ranking charter member, were expelled.

Stalin took a personal interest in the American situation. Speaking in May, 1929, to the American Commission of the Presidium of the Executive Committee of the Communist International, he started the line that the communists were to revive after World War II, and asserted that the United States was heading toward a depression that would develop a revolutionary situation.

> I think the moment is not far off when a revolutionary crisis will develop in America . . . It is essential that the American Communist Party should be capable of meeting that historical moment fully prepared and of assuming the leadership of the impending class struggle in America. Every effort and every means must be employed in preparing for that, comrades. For that end the American Communist Party must be improved and bolshevized. For that end we must work for the complete liquidation of factionalism and deviations in the Party. For that end we must work for the reestablishment of unity in the Communist Party of America.

The Russians, by disciplinary purges, were hammering out a Party "of a new type," or, in the words of Stalin, bolshevizing it.

In the 1930's, with the beginnings of the depression, the Communist Party broadened its propaganda-agitation work. Economic disorder was exploited. The Party organized parades, hunger marches, petition campaigns, mass demonstrations. It plunged with vigor into strikes such as the San Francisco general strike of 1934 and the textile and bituminous coal strikes of 1934-35. In November, 1935, the Congress of Industrial Organizations (CIO) was launched, and communists attempted to burrow themselves in its member unions. In addition, they attempted to convert members of other labor unions, minority groups, especially Negroes and individuals recently arrived in the country.

The Party increased in numbers. By 1930, after the great "purges," membership stood at 7500. By 1935 it had jumped to 30,000, and to 80,000 in 1944. The Young Communist League, the youth organization of the Party, reached 20,000 by 1938. Communist "cells" were being formed in industrial plants, and Party members had infiltrated governmental positions, some even carrying out espionage. Intra-Party struggles had ceased, with Earl Browder, a native of Kansas, being elected in 1930 as General Secretary. He was to remain "in power" until 1945. Step by step the Party was becoming stabilized, developing its agitation and propaganda functions. Disciplinary machinery maintained "unity" and "correctness of views." This was a period of accepting new members, broadening struggles, and strengthening organizational structure.

In 1935 the Seventh World Congress of the Comintern, meeting in Moscow, initiated the "united-front" policy, which provided that communists should work with other groups against fascism. Since 1933 Hitler had become the principal target of Soviet Russia. The Bolsheviks, fearing German military power, desperately attempted to enlist the support of the noncommunist world against the Nazis. Russia joined the League of Nations and became a strong supporter of the "collective security" program aimed at holding Hitler in check. Fascism, the communists shouted, represented a danger to everybody, communist and noncommunist. All must work together.

The "united front" is an old Leninist tactic designed to prepare for revolutionary situations. Internationally, the aim is to protect the Soviet fatherland. On a local level it gives the communists an opportunity to infiltrate, manipulate, and take over organizations. Noncommunists are encouraged to participate in communist campaigns with the Party, which always keeps in mind the best way to advance its own interests. If a united-front tactic does not promote communism, it is dropped. A new approach is then developed.

The prewar period was the time of great communist fronts in which so many innocent victims were caught. Literally hundreds of organizations, such as the American Youth Congress, American League Against War and Fascism (later known as the American League for Peace and Democracy), the American Peace Mobilization, and the National Negro Congress sprang into existence. They were created or captured by the communists. All were tailored, through high-sounding names, to attract as many people as possible; the communists had something to offer everybody. The Party during these years moved literally thousands of Americans, causing them, in some way or other, to support the communist cause. Their thought-control nets were busy at work, as will be shown later.

In 1936 the Spanish Civil War erupted, and the communists in the United States, amid great fanfare, sent about 3000 "volunteers," commonly known as the Abraham Lincoln Brigade, to aid the Spanish Loyalists. Front groups of many types were formed to collect money, supplies, and medical aid. Those Americans who were the leaders in the movement to send other Americans, of whom some 50 per cent never returned, had no interest as such in either the Franco group or the opposing Loyalist government. They were acting, along with international communism, to advance the Bolshevik cause.

American communists used glittering promises, underhanded tricks, and downright fraud to coax young men to go to Spain. An enlistee might be promised a lucrative position in Spain, cash rewards, or travel accommodations. A young girl would entice unsuspecting men; in return for her favors they would promise to enlist. If necessary, fictitious passports were obtained or enlistees were stowed away on boats. An elaborate "convoy" system was established, individuals being taken from the United States, usually through France, to Spain. Any tactic was used to gain fighting manpower for the communist cause.

The events of World War II were to demonstrate clearly the loyalty of a now disciplined Communist Party to Soviet Russia. In August, 1939, the entire world was shocked: Hitler and Stalin had signed a "nonaggression" pact! Here was Moscow making an agreement with that "Fascist beast," Hitler, whom it had denounced in bitter terms.

In a few days the pact's full meaning became clear. Hitler had made a "deal." German forces invaded Poland. The Russians, much more quietly, moved from the east. Poland was partitioned and Russia annexed a large slice of Polish territory. Hitler now turned toward the west, his "back" secure.

The Soviets were now in the role of "defenders of the peace" and everyone else was an "imperialist warmonger." If Stalin did it, well, it was right. Hitler, the former enemy, now became a friend and ally. The war between Germany and the Western Allies was termed an "imperialist" war, with no support for the Allies. There was opposition to lend-lease, the draft and military production, support of strikes, circulation of antiwar literature. "The Yanks Are Not Coming" was the slogan. Russia's war on Finland in 1939-40? That was different. That was not imperialism, said the communists. Round-the-clock marchers picketed the White House, urging that the United States stay out of the European war. The pickets were suddenly disbanded on June 21, 1941. A change in tactics seemed imminent.

The next day, June 22, 1941, the Germans attacked Soviet Russia. The European conflict now became a "patriotic war," a "people's war." The United States must lend support: war matériel, money, and manpower. Russia was being overrun. The revolution was in danger. A virtual nightmare gripped the communists. Employ anything to help the land of Stalin: lend-lease, a second front, immediately. Strikes must be stopped. Send relief to Russia.

All these moves and countermoves are not just history. They stand as an everlasting warning of the way in which communists in America, whatever their claims, serve only one master: Moscow.

Other events in Russia had repercussions in the Communist Party, USA, as they still do today. In 1943 Moscow dissolved the Comintern. One purpose was to mollify Western fear and distrust of communism. Russia, the communists claimed, wanted to be a genuine friend. In 1944, following the new line, the Communist Party, USA, under Browder's leadership, "dissolved"; actually it merely changed its name to the Communist Political Association (CPA), a "political-educational association." Here again the idea was to "soften" opposition to communism, make it sound a "little better" to Americans. This was the period when Russia was a military ally and the communists were trying to extract as much as they could from this country. The best tactic, of course, was to be "friendly." The Communist Political Association did not have the harsh, bugaboo connotations of the "Communist Party," but it was the same faithful lackey of Moscow.

In 1945 the war was over. Hitler was defeated. Moscow reverted to its former hostile "line"; she denounced the Allies and claimed full credit for destroying Hitler, and Japan too. Communist Parties, including the one in America, were told to be more defiant.

This meant another change for the communists in the United States. In April, 1945, an article was published in a French communist journal, *Cahiers du Communisme*, by Jacques Duclos, then Secretary of the Communist Party of France. Duclos condemned "Browderism," the so-called policy of "collaboration" with American capitalism as shown in the CPA. This was "revisionism," "opportunism," and a betrayal of Marxism-Leninism. What was needed, according to Duclos, was a militant attack on "capitalism," not cooperation with it.

The Duclos article initiated a purge in the Party, the greatest since the days of Lovestone and Gitlow. Browder became the scapegoat. An emergency convention of the Communist Political Association was hastily called and by "unanimous vote," except Browder's, re-established the Communist Party. Browder was suspended from office and later expelled. This man from Kansas, twenty-five years a faithful servant of the Kremlin, had served his purpose. Foster became Chairman.

"Browderism" was regarded by communists as a direct outgrowth of the Lovestone-Gitlow period. Lovestone had been accused of espousing "American exceptionalism." By this the communists meant that he viewed American capitalism as something "exceptional," not obeying the Marxist-Leninist laws, which teach that capitalism, because of internal contradictions, will decay. Lovestone believed that American capitalism was too strong to follow these Marxist rules.

Browder, according to his communist critics, also fell into a similar error. He overestimated the power of American capital and believed that, through planning, America could overcome for some time its economic problems. This theory of "organized capitalism," these opponents said, was wrong. It revised Marxist principles, weakened the communist movement, and betrayed the "socialist future."

After 1945 the Communist Party, using Browderism as a weapon, entered into a new period of consolidation and loyalty to Soviet Russia. The Party apparatus was tightened and discipline strengthened. Security commissions, with almost unlimited powers, tested the "loyalty" of members and many were expelled. Increased restrictions on the admittance of new members were set up. The Party press, following the Moscow tack, inveighed against American "imperialism" and heaped abuse on the Marshall Plan, the Greece-Turkey Aid program, and the organization of a West European defense organization. The old-time Stalinist, William Z. Foster, was welding the Party into an anti-American weapon of the cold war.

In 1948, for the first time since the 1920's, the Party found itself on the defensive when the Department of Justice initiated prosecution against its leaders. The twelve members of the Party's National Board were indicted under the Smith

Act (enacted in 1940), which prohibits any conspiracy that advocates the overthrow of the United States government by force and violence. Previously, in 1941, the government had instituted prosecutions against members of the Socialist Workers Party (Trotskyites) under this statute. Other statutes since used by the government in the attack on the Party include the Internal Security Act of 1950 and the Communist Control Act of 1954.

In a long trial, running through most of 1949, eleven members were convicted, the twelfth, William Z. Foster, having been severed from the trial because of illness. In June, 1951, the Supreme Court upheld these convictions, and the government subsequently took prosecutive action against additional Party leaders.

This government prosecution was a strong disabling blow against the Party. Many of its top leaders were arrested and convicted. Others lived in fear of arrest. As a result the Party to a large extent went underground in the first large-scale underground operation since the early 1920's. Party offices were closed, top Party leaders went into hiding, records were destroyed. Courier systems were instituted and clubs broken up into small units, if not completely disbanded. For about four years, from mid-1951 to mid-1955, the Party in protecting itself spent energy, time, and money that otherwise would have gone into agitation and propaganda.

Again, as in previous years, events in Russia determined communist policy in America. The death of Stalin in 1953 and the advent of Malenkov brought the "Big Smile" policy from the Soviet bear, which was continued by Bulganin and Khrushchev. The Communist Party, USA, weakened and largely immobilized in its underground haunts, welcomed the new line. Then, in the summer of 1955, came the Geneva Conference. The Party, sensing a new "political climate," began to come above ground. Quietly communist leaders reappeared in public, many courier systems were discontinued, and most underground hideaways abolished. By the spring of 1956 most of the Party's underground had been curtailed and even the communist leaders who had become fugitives from justice began to surrender. This experiment in underground strategy had cost the Party severely.

Now, however, the Party was faced with severe problems of internal disorganization and factionalism. Many Party members had left the movement. Administrative affairs were in a state of chaos. Invaluable records had been destroyed. Party leaders, returning from underground assignments, found that they were often ignored by the ruling hierarchy. Money was scarce. Footholds in noncommunist organizations, such as labor unions, had largely been lost.

Then came Khrushchev's denunciation of Stalin and charges of anti-Semitism in Russia. In the fall of 1956 came the bloody Soviet intervention in Hungary. No events since the German-Russian nonaggression pact of 1939 had so gravely shaken the Party. Stalin, the man the comrades had revered so long, was proved to be a murderer, thief, and liar. Communist leaders in the United States were stunned and aghast. Immediately, different opinions developed as to the Party's future policy—opinions that gave rise to severe leadership differences.

One group, headed by William Z. Foster, although accepting Khrushchev's denunciations, emphasized what "good" Stalin had done for the communist movement. These were the so-called Stalinists, who wanted as few changes as possible in the Party organization. Opposing Foster was a faction headed by John Gates, editor of the *Daily Worker,* who openly advocated disbandment of the Party and establishment of a political association. This action, he argued, would make the Party more palatable to the general public in light of the severe criticisms. In between, many middle-of-the-roaders, led by Eugene Dennis, were not sure just what the Party should do in this, one of its most severe crises.

In February, 1957, the Party assembled in its Sixteenth National Convention, the first since 1950. The convention was under the dictatorial control of a few Party leaders. Much deceitful publicity was released to demonstrate that the Party had declared its "independence" of Moscow, that a new leadership had been installed, and that the Party was entirely American in character. However, Foster and his associates so effectively manipulated the sessions that the same old Stalinist line prevailed.

The Party retained its same old name, continued the majority of its old leadership; it reaffirmed its adherence to the basic tenets of Marxism-Leninism; it reaffirmed its acceptance of "proletarian internationalism"; it refused to condemn or even take a stand on the Soviet rape of Hungary; it refused to condemn the tyranny and proven anti-Semitism of the Soviet Union; it did not take a single affirmative step to declare its independence of the Soviet Union; and, in fact, the Soviet-controlled press hailed the Communist Party, USA, for remaining loyal "to the principles of Marxism-Leninism."

The Communist Party is a highly disciplined tool of the Soviet Union in the United States. In the thirty-eight years since it came into being, it has developed a trained and potentially effective leadership that overnight, should the situation become favorable, could expand into a mass organization of great potential power. No longer does it need to send its promising young leaders to Moscow for training, because its own educational system is now performing that function.

The present menace of the Communist Party in the United States grows in direct ratio to the rising feeling that it is a small, dissident element and need not be feared. As we relax our protection and ease up on security measures, we move closer and closer to a "fool's paradise."

Through the Communist Party, the mentality of the Russian Bolsheviks is being transmitted to America, together with the belief that man can be completely redesigned from a child of God into a soulless social cog. The Party member, whether he be a farmer in Missouri, an automobile worker in Michigan, or a lawyer in California, must be made to think, act, and be like other Party members. Many techniques, such as discipline, education, the Party press, recreation, literature, organizational structure, the arts, are used to fashion the "communist man," the terror of the twentieth century. This is the "man" the Kremlin hopes will place the hammer and sickle above the White House and establish a Soviet America as part of a world empire, with Soviet Russia as the master of all. This is the "man" who, in a recent secret Party meeting, admonished the comrades present that a search of history would show that there has never been a revolution without force and violence and when the time comes, "We will hang and shoot those responsible for the type of government we have today."

THE COMMUNIST APPEAL
IN THE
UNITED STATES

6.

Who Are the Communists?

THE COMMUNIST PARTY, USA, works day and night to further the communist plot in America. Virtually invisible to the non-communist eye, unhampered by time, distance, and legality, this bolshevik transmission is in progress. The Communist Party, USA, is bolshevizing its membership and creating communist puppets throughout the country. The American Party, in the Kremlin's eyes, has for its objective the ultimate seizure of power in America and, to accomplish this purpose, it seeks to "educate" in the ways of communism all who will listen.

To appreciate the deadly seriousness of this process, the American citizen must see how the Communist Party, USA, by its every act, often without fanfare or newspaper headlines, is creating a corps of dedicated Party members, supported in many ways by United States citizens who have been infected or misled in one way or another.

Millions of Americans have wondered how the communists gain support. Frequently they seem to wield influence entirely out of proportion to their actual numbers.

Party influence is exerted through the communist device of thought control (controlling, in various degrees, the thinking of many Americans). The communists quickly accuse anybody who disagrees with them of being guilty of thought control; it is a favorite communist expression. Yet this same technique, applied in varying degrees to different groups of our population, is the key to communist strength in America today.

The Party's objective is to drive a wedge, however slight, into as many minds as possible. That is why, in every conceivable way, communists try to poison our thinking about the issues of the day: social reforms, peace, politics, veterans', women's, and youth problems. The more people they can influence, the stronger they will be.

Top Party officials have a definite assignment: to capture positions of power. They are the Party's front-line commanders. Communism is at war with America. The United States is a vast battlefield. A school, a labor union, a civic group, a government official, a private citizen—all are important in the never-ending struggle for power.

The whole nation, to the communists, is a gigantic checkerboard. The communist high command is constantly moving, jumping, switching, and retreating to get communist members in positions of influence. They are outnumbered; they know that. That is why they must depend on skill, maneuvering, and deception.

The communist official in our country realizes that his supporters often form a motley collection, varying greatly in loyalty: some are fanatically loyal; others are half-timers or "single-nighters." Many are "tremblers," needing constant encouragement, whereas some are just victims unwittingly caught in the Party net.

But time after time the communists are able to weld these seemingly ill-assorted supporters into a unified instrument of power. They have succeeded in creating and dominating different areas of thought control. Each area contains supporters who, under Party guidance, can quickly and effectively be mobilized. The result of this manipulation, as applied to diverse personalities, groups, and issues, is a tribute to the communists' deceitful skill. By this technique, using its own membership as a base, the Party is today influencing literally thousands of Americans.

There are five principal areas, or circles, of thought control that should be thoroughly understood. These are the keys to communist mobilization to achieve control of the United States.

1. *"Open" Party members.* The area of highest thought control, which is the core of communist strength, is the Party membership. These individuals, after indoctrination, become full-fledged revolutionaries, pledged to stick with the Party at all times.

Normally they make no effort to conceal their membership. They may be high-ranking officials, such as a state chairman, a section organizer, a club chairman, an educational director, or mere rank-and-file members. They are enrolled, pay dues, and accept Party discipline.

The Party member must be completely obedient; that is the hallmark of Party life. The constitution of the Communist Party, USA, sets forth specifically this definition of a full-fledged member:

> A Party member shall accept the Party program as determined by the Constitution and conventions of the Party, belong to a Party club and pay dues.

Very clearly, he is a tool of the Party.

Party policy is built around Party membership. The trained member is one on whom the Party depends to commit espionage, derail a speeding train, and organize riots. If asked, gun in hand, to assault the Capitol of the United States, he will be expected to obey. These members are today working to promote a Soviet America: some in undercover assignments, some in communist-front organizations, others as Party officials. They are the offensive shock troops—confidently expecting that the precise moment will arrive when conditions will make feasible the revolutionary overthrow of our government.

If the Party desires to undertake a certain task, Party members, seen or unseen, will be the leaders. Suppose that a communist front is to be started; that is, an organization which is to be maneuvered by the Party. A communist sympathizer may be named president, but a Party member will probably be executive secretary, placed there to control policies. Or suppose a giant rally for "peace" is to be held. The platform will glitter with noncommunists. But a communist member on hand will control the agenda.

The strength of this inner circle, the real backbone of communist striking power, lies not in numbers but in organized deception. Following Lenin's teachings, the Party is a small, compact, and highly mobile group that can strike quickly with great fury, often achieving objectives unwarranted by its numbers. Today's membership is hard, well trained, and disciplined. The weak, fainthearted, and skeptical have been purged. Those who remain faithful to the Party are dedicated to the communist revolution. They are willing to sacrifice everything for it. Here is an actual case:

> A Party member was given a special assignment. The first step was to drop everything and go into hiding. That was all he was told. He obeyed. He took another name, moved away. Time passed. The children began to ask, "Where is Daddy?" The mother's answer: "He is dead. You don't have a daddy!"

This is the fanaticism of the trained member.

To be obedient, however, is not enough. This select group of Party members must be made superobedient, meaning subservient beyond the hope of return. They must be constantly whipped into a state of frenzied enthusiasm and never allowed to relax. The moment a member "lets up" he is endangered; a noncommunist thought might slip in. He must be made to think exclusively in Party terms and nothing else. Some Party members are old-timers; others are new recruits. All of them grew up in capitalist society. Many still show the effects of their "enemy upbringing," especially the younger ones. That is why they slacken once in a while. They think for themselves; they put self before Party. These instincts must be pounded out and communist thoughts instilled. Communists are not born; they are made. For example:

Is this a moral thing to do?
Do C. know morality?

A Party leader in the Deep South was angry. He was talking to a member who had "slipped" a little. This individual was not giving his best effort to the Party, although he had been in the Party for twelve years and had fought in Spain with the Abraham Lincoln Brigade.

"Work harder for the Party," was the leader's theme. "You've got to give more time to the Party than you're doing now."

"And starve," answered the other man. "I've got to keep my job. I can't make a living just doing Party work."

"Let your wife work," retorted the official. "That'll hold you for a while, or borrow money if need be."

"But she can't make enough. Besides, she wants to keep house."

"She's a drawback," flashed the leader, "a definite hindrance. What are you going to do, stand up for the Party or your wife?"

The question was direct. The individual answered, "What do you want me to do? Divorce my wife?"

"If your marriage is such that you can't work for the Party," came the reply, "I'd seriously consider divorce. Your wife is selfish, simply self-centered. She wants all your time. She doesn't understand the movement. She's interested in her own happiness and security."

The communist leader rammed home his point. "I'm working all the time, so much that I can hardly sleep nights. You can't allow personal problems to take your mind off the Party. You've got to fight that kind of pressure. Your allegiance to the Party comes first. I never let my wife interfere. She knows her place."

2. *Concealed Party members.* Another area dominated by communist thought control consists of the concealed communist, the individual who, though accepting Party discipline, does not wish his affiliation to be publicly known. These two areas, open and concealed members, in fact, are closely related, often interchanging and always cooperating with each other. The concealed communist, because he is not known as a

communist, can often advance the Party's cause among people and in organizations where an open member would be scorned.

The number of concealed communists is high. They vary in degree of concealment. Some are concealed from the public and are not openly identified as communists. Others are concealed even from the membership, and a few are so deeply hidden that only top leaders know their identity. Usually the more prominent the individual, the more concealed he must be.

Concealed communists are found in all fields. They may be enrolled members, although secretly and usually under an alias or assumed name; or their names may never appear on official rolls. It does not matter. They are viewed by Party leaders as members. They are equally as dangerous as the open member, if not more so. They are difficult to identify and, being concealed, can operate freely in noncommunist groups.

A physician, a lawyer, an educator, a personnel manager in a business firm, a television script writer—each may be a concealed communist of great value to the Party. Suppose that a Party member is in hiding. He becomes ill. The doctor, a concealed communist, is called. He can be trusted. Or a study group is formed on a campus. The professor "guides" the discussion and subtly engenders communist doctrine. A personnel manager hires communist sympathizers, working them into key positions. Party influence increases, almost without anybody's knowing it. Here is an example of how the system works:

Two men huddle in conversation. One is a top Party official; the other, a high-ranking labor union leader who is a concealed communist, although his union has since ousted him from his post.

The national convention of the union is about to open in Philadelphia, Pennsylvania. The Party official is issuing instructions. Support this, support that. He talks in great detail, laying down the over-all Party policy. Then he becomes more specific, even going so far as to dictate the wording of resolutions, suggesting the order of convention business, and advising how certain personalities should be handled. Nothing is to be left to chance.

The union leader listens. He can go on the convention floor, since nobody knows that he is under Party discipline, and carry out the communist program. This concealed communist is essential to the Party's thought-control technique. There are thousands like him always seeking to penetrate the healthy body of American life and to corrupt it.

In another case, a top communist leader, long before he fled into the communist underground, was confronted with the problem of being identified, for he was well known and his picture had been widely publicized in the press. He could dye his hair, shave off his mustache, and lose weight, but he still could be readily identified by a mole on the right side of his jaw. He went to a physician in a Midwest city, a reported communist, who operated on the Party leader to remove the mole from his face.

Another concealed member of the Party was the editor-in-chief of a conservative book-publishing house. This editor, having an excellent educational background, was highly regarded by his company. On one occasion, after this publishing house had been criticized by a newspaper columnist for publishing procommunist books, the president discussed the problem at a meeting of the board of directors. He reported that he had asked the editor if, in fact, he was a member of the Communist Party. The editor entered an emphatic denial. The president then advised the board that since the editor was a gentleman, the allegations that he was a communist were false.

The president of the publishing house simply did not know the facts. The editor's usual procedure was to have the manuscript of a communist author submitted directly to him on a personal basis. He would review it, be sure it was in publishable form, then have the author submit it to the publishing house through routine channels. Receiving the manuscript later through the company, he would recommend its publication. Through this technique, the editor was eminently successful in circulating communist literature.

When noncommunist authors complained and several terminated their relations with the publisher, the editor was later quietly eased out of his job.

There are occasions when a member of the Party will drop his open Party activities, move to another section of the country, and become a secret, concealed member. Such was the case of a talented young man who became active in the Communist Party in New York City before World War II when he was employed by a motion-picture company. After work he functioned as a Communist Party organizer, later as a membership director of a Party club, and, for a while, worked on the paid staff of the American Labor Party. In the meantime he obtained a job in television and in 1953 became program director of a television station in a large Southern city.

Soon after his arrival in the Southern city, the TV program director started to meet secretly with the Party's "white-collar" professional group. Word came through that he should sever even these connections, according to a Party functionary, who said, "We want them [him and his wife] to be secure for the Party." He was too valuable a member to be compromised. The Senate Internal Security Subcommittee, however, uncovered the white-collar professional cell, and when the TV director declined to answer Committee questions, he was promptly fired by his employer.

3. *Fellow travelers.* The third area in which communist thought control works is that of the fellow traveler and sympathizer. These two terms are distinct but related. The fellow traveler, while not a member, actively supports (travels with) the Party's program for a period of time. The sympathizer is more passive, sympathizing with the Party or individual members on specific issues, and may or may not give active aid. These individuals are not Party members, but, in some degree, have come under Party control.

This control is sufficient to make them work willingly for the Party. Many consistently follow the Party line, even maintaining personal contacts with Communist Party officials. Others, the so-called "intellectuals," may never have attended a communist meeting and may know nothing about Party organization. Yet, because of the spell of communist thought control, they knowingly do the Party's work. Perhaps they have been influenced by Marxist writings or the professed aims of the Party on certain issues. In any case, deluded by communist propaganda, they desire to render active assistance.

Fellow travelers and sympathizers, unlike open or concealed communists, cannot be disciplined. A Party leader may request a favor. If the fellow traveler or sympathizer agrees, fine; if he doesn't, the Party cannot do much except hope to exert more influence next time.

Moreover, these people are often undependable, donating money, for example, to one Party function but not another. Sometimes they may be "hot," doing just about anything asked. Then suddenly they grow "cold," lose interest, and become inactive.

The value of fellow travelers and sympathizers lies in their alleged noncommunist affiliation. That is why, in most instances, communist leaders do not attempt to recruit them into the Party. They are more valuable outside: as financial contributors, vocal mouthpieces, or contacts between Party officials and noncommunists. They constitute, in fact, fronts for, and defenders of, the Communist Party.

The role these individuals can play for the communists is clearly illustrated in front organizations, where they serve as sponsors or officials. Behind the scenes is a communist manipulator. Consider, for example, one such organization. In October, 1951, the *Daily Worker* announced the formation of the Emergency Civil Liberties Committee with one hundred fifty founders (from thirty-nine states), including fifty who were educators, clergymen, and professionals.

One of the Committee's first official moves was to petition the New York State Commissioner of Education to "forbid the New York City Board of Education from enforcing its newly-enacted ban on suspected communist teachers. . . ." Gradually, as the old Civil Rights Congress, a well-known front, became discredited, the Emergency Civil Liberties Committee took over its work. In 1956 the Senate Internal Security Subcommittee, after identifying the Emergency Civil Liberties Committee, stated, "When the Communist Party itself is under fire these fronts offer a bulwark of protection."

The names of the group's one hundred fifty founders have been exploited by the Party to fight its battles.

To make a known Party member president of a front would immediately label it as "communist." But if a sympathizer can be installed, especially a man of prominence, such as an educator, minister, or scientist, the group can operate as an "independent" organization. This trick has worked time after time and is still working today. By allowing themselves to be used as tools, fellow travelers and sympathizers have immeasurably advanced the communist cause.

In Chapter 17 we shall discuss communist fronts in greater detail.

Of particular interest to the communists is the influence of fellow travelers and sympathizers in the "thought-molding" field: teachers, script writers, newspapermen, news analysts. If these individuals can be subjected to the slightest bit of communist thought control, the Party will have won a major victory. College particularly

One individual in New York City, for example, once occupied an important role as a news commentator and author. His views were consistently procommunist. He represented himself as an authority on international affairs. He claimed to have talked personally to many of the world's leaders. Just as the communists would want, everywhere he went he built himself up as an individual who could give the American people guidance in their thinking.

This sympathizer was simply irreplaceable in the communist scheme. No open communist could discuss current events before lecture audiences, behind the microphone, or through the written word with his degree of "objectivity" and "independence." He was able to fool many noncommunists and exert considerable influence. His lecture tours were often arranged by communist-front groups. A concealed communist contributed money to his expenses. Wherever this "world observer" went, he preached communist-line and pro-Soviet propaganda. When his influence began to slip, he then changed his ways and sought his livelihood elsewhere.

Men and women of this caliber can do much to bring others into the communist thought-control net. No wonder the Party works to support them.

4. *Opportunists.* Another group that falls, on occasion, under communist thought control consists of opportunists, individuals who, if they can benefit personally, will knowingly support the Party in return for support or favors from it. Opportunists are cynical and self-seeking, not caring that by cooperating with the communists, even though temporarily, they are injuring the nation.

In a large Midwestern city a noncommunist labor leader had aspirations to become president of a union council. A group of communists, opposed to the then president, decided that this labor leader could be controlled. They drafted him as a candidate and, of course, on the election slate placed also some Party members. The labor leader won the election, and so did the communists, because they gained a man over whom they had a hold and whom they could therefore expect to use.

The opportunist was then pushed into various front organizations: he was put on the board of a communist-sponsored school; designated as a delegate to a convention of a front group; enlisted to join a campaign to oppose the "anticommunist clause" in a state-wide labor convention. He was besieged constantly to "do this" and "help us." His value to the Party was shown, for example, when, even though he refused on a certain occasion to cooperate with a Party front, his position was defended by the Party. The opportunist, in the Party's eyes, was more important to it as a labor leader than as a supporter of the front.

For some time the deal paid off. The opportunist received the prestige and the communists had a champion. Then things began to change. The opportunist had his own ideas and ceased to follow the Party lead. Relations became strained. When the communists wanted the city-wide council to endorse a well-known comrade as a candidate for the board of education, they brought up the motion at a meeting when the opportunist was absent. The communist candidate was endorsed. That was too much for the opportunist, who promptly issued a public statement denying that he was backing the communist candidate. A special meeting of the council was called to reconsider its action.

The communists now moved into high gear. Word went out that the opportunist would have to be "put in his place" for publicly denouncing the communist candidate. At a special meeting the opportunist took the floor and successfully led the fight to reverse the council's endorsement of a communist. The communists were bitter in their condemnation of their one-time protégé; he was a "traitor" and a "hypocrite." Deciding he had had enough, the opportunist resigned the presidency.

In such a case who is the ultimate winner? The communists, for they have advanced their program. When he, the opportunist, faltered, he was dropped.

Communists watch eagerly for such opportunists; they are usually easy to influence and exploit. The self-seeker, fighting to win an election or wanting to earn some easy money, may listen to communist double talk and cooperate. Not that the Party is under any illusions; the opportunist is not going to be converted. He will denounce communist support just as quickly as he accepted it. Relations are strictly "dog eat dog," each trying to exploit the other. But the opportunist can be used.

5. *Dupes.* The final area is that of the dupe, or innocent victim, the individual who unknowingly is under communist thought control and does the work of the Party. A tragedy of the past generation in the United States is that so many persons, including high-ranking statesmen, public officials, educators, ministers of the gospel, professional men, have been duped into helping communism. Communist leaders have proclaimed that communism must be partly built with noncommunist hands, and this, to a large extent, is true.

Communist propaganda is tailored to attract noncommunists. Communism offers a bogus "spiritual appeal," a "Kingdom of God on earth." Its tactics and strategy are covered with attractive, appealing words, such as "freedom," "justice," and "equality." The communists claim they are working for a "better world," that they have the answer to discrimination, exploitation, and economic want. To fight for communism, they say, is to become part of the most sacred crusade in the history of man.

Many well-meaning citizens, attracted by these words and not seeing behind the communist intentions, have been swept into the communist thought-control net. Most are sincerely interested in improving society, and there are many ways in which our society can and should be improved. They are willing to devote their time, talents, and energies to a "sacred cause." That is how communist thought control works. If it can influence you on any matter, regardless of how minor, making you think favorably toward communism, it has gained. It has something to sell everyone.

"Fool the noncommunists!" That is the slogan. And, better still, make noncommunists fool each other! Encourage the support of as many dupes as possible. These individuals see only the exterior, or false face, of communism. They are never shown the inside, the real communism, the terror, injustice, and slavery. Time after time, in almost unbelievable fashion, victims, somehow or other under communist thought control, do communism's work: signing communist election petitions, contributing time or money to communist fronts, issuing statements in support of communist-sponsored campaigns.

Elizabeth Gurley Flynn, a member of the National Committee of the Communist Party, USA, quite recently was a candidate for the New York City Council under the emblem of the People's Rights Party. Communists canvassed to obtain at least 3000 signatures on petitions required by law to place her name on the ballot. They went over the goal with the help of noncommunists. In the November 5, 1957, election, however, Flynn received fewer than 1000 votes.

The People's Rights Party is a sham political party created to give the Communist Party the legal right to run communist candidates. In 1946, 1952, 1954, and again in 1957 communist candidates have run for municipal, state, or national office in New York City under the banner of the People's Rights Party. Each time signatures had to be obtained to secure the right of the PRP to place its candidates on the ballot.

Another instance of Party manipulation to gain the support of noncommunists was the campaign in the summer of 1957 to solicit signatures for petitions opposing the further testing of nuclear weapons by the United States government. Most of these signatures, of course, were those of noncommunists. On this issue the Party was slavishly following the line of international communism. Communist strategy is to provide the leadership, encouraging noncommunists to do the work.

Not that these individuals are communists. The great majority of them are loyal, but deceived, citizens. Sending five dollars to a front organization with a patriotic-sounding name; signing a communist-inspired petition urging "world disarmament" (isn't that a worthy cause?); attending a giant Party-manipulated rally in support of the "Bill of Rights": the noncommunist does not realize these campaigns are being operated out of downtown communist headquarters. He is fooled because he believes in the aims they profess and does not recognize the hidden motive.

But, from the communist point of view, a dollar is a dollar. A victim makes a contribution. His money is just as good as money from an open member. A noncommunist allows his name to be used on a letterhead. Suppose he *was* fooled? The name is still there. Thus the communists assemble support from all quarters, whether given intentionally or not, and apply it toward their objectives.

Party officials, like fishermen, are constantly watching their "nets" to see what the fishing will bring. Each day, unfortunately, communist thought-control nets, sweeping through American life, catch new supporters, maybe two or three new members, several sympathizers, an opportunist, many victims. A "big-name" sympathizer is worth a great deal and so is another fellow traveler. Each can be put to work. The strength of the Communist Party depends, at any given time, on the number of fish in the net.

How can we, as Americans, protect ourselves from becoming "innocent victims" of the communists?

First, we should not fall for "fronts." In Chapter 17 you will find a detailed description of how communist fronts operate, together with a twelve-point list of ways to spot them so that we will not be fooled into giving them our support. (The Attorney General of the United States has issued a list of subversive organizations, and the House Committee on Un-American Activities has also issued a *Guide to Subversive Organizations and Publications.*)

Second, we should know the answers to the *Five False Claims of Communism.* In the next chapter we shall learn what those claims are and how United States communists use them to disarm and confuse loyal Americans. We should learn to spot those claims, and know the answers.

Finally, we should not permit the use of our names unless we know the true identity of the soliciting group. We should use our right of petition to further the American way of life, and not allow the communists to steal it from us.

7.

What Do U. S. Communists Claim?

I HAVE SAID that one of the chief strengths of the Communist Party has been its ability to appeal, by trickery, to many Americans who are sincere, idealistic, and well-meaning.

A first step in arming ourselves against communism is to know how those appeals are made and how to see through them. So now let us consider five of the most deceptive claims made by the Communist Party, USA, in its effort to lure "innocent victims." Let's see what communists pretend to be and what they really are:

1. *Communists are not liberals.* The concept that communism is a new world of liberalism is false, a trap used to catch noncommunists. The word "liberal" has a fine, upright meaning and is symbolic of a great historic tradition. That is why the communists appropriate the term for their own use. *Communism is the very opposite of liberalism.* Liberalism means increased rights for the citizen; a curb on the powers of the central government; freedom of speech, religion, and the press. Communism means fewer and fewer rights for the private citizen, curtailment of freedom of speech and press and worship of God. The state becomes all-powerful, the absolute reverse of American tradition.

Make no mistake, communists do not like liberalism; that is, the genuine liberalism of Western civilization. They denounce liberals ("liberal blockheads" Lenin called them) and attempt by every means to destroy them. The communists realize that true liberalism is a bitter enemy, a fighter for the things that communism opposes.

A derisive poem entitled "March of the Liberals" published in the July 16, 1935, issue of *New Masses* (a now-defunct communist publication) makes clear this communist attitude, depicting liberals as weak, vacillating, and incapable of any affirmative action:

> a conclusion is something
> we never can find. . . .
> . . . One step forward
> and two steps back:
> that's the method
> of our attack.

"You see here," *New Masses* comments, "the rhyme and reason of why a liberal looks so poisonous to a sincere and active radical. . . ." The "antidote" for such liberalism? "Weekly doses" of Marxism-Leninism, or, in the words of the editors, "If you know one of these 'open-minded' marchers, you can save him! Give him a copy of NEW MASSES quick. . . ."

The liberals do not want revolution but genuine social re-forms. That is why the communists detest them. But if they can be exploited, so much the better. Like everybody else, they are fuel for the communist engine of revolution.

2. *Communists are not progressives.* "We of the Communist Party are fully and completely in the camp of progress. . . ." A prime tenet of communist propaganda is that communism is the latest word in social progress. All other forms of government, especially our constitutional government, according to the communists are outmoded, old-fashioned, and antique. Communism is the wave of the future, they like to say, bringing all the good things that man has been dreaming about for years. Religion, the "opium" of the people, must be destroyed, God cast out, and the "oppressors" liquidated. The road ahead is clear. Join the Communist Party and see "progress." Those who do not join are "reactionaries," "fascists," and "warmongers."

Everybody likes progress. If you are a farmer, you want to grow better corn and more of it. If you have a lawn, you want to weed out the dandelions and have better grass. If you are a manufacturer, you want to develop a better product. This is a natural human trait. The communists, identifying themselves with this idea, have convinced many people that they are the "progressives" of the twentieth century.

The exact opposite is true. Communists are barbarians in modern dress, using both club and blood purge.

Shortly before 1700 Peter the Great came to the throne in Russia. He was ruthless and dictatorial. He was interested in making the Russian state strong. The church, the nobles, the peasants, everybody must be subjected. The most minute details came under his supervision. The army was reorganized, a new civil service put into operation. He even ordered men to shave their beards and women to dress in modern clothing. The law was what he said it was.

Communists have inherited this tradition. With modern, efficient tools, such as the secret police, the army, and control of communications, they have increased the tyranny of the state. The individual under communism is a mere number with two shoulders to carry a bale of hay or a couple of feed sacks, two hands to pull a wagon or drive a tractor. This is not progress but a turning backward, throwing away the fruits of history, religion, and free government.

3. *Communists are not social reformers,* people working for the betterment of living conditions. "The Communist Party . . . champions the . . . interests of the workers, farmers, the Negro people and all others who labor by hand and brain. . . ." This theme, here quoted from the 1957 Party Constitution, is exploited time after time, to attract noncommunist support.

Some years ago a very distinguished person, after reading a summary of the program of a communist-front organization, commented that if communists worked for desirable objectives, that was praiseworthy. However, in this individual's opinion, such action could hardly represent much of a gain for communism, except perhaps to make it more like democracy.

This is a complete misunderstanding of communism and is just what the Party desires. The communists detest democratic reforms. These changes, they know, will make free government stronger, hence less likely to be overthrown by revolution. Their espousal of reforms (higher wages, better working conditions, elimination of racial discrimination) is strictly a revolutionary tactic. That communism, by such mass agitation, might gradually change to democracy is a false and dangerous illusion. Communism's goal is world revolution. Any device that will advance its cause is urgently pursued.

Lenin himself is frank:

> The strictest loyalty to the ideas of Communism must be combined with the ability to make all the necessary practical compromises, to "tack," to make agreements, zigzags, retreats and so on. . . .

4. *The Communists do not believe in democracy.* Communist leaders of all ranks, from N. S. Khrushchev to William Z.

Foster, from Lenin to the communist agitator on the corner of 12th and Market Streets, have proclaimed that communism is the most highly developed form of democracy. Lenin stated that the Soviet Union was "a million times more democratic" than the most advanced capitalist democracies of the West. William Z. Foster in an official statement commented, "The Communist Party is a democratic movement," adding:

> And in the Soviet Union . . . there exists a higher type of democracy than in any other country in the world.

Mention must be made, to understand this double talk, of a communist deceptive device called *Aesopian language.*

Nearly everyone is familiar with the fables of Aesop, such as "The Fox and the Crow" and "The Lion and the Mouse." Often the point of the story is not directly stated but must be inferred by the reader. This is a "roundabout" presentation.

Lenin and his associates before 1917, when living in exile, made frequent use of "Aesopianism." Much of their propaganda was written in a "roundabout" and elusive style to pass severe Czarist censorship. They desired revolution but could not say so. They had to resort to hints, theoretical discussions, even substituting words, which, though fooling the censor, were understood by the "initiated," that is, individuals trained in Party terminology.

The official *History of the Communist Party of the Soviet Union (Bolsheviks),* telling how Bolshevik agitation in Saint Petersburg in 1912-14 was led by *Pravda,* the communist newspaper, explained that the periodical could not openly call for revolutionary action. That would have brought government suppression. Rather, "hints," understood by the communists, were used:

> When, for example, *Pravda* wrote of the "full and uncurtailed demands of the Year Five," the workers understood that this meant the revolutionary slogans of the Bolsheviks, namely, the overthrow of tsardom. . . .

In 1914 labor troubles sprang up in the capital of Russia. The communists wanted mass meetings and demonstrations. *Pravda* couldn't publicly sound the call, so it resorted to Aesopian language.

> But [the communist *History* reads] the call was understood by class-conscious workers when they read an article by Lenin bearing the modest title "Forms of the Working-Class Movement" and stating that at the given moment strikes should yield place to a higher form of the working-class movement— which meant a call to organize meetings and demonstrations.

Lenin himself told how he was compelled to write:

> with an eye to the tsarist censorship. Hence, I was not only forced to confine myself strictly to an exclusively theoretical, mainly economic analysis of facts, but to formulate the few necessary observations on politics with extreme caution, by hints, in that Aesopian language—in that cursed Aesopian language—to which tsarism compelled all revolutionaries to have recourse, whenever they took up their pens to write a "legal" work.

In one propaganda tract Lenin, writing about world problems, mentioned "Japan." However, as he later explained, that was merely a trick to pass the censor. "The careful reader," Lenin said, "will easily substitute Russia for Japan. . . ."

So it is with the word "democracy." Communists still use Aesopian language; they say one thing and mean another. In this manner they fool noncommunists, encouraging them to believe that communism stands for something desirable. The trained communist knows otherwise: it is mere double talk with a completely different meaning.

The word "democracy" is one of the communists' favorite Aesopian terms. They say they favor democracy, that communism will bring the fullest democracy in the history of mankind. But, to the communists, democracy does not mean free speech, free elections, or the right of minorities to exist. Democracy means the domination of the communist state, the complete supremacy of the Party. The greater the communist control, the more "democracy." "Full democracy," to the communist, will come only when all noncommunist opposition is liquidated.

Such expressions as "democracy," "equality," "freedom," and "justice" are merely the Party's Aesopian devices to impress noncommunists. Communists are masters at getting other people to do their work. They clothe themselves with everything good, noble, and inspiring to exploit these ideals to their own advantage.

5. *Communists are not American.* The Communist Party, USA, endeavors, in every possible way, to convince this country that it is American. "The Communist Party is American," one of its top leaders recently proclaimed. ". . . We take second place to nobody in our devotion to the United States and its people."

This is a typical Aesopian trick. Communism stands for everything America abhors: slave camps, rigged elections, purges, dictatorship. As we saw in Part II, the communist movement was born abroad, was imported into the United States, and grew up under the personal direction of Russian leaders in Moscow. How can communism be American when it employs every form of treason and trickery to bring about ultimate domination of the United States by a foreign power?

The American people, fortunately, are now more than ever aware of the danger of communism. The hostile attitude of Soviet Russia in international affairs, the Canadian spy revelations, Khrushchev's denunciation of Stalin, Soviet intervention in Hungary, the aggression in Korea—all these events, and many more, have taught Americans that the communist is not an angel of mercy, ministering to the weak, oppressed, and wounded, but a menacing demon spattered with blood and wielding a hammer and sickle of iron.

Nevertheless, great damage has been done, and is still being done, in miscalculating and failing to understand the true nature of communism. In the 1930's, and especially during

World War II when Russia was a military ally, this foreign ideology gained tremendous strength.

The Party in 1944 claimed a membership of 80,000. Communist fronts welcomed overflow crowds; distinguished citizens flocked to do their work. A great backlog of influence was built up upon which the Party is still drawing. Thought-control nets touched, in one way or another, literally thousands of sympathizers and victims. Many individuals, people who should have known better, went completely overboard, hailing communism as "Twentieth-century Americanism," a term widely publicized by the communists themselves.

Henry A. Wallace, in a frank and forthright article entitled "Where I Was Wrong," published in *This Week* magazine on September 7, 1952, graphically pictured the communist power of deception, how he incorrectly interpreted communism and its counterpart, Russian imperialism.

While Vice-President of the United States, and even later, Wallace thought Russia "wanted and needed peace." He visited the Soviet Union in 1944 and was favorably impressed. But, as the article relates, he did not realize during his tour the feverish efforts being made by the Soviets to hoodwink him. For example, he visited Magadan, a city in Siberia, which was one of the Soviets' most notorious slave labor camps. "Nothing I saw at Magadan or anywhere else in Soviet Asia suggested slave labor." Later he learned of the Soviet actions

> . . . to pull the wool over our eyes and make Magadan into a Potemkin village [an ideal show city especially built for visitors] for my inspection. Watch towers were torn down. Prisoners were herded away out of sight. On this basis, what we saw produced a false impression.

Mr. Wallace then added these important words:

> . . . what I did not see was the Soviet determination to enslave the common man morally, mentally and physically for its own imperial purposes.

The communists claim to be many things they are not. All

over the world and in every field of human life they have erected false fronts, Potemkin villages, to fool and enslave mankind.

8.

Why Do People Become Communists?

IN THE LAST CHAPTER the Five False Claims of Communism showed how, in truth, communists stand for everything that is abhorred by normal Americans.

Why, then, do Americans turn communist?

The answer involves many details and is not simple. Most communists are ordinary-looking people, like your seatmate on the bus or a clerk in one of your neighborhood stores.

Most communists in the United States are now native-born. Others are naturalized citizens; a few are aliens. Some have never gone to school and have difficulty reading and writing. Many are well educated and have college and university degrees. Often they possess special talents in one field or another.

A member may earn his living in practically any occupation or profession. Not long ago a large Communist Party section listed members in these categories, tabulated as "professional and white collar": artists, actors, doctors, dentists, educators, engineers, draftsmen, lawyers, musicians, nurses, newspaper writers, office workers, salesmen, social-service workers, pharmacists, clergymen. Or a member may be a butcher, carpenter, mechanic, truck driver, plumber, or laborer.

Members are recruited from all nationalities, races, and areas of the country. They may live in expensive mansions or tumble-down homes. They are of all ages. Never can a communist be identified simply by his physical appearance, occupation, or clothes.

Why, you may ask, do these individuals join? And why, especially in this country, which, under democracy, has such a long and heartening record of expanding privilege and opportunity for so many?

Perhaps we can better understand why members join if we look at an actual case, which we can call the Case of Lost Faith.

Jack was born in a Midwestern city. He was tall, brown-haired, and possessed a pleasant disposition. He liked school and endeavored to please his teachers. He was intensely curious concerning the world about him, especially the physical sciences.

Then something started to happen to him, slowly but surely. His faith in God and religion seemed to be fading. As he later told FBI agents, he felt this loss already in high school. By the time of his graduation his faith in religion, which as a small child had been most sincere and tenacious, had completely disappeared. There was now inside him a spiritual vacuum.

Upon entering college Jack found himself with an exceedingly curious mind but one uncontrolled by any spiritual faith. In a class on government he made the acquaintance of the *Communist Manifesto*. Later he read sections of Engels' *Anti-Dühring*, which, among other things, discusses Marxist theory in relation to science. He was impressed. Here were some ideas that seemed to offer something positive and new.

Then one day, almost by chance, he came upon a leaflet distributed on the campus by a communist club. Jack became interested and made contact with the Party. Here, for the first time, he seemed to find an "answer" to the problems that had plagued him. Here, in the Party's claim to be working for a better world, Jack believed he had found a new "faith," which would give meaning and validity to his life. Though later he was to realize his tragic error, Jack joined the Communist Party.

In many instances we know, joining the Communist Party

comes from a loss of faith, so to speak, in our Judaic-Christian heritage and earnest, though perverted, seeking for a new faith. The individual is trying to find solutions to problems, real or fancied, that disturb his life. Many reasons cause individuals to join the Party, but undoubtedly most important is the Party's appeal to idealistic motivations, to a "bright new world" where justice, peace, and freedom will replace strife, injustice, and inhumanity. "I believed that in the Communist Party was the beginning of a true brotherhood of man, working with devotion for socialism, peace and democracy," wrote Howard Fast, one of the Party's best-known writers, later to become bitterly disillusioned. ". . . I believed, as did millions of men of good will, that the only truth about the Soviet Union was the picture presented by friends of the Soviet Union."

Communism with its deceitful double talk exploits these basic human yearnings for better social conditions, racial equality, justice, and peace, and places them in the service of tyranny. In this way, strange as it may sound, communists are able to entice free men to fight for slavery in the name of freedom.

Unfortunately, this idealistic motivation has given thousands of members, from brilliant scientists like Klaus Fuchs to ordinary laboring men, undaunted zeal and enthusiasm. Members driven on by this idealism have been willing to sacrifice their homes, families, and lives for the cause. They have become inflamed with a passionate, though twisted, courage. This is the motivation of the New York functionary who thought that five or six hours of sleep a night were sufficient for any member and regarded any request for time off as traitorous. "You can get your recreation after the revolution," she once snapped at an associate.

The Communist Party, in a very true sense, becomes as in the case of Jack a new but bigoted faith.

The FBI has interviewed many hundreds of Party members. A few case histories will illustrate why many joined. By understanding these influences we can do much to defeat the Party's present recruitment drive.

Let's take the case of Eric. He is typical of the many who

joined the Party during the economic depression. He remembered his youth as days of "deprivation." He worked at odd jobs, such as helping the milkman and caring for chickens. But everywhere he went he met bitter frustrations. He became more and more dissatisfied with existing economic conditions.

Then one day at a secondhand bookstore he came upon some documents that alleged very unsatisfactory conditions in American economic life. Eric bought and read these documents. "The effect upon me was profound; I don't believe that anything I have ever read has had the same impact upon me since." In his own words, he felt a "terrific compulsion . . . to do something to help better the conditions brought out in the report." He was swept up by a desire to wipe out prejudice, to "help bring the underdog of our civilization up to a place of dignity."

Eric had never talked to a Party member. He had no personal knowledge of communism. Yet somewhere he had formed a false impression of the Communist Party, based on communist propaganda. "I knew that it . . . somehow had come to believe that it considered all men equal, that it was fighting for the underdog, that it had no prejudices against color of skin or religion."

Motivated by these errors, Eric on his own initiative went to a corner drugstore, looked up the Party's address in the telephone directory, and called headquarters. He told how Party officials seemed "surprised" when he stated his desire to join.

With determination in his heart, Eric went to Party headquarters, climbed the brownstone steps to the front door, and rang the bell. A young lady answered. He asked if this was Party headquarters. She said no but pointed to a basement entrance. There, in the presence of an eighteen-year-old girl and a dark-haired, stooped man, Eric signed an application card for Party membership. His tragic decision had been made with gusto and enthusiasm.

Karl as a young man, like Eric, was deeply affected by the depression. He told how he had seen people eating out of garbage cans. He felt that something had to be done to remedy conditions. Moreover, in his opinion, the incumbent government was not adequate to cope with the problems.

Soon he began to read communist literature and in 1934 joined the Young Communist League. But this was to be only the beginning.

In 1936 came the Spanish Civil War. Karl, because of communist agitation, became deeply interested. He detested Hitler and fascism. Mussolini and his Black Shirts were even more detestable. The more he thought about international developments, the more he had the urge to take a personal hand in the situation. His hatred of fascism was intensified when some of his relatives had to flee from Europe because of Mussolini's persecution.

Full of youthful vigor, Karl went to Spain as a volunteer in the Abraham Lincoln Brigade. Here on the front lines he was wounded and to this day bears the effects of the injury. This impetuous decision, taken against the advice of his family, represented a contribution of the Communist Party of the United States to international communism. Karl's idealistic fervor against fascism and injustice was translated into shot and powder for the furtherance of communist aims.

Many thousands of Americans joined the communist movement during these early days of the fight against fascism. The hardships of depression days contributed to the deceptive appeals of communism. These men and women, seeking solutions, thought incorrectly that the panacea lay in communism. They labored under the illusion that the Party and Soviet Russia represented a better democracy. As one disillusioned member was later to complain, "At this time the Communist apologists stressed idealistic goals, and bragged of a growing democracy in Russia."

Many individuals have joined the Party in the vain hope of improving social conditions, gaining better housing, or achieving better relations between the races.

Ralph was typical of many. He was a Negro, proud of his race and eager to help better its status in America. While in school he prepared a thesis on this subject. Wanting to secure various opinions, he asked several friends to read his manuscript. One of these, a fellow student, remarked after reading the paper that Ralph's approach had been very naïve and that further study should be undertaken. Thereupon he furnished Ralph with information about Karl Marx and the communist viewpoint.

The communist position appealed to Ralph. Here was an organization that claimed that it was working zealously for the betterment of the Negro. The propaganda appeals seemed to point the direction that Ralph should take. He succumbed and joined the Communist Party. He was to learn that the Party has no sincere concern for the Negro but was and is using deceptive propaganda appeals to advance the communist cause.

The very same communist tactic applies in the field of labor unions. Edward was an active member of his union. In the early 1940's he was recruited into the Communist Party and assigned to a club in the industrial section of the Party. Why had he joined? "When I joined the Communist Party I believed that I was joining a political party that would benefit the workingman." Three years later he dropped out of the Party; it was *not* for the workingman. Rather it aimed at killing individual rights, making unions subservient to Party orders, and using union strength, influence, and finances to further communist goals.

The Party today is still busily at work trying to infiltrate unions. Historically, communists, including Lenin, have taught that communists must infiltrate unions. Every union member must realize that the communist interest in labor organizations is insincere. Past communist appeals have been recognized as false by patriotic union leaders themselves. Today's communist appeal is no less false or dangerous than those of previous years. Our knowledge of how the Party operated in the past is one of our best weapons in defeating its techniques today.

The list of specific reasons for joining the Party, growing out of a desire to improve our nation, would be long. One woman was interested in social problems, such as slum clearance and better housing. Communists claimed to favor the same things as she. She believed and joined. Another individual, as a young minister, saw many injustices in a Northern state. Still another, arriving home from overseas, felt that the war had not accomplished any semblance of peace; he was displeased with American policy. He walked into Party headquarters on his own initiative and signed up.

Over the years thousands of Americans have entered the doors of communism. The turnover of Party membership has been great. Besides those motivated from idealistic reasons, there have been curiosity- and adventure-seekers, opportunists, disgruntled misfits, and power-hungry personalities. Some of these have consciously sought out the Party; others have just drifted into it. Many were youngsters, wanting to dance and sing. Some wanted social companionship. In others, sexual appeal played a role.

The Party, falsely representing itself as the final answer to *all* of society's problems, economic, social, political, and religious, makes ready use of the various hopes, fears, and aspirations of recruits. This dynamic deceit of communist action provides an immediate channel for energy and enthusiasm. Within hours a recruit will be handing out leaflets or running errands. He gets the feeling of being in action *now* and not having to wait to participate in the fight for what he conceives to be a better world. Many recruits to the Party, when asked later why they didn't offer their talents to legitimate organizations concerned with reform, said such groups were "too slow." In the Party they found that "immediacy" which so satisfied them.

Then, in working in the Party, the recruit is promised a "belongingness," a feeling of comradeship that can be won only in day-to-day battles for the greatest of causes. The member is told that he is part of a world-wide movement based on the most "enlightened," "advanced," and "scientific" principles. Unfortunately the Party has been able to generate great enthusiasm through this teaching. One member told the FBI that the slogan, "vanguard of the working class," had appealed to him. He felt that not only was he contributing his own talents to the cause but he was "leading," "educating," and "guiding" others. "I think this activity was satisfying something in me," another stated. Such an approach often deceives recruits, especially those of an egotistical nature, who appreciate the prospect of achieving personal "power" inside the Party structure where the chief qualification for advancement is not ability, education, or talent but loyalty to the Party. One high Party leader whose authority over Party disciplinary matters extended across half a continent was in ordinary life a day laborer. The flattering of his ego from his Party position can well be imagined.

In particular the communists have made an appeal to the so-called intellectual. The seduction of many intellectuals over the years by the Party stands as a disgrace. Thinking men and women, trained to analyze critically, all too often have been duped.

Our experience has shown that members joining the Party for idealistic reasons are more likely to stay in the movement than those not so motivated. Of course, this is not always true. Though joining the Party in a sincere attempt to better society, a member may quickly become disillusioned. However, time after time members who join for curiosity, for social reasons, or for sexual pleasure soon drift out. They are usually not the material from which hard-core communists are made. Here is an example:

Gladys was a college girl, rather gay, not too serious, with a great deal of leisure. She attended some Marxist study groups. Here Russia and communism were painted in rosy colors. After several meetings she was invited to join the Party. She accepted, 80 per cent, she said, out of curiosity and partly because she felt that if the communists could achieve a "peaceful" world about which they talked, it would be a "nice thing." Other reasons Gladys gave for joining: to have something to do and to alleviate "boredom." She described Party literature as more amusing than educational. Needless to say, she did not stay in the movement. Even Party officials, in her opinion, never seemed to trust her.

A sad group of recruits are simply the twisted, mixed-up neurotics. Perhaps as sons and daughters of well-to-do parents they harbor a "guilt complex" about the very privileges that

America has given them. Or, because of some setback in life, they are angry at society and turn to communism as a way to "get even."

Let's look at Larry, a communist in a Midwestern state. Ever since youth, he had felt a "persecution complex." Everywhere he looked he seemed to see despair and strife. The whole of society, he concluded, was strictly a dog-eat-dog affair, with life being divided between the have's and the have-not's. Such an attitude was intensified by an "artistic" and "sensitive" temperament. Seeing these "injustices," he felt compelled to help the "persecuted." At first he became just a "reformer"; then, after reading Marxist literature, he joined the Party. Twisted, distorted, and maladjusted, he is today even more confused. He found that the Party only exploited his neurotic condition to make use of his services.

The techniques of actual recruitment vary. In most instances indoctrination comes slowly. A fellow union member, worker, or associate who is a Party member will "work" on the prospect. First come conversations about mutual interests such as union activities. Deftly the communist slant will be emphasized. Perhaps then will come communist literature or an invitation to a "study group." Step by step the recruit becomes enmeshed in the Party's efficient recruitment apparatus.

A former member told how she first became acquainted with communism, which she was later to reject. She was living a lonely life in a boardinghouse. She noticed that some of her neighbors had many friends who laughed and chattered gaily. Apparently they had common interests that drew them together. One night she heard the muffled overtones of what sounded like a meeting next door: "Overcome by my growing curiosity about them, I snooped as no lady should. I sat on the bed and pressed my ear against the plaster wall. As their subdued voices rose and fell, I caught words and snatches. I don't know now what I heard, or what could have convinced me in my great ignorance of that time. But before the meeting adjourned, I believed my jolly neighbors were Communists, and that I was listening to a secret meeting of a Communist cell of

Government workers! They did not look as Communists were pictured, and they were not plotting bomb-throwing or assassination, but some much duller discussion with long words." In her loneliness this woman joined the Communist Party but found neither "happiness" nor a "sense of direction"—only bitter disappointments.

Party fronts offer excellent means of recruitment. Be assured that every noncommunist who actively participates in a front is under the Party's close scrutiny. Sometimes, of course, as we have seen, an individual is more useful to the Party by remaining a nonmember, a sympathizer, or a fellow traveler. At other times, if the prospect seems to offer a fertile field of recruitment, pressure is applied. Thousands of Party members were recruited through the many fronts operating in the 1930's and 1940's.

Of special interest to the Party are young people. The Party's youth organizations, such as the Young Communist League and its successors, are largely recruiters of young people for communism. Many Party-sponsored activities—dances, parties, and picnics—are aimed to win the allegiance of boys and girls. Time after time members join as teen-agers —the age at which the Party would like to capture minds.

Many Party members have been recruited from communist homes, the children of Party members. In America today many hundreds of children, growing up in communist homes, are captives of this alien ideology. These youngsters are taught from the earliest years that God does not exist. One communist mother in a Northern state taught her children that God was not real. She said that it was fun to watch Superman on TV but that a person must recognize that he doesn't actually exist. It's the same way, she said, with God. In another city a communist father noticed a religious program on the family television set. He uttered a derogatory remark and turned off the program with the exclamation, "I'm a Marxist."

Party parents provide special Marxist instruction for their children. One father would sit down with his youngsters and discuss items appearing in the *Daily Worker;* another gave regular quizzes on Marxist literature; still another lectured on

Marxist economics every morning at the breakfast table. When the child grows up, he is given Party tasks: distributing literature, taking up collections at rallies, walking in picket lines. He begins to get the "feel" of Party life. In one instance a communist family gathered around a table and spent an hour or two in Party self-criticism and promising to do better. Party morality is constantly being inculcated in these youthful minds, a belief that whatever helps the Party is good, whatever hinders it is immoral. In one instance a communist father denounced a federal law that restricted the activities of the Party. His teen-age son, confused by the statement, pointed out that the Act was part of the law of the land. "Son," the father replied, "if a law is bad, you do not have to obey it."

No wonder many hundreds of recruits spring from communist homes as devotees of Marxism-Leninism.

Our experience has shown that reasons for joining the Party are many, varied, and complicated. Each individual has his own personal problems, hopes, and aspirations. Any attempt to apply generalized, ready-made stereotypes is to leave the problem unsolved. Moreover, we must try to see the *total man;* that is, all the forces, events, ideas, and motivations that brought about his tragic decision. For that reason each member deserves careful study. In the next chapter I shall discuss the reasons why members leave the Party. Here again we must understand each member as a human being, as an individual, always remembering that even though still a bigoted devotee he is convertible. Any thinking Party member will soon recognize the basic contradictions of communism.

We should be alert to help any communist back on the road to good American citizenship as soon as he shows the slightest indication that he is disillusioned with what he has found inside Party circles.

What lesson can we as a society learn from the Party's methods of recruitment? Most important, I think, is to realize that the Communist Party is attempting to exploit the rise of materialism, irreligion, and lack of faith in our society. In an era when moral standards have been lowered, when family life has been disrupted, when crime and juvenile delinquency rates are high, communists have tried to set forth a goal—dressed in attractive phrases—that would captivate the longings and hopes of men and women. They have, in truth, tried to "steal" the nobility, the fervor, the enthusiasm of a free government under God.

9.

Why People Break with Communism

JUST AS IMPORTANT as knowing why people join the Communist Party is understanding why they leave. Here again, by recognizing the influences that cause them to reject this alien doctrine, we can do much to defeat the communist conspiracy.

Always we must keep in mind that communists, even hard-core members, potentially can be converted. To the individual who asserts, "Once a communist, always a communist," I say: "No. Every communist can be made to see the errors of his way. He must not be despised, belittled, or rejected as hopelessly lost. He can redeem himself by actively taking a stand for freedom. Every patriotic American must do what he can to bring these persons to see the truth. The ex-communist is today one of our most potent weapons against communism."

On September 9, 1957, the *Daily Worker* published a story which stated: "Joseph Clark has resigned from the Daily Worker, of which he was foreign editor, and from membership in the Communist Party."

Clark was a Party member for twenty-eight years, always known as an ardent one. When Stalin died, Clark was his paper's correspondent in Moscow. Yet, by his own current processes of thinking he saw the futility of the Party.

Howard Fast, well-known communist author, was mentioned in the last chapter. After years of Party membership and thousands of words of communist propaganda, he quit. The revelations of Khrushchev about Stalin's murderous regime were too much. "The dimensions of this horror were not only beyond anything we could have dreamed of . . . I was filled with loathing and disgust."

On the West Coast Barbara Hartle, because of her fiery energy and zeal, was recognized in Party circles as the outstanding woman communist in the Pacific Northwest. So active was she in Party circles that she was indicted, tried, and convicted under the Smith Act. But she, too, became disillusioned. Like Louis Budenz, Bella Dodd, Howard Fast, and Joseph Clark, she added her name to the growing list of communists who have said, "We've had enough. We're quitting."

To understand why members break with the Party, let's examine the case of Barbara Hartle, who exemplifies the anguish of a Party official desperately seeking her way to freedom. Her experiences may enable members still in the Party to look into their own hearts. Are they being beset by the same doubts? Why have these doubts arisen? What is working to increase or to quell them?

On the other hand, Barbara Hartle's story will give the patriotic citizen an appreciation of the anguish experienced by Party members on their journey to freedom. He can learn to be understanding, patient, and helpful. He will see, for instance, how a sympathetic citizen helped Barbara free herself from communist entanglement.

On March 12, 1954, Barbara Hartle walked into the Seattle office of the FBI. She didn't need to identify herself. The previous October she, along with four other top Party leaders, had been convicted in Seattle under the Smith Act.

Barbara Hartle told her story: She had been graduated in 1929, Phi Beta Kappa, from Washington State College, majoring in English; then she went to Spokane, trying to find a job. Those were depression days and her story is all too typical. Hoping for a "better world," she began to read Karl Marx. Deeply impressed, she joined the Socialist, then the Communist, Party. Her rise was rapid. Later she was transferred to Seattle where she occupied some of the highest Party positions in the Washington State organization. "I'll go to jail if I must," she once declared, "but I'll remain a communist."

One day in 1945 Barbara Hartle sat writing an article for the communist press. Earl Browder was on his way out as head of the communist movement. By force of habit she defended him. But Party experience taught otherwise. Foster was now the "boss." Confused by the sudden Party shift, she tore up the article.

Later, back on the Party line, she wrote another article supporting Foster. But something had happened. Out of this confusion, this "great surprise," as she termed it, of the Party switch, she seemed suddenly to have seen something new— that the Party was not what it claimed to be, but a fraudulent deception. To Barbara Hartle, as to many communists, doubt had come, an indication that the breath of freedom was still alive in her.

As in many such cases, this confusion and doubt quickly disappeared, swallowed up in the rush of Party life. In 1939 she had become disturbed by the Party's position on the Hitler-Stalin pact, but this also had passed. She soon became the same fanatical Barbara Hartle, attending meetings, issuing orders, making speeches.

Yet these doubts were to be followed by other doubts. Now she began, as she later explained, to become conscious of certain features of Party life that she had not previously noticed. She listed some of them:

1. The constant factional struggle for leadership.
2. The hand-picking of leaders from the top.
3. The arbitrary handling of funds by some of the top officials.
4. Finding the "self-criticism" of leaders to be mere "empty promises."

5. The "furious resistance" of Party leaders to criticism or guidance offered by rank-and-file members.
6. The expulsion of members by "rigged trials."

Like a searchlight, these doubts began to search out other doubts, inconsistencies, and contradictions. The fissure of doubt was widening.

Now Barbara was to experience a phenomenon that affects every Party member trying to break the communist spell: *the counterattack of the unconscious Party discipline.*

Doubts would suddenly arise, then disappear. They would arise again but again disappear. When she seemed to want to slow up in her Party work, her old enthusiasm would return. She found, as she later explained, that her "process of mental reorientation was impeded by the study and teaching of Marxist-Leninist works, which is the Communist Party's antidote for such an eventuality."

> Over a long period and through a slow process of constant discussion, schools, and self study the Communist Party builds a conscience of responsibility upon which it then relies to keep a member functioning, even though any real desire to do so has passed.

That's why the Party keeps stressing Marxist-Leninist education: Party schools, reading the communist press, self-study. It builds up a discipline that automatically attacks doubts, rationalizes contradictions inside the Party structure, and guides every decision in the Party's favor.

Then, in mid-1950, an important event occurred for Barbara Hartle. She received instructions to attend a secret meeting in Woodland Park, Seattle. There she was told to change her name, leave Seattle, and enter the Party's underground. For the next two years she lived under assumed names in various Washington State and Oregon cities.

The unending hustle and bustle of everyday Party activity ceased. As she sat in a lonely room or stood on a dark street corner waiting for an underground meeting, she now had time to think. Suddenly all the doubts that had been slowly accumulating came together. At the same time the restraining influences of Party discipline became weaker.

> A more rapid disillusionment on my part took place when I left the active Communist Party upon leaving Seattle to enter the Communist Party underground movement. Without direct day to day pressure, with less reading of Marxist-Leninist works and with increased reading of other material, and through coming into contact with average people my mental processes were hastened. The culmination of this process was my decision to leave the Communist Party and to live my own life.

She became convinced that the Communist Party was an evil; that it did not represent a way to better social or economic conditions; that it was a fraud and a deception.

> I never realized that this discipline and this mental and physical domination of the Communist Party over its members is necessary to it in order to continue its double life of posing as one thing and being another. I had never before realized that the many unsolved problems I had noted while still a Communist Party member were products of this double existence.

It was one thing, however, to break intellectually with the Party, another to break openly. That was now to be Barbara Hartle's anguish and the anguish of so many members still in the Party today.

Barbara was living in a no-man's land: she had broken with the world of tyranny yet was held by the power that had robbed her of freedom. The indecision began to tear her apart. She was spiritually sick. At first she kept saying to herself and the Party, "I'll be all right. Just give me a little time. I'll work this out." She just couldn't realize that these doubts were permanent signs of a new life, not temporary confusions in an old allegiance. Merely to drift away quietly wasn't possible.

The Party wouldn't allow that. The only way was to redeem herself by walking boldly forward.

This she did in March, 1954. And here is what a sympathetic citizen can do to help. Mr. Traynor Hansen, a reporter for the Seattle *Post-Intelligencer*, had covered the 1953 Seattle Smith Act trial. He noticed, as did others, that Barbara Hartle lacked the fiery disposition of the other defendants. Later, while on bond, she had long visits with him. It was his counsel that she go to the FBI since it would have been improper under the circumstances for us to go to her.

To Barbara Hartle's lasting credit, she did not try to evade responsibilities for her past errors. The information that she furnished the FBI is now at work against the very Party that for almost twenty years duped her. And she, with a clear conscience, is winning back the respect and esteem she had before the Party stole her away. She deserves aid as she reconstructs her life.

Many interviews with Party members reflect numerous men and women inside the movement today in various stages of disillusionment. Such doubts are good omens. They indicate that not all members are lost beyond recall. By the very nature of Party discipline doubts are inevitable. Any member in the Party today without doubts is indeed a complete slave.

What causes doubt to arise in the minds of members? Our experiences reveal these major categories:

1. *The absence of freedom inside the Party.* The greatest single factor making for doubt is the lack of democracy inside the Party. "I was constantly whipped into line," one member said, "on policies and issues with which I disagreed." "Discussions at meetings were not open. . . ." Party organizers would come and tell the club what to do. "Why Writer Quit Reds: They Frown on Thinking," read a headline in a New York City newspaper. This member could no longer force himself "to live in the stifling atmosphere of the party line with all its ruthless intolerance for the processes of the mind." In another instance a woman told us how she had voted "no"

in a Party meeting. "People literally moved their chairs away from me. I walked out of the meeting and never attended a Communist Party meeting again."

More and more intellectuals are realizing that the Party is simply exploiting their prestige and talents, without trusting them. Intellectuals are encouraged to think, if they think the "right" way; but any independent thinking is not allowed. That is why, in the final analysis, the Party keeps the pressure on its members who are intellectuals. It fears that they might start thinking for themselves. As one intellectual stated, "I think that the Party was using me, as they were many other intellectuals . . . I always had the feeling that they never trusted intellectuals beyond a certain limit. . . ."

2. *The inability to live a normal life.* Closely allied is the impossibility of living as a decent human being. One member said he resented the Party's constantly demanding his time. There was no end of assignments: distributing literature, attending meetings, getting petitions signed. Another member complained that she was "sick and tired" of her husband's putting the Party before her and the children. The Party's instructions must always take precedence. This constant stealing of time, never allowing the member to relax, develop a hobby, or enjoy a family, provokes the most searching doubts.

3. *The Party's callous disregard of members' personal problems.* A Party official's wife was sick. He asked for time off. It was refused. Or, a member's home must be mortgaged in a fund drive. And if he cannot make payments, it's his hard luck. Again, an old-time member was sent underground. He was instructed to change his name, sell his car and personal belongings, leave his wife and not contact her. He asked Party permission to visit his family. The answer: no. He came home anyhow and was severely disciplined.

No wonder more and more members are asking, "Why continue to be exploited?"

4. *Discrepancy between Party practices and claims.* As we have seen, many members join in the mistaken belief that the Party will improve some social evil, such as racial inequality or inadequate housing. "It is frankly recognized in Communist theory," one disillusioned old-timer confessed, "that the whole strategy is not for the main purpose of Negro liberation, but for the purpose of the proletarian revolution." "My dissatisfaction with the Party and my break with the Party came about through a gradual process as a result of the realization that Party policy was a detriment to true trade unionism."

Like Barbara Hartle, dubious communists see the internal squabbles and feuds, rigged elections, trumped-up evidence, the striving to be little commissars. Party leaders stay in fancy hotels or take vacations, while rank-and-file members are hounded to donate the last dollar. All this is disillusioning, especially in an organization that claims to be working for a just society.

5. *Communist tyranny in Russia and behind the Iron Curtain.* The sensational revelations of Khrushchev concerning the crimes of Stalin rocked the Party apparatus. Then came indisputable evidence of anti-Semitism in Russia and in November, 1956, the capping blow, suppression of Hungary by Soviet troops, the spectacle of a self-proclaimed leader of "people's rights" physically strangling a people's demand for liberty.

This caused Howard Fast to strike violently at the Party that could give birth to "the explosive and hellish revelations of the Khrushchev 'secret report' " when he said:

> I felt a sense of unmitigated mental nausea at the realization that I had supported and defended this murderous bloodbath, and I felt, as so many did then, a sense of being a victim of the most incredible swindle in modern times.

About Hungary: "From Hungary and its tragedy we learned of a new kind of socialism—socialism by slaughter and terror."

No wonder Fast laments, "A life-long structure of belief lies shattered around me. . . ."

Another member who had been in the Party almost twenty years told our agents that she was quitting. If what happened in Russia, as revealed by Khrushchev, was true, she wanted "no part" of it. Still another member with over twenty-five years in the movement admitted that Soviet intervention in Hungary brought things to a head for him. If he were in Hungary, he said, he would be a Freedom Fighter.

Every abrupt change in the Party line, such as the 1939 Hitler-Stalin Pact or the 1945 ousting of Browder, jars many members. However, no event in Party life has been so conducive to raising doubts among members as the Khrushchev report and its sequel.

6. *Communist opposition to religion.* Member after member has related that the Party's claims that God doesn't exist and that religion is a myth have raised doubts. Many members carry within their hearts the influence of religious training received while they were young. They inwardly rebel at a materialist solution to life.

Then there is the protest against the Marxist doctrine, which, in the words of one former member, "purports to reduce man's problems and destiny to an economic formula." In deeply emotional terms he added, "I want my children to approach their world and the history behind it, with the curiosity and objectivity it takes to learn. I do not want them to feel that the questions are answered, that this or that little system is the slide rule for answering all their questions."

These, then, are some of the reasons why doubts concerning communism arise in members' minds. Why do many still hesitate to break with the Party? The answer: They are still under the influence of false fears.

1. *Fear of the FBI.* One member, when interviewed by the FBI, expressed amazement at the cordial treatment accorded him. "I thought you fellows would drag me from my house."

Communists for years have poured scorn and contempt on the FBI. They try to paint our agents as brutal thugs in the hope of driving a wedge between their members and the government. One highly placed member, visited by the FBI, turned what was expected to be a fifteen-minute interview into a five-hour discussion, during which he said, "The Party considers the FBI its prime enemy and Party members are expected to denounce the FBI." The FBI wants sincerely to help these individuals. They should feel free to counsel with us. Members can be assured that they will be cordially received, not embarrassed, and that their information will be kept strictly confidential, should they so request or if there is good reason to protect their identity.

2. *Fear of being a "stool pigeon."* This false belief, inspired by Party discipline, is today keeping many lost souls silent. Our agents asked one Party member, "Suppose a criminal gang kidnaped one of your children. What would you do?" The answer: "Call the FBI." "Would you want the FBI to make inquiries to locate the youngster?" "Yes." "Would you expect citizens having pertinent knowledge of this criminal conspiracy to give that information to the FBI?" "Certainly," he said.

The communist member furnishing information to the FBI is also doing his moral and patriotic duty in helping crush a criminal conspiracy. To remain silent is to assist the Party. Communism, like a criminal gang, thrives when people able to combat it refuse to do so. "Stool pigeon" is a Party-defined term used as a weapon to enforce communist discipline. The Party is enabled to reach into men's minds, censor their thoughts and words, and thereby buttress tyranny.

3. *Fear of personal safety and reputation.* Some members fear the rabid hatred that the Party spews out at members leaving the movement. A West Coast communist, though disillusioned, didn't break with the Party. He feared that his communist friends would ostracize him. Finally, though hesi-

tantly, he said he was now willing to "risk" being with the majority of Americans!

Party members should not fear the hostility of their former Party associates. To be denounced by communists is an honor. Remember, the example of a Party member breaking with the Party may influence others to do likewise.

4. *Fear of disgracing their families.* Many members trapped in the Party dread that their loved ones will know of their involvement. One man, asked if his wife and children knew of his communist background, began to cry. Another said he would do anything to keep his young son from knowing. Not long ago our agents contacted a Party member. "Don't talk to me at home," she said. "I don't want the children to know. Call me on the phone." Her wishes were respected.

To remain silent is not to improve the situation. There is no way in which such cooperation will injure the family. One member, very thankful that he had cooperated with the FBI, said he was happily married and simply would not allow his communist background to injure his innocent family.

5. *Fear of not being received as a loyal American.* The answer lies largely with the Party member himself. It is within his power alone to break completely with communism. He will be judged by his actions, not alone by his words. The biblical advice holds true: ". . . by their fruits ye shall know them."

In addition, patriotic Americans must do their share to help these Party members. Many are driven back into Party tyranny by the inexcusable ignorance, rancor, and pride of noncommunists. Moreover, it does not help when the truly reformed communist is characterized as a "renegade" and "traitor"—terms which would normally be used by communists themselves and not by good Americans.

In November, 1953, I wrote an article entitled "Breaking the Communist Spell," which appeared in *This Week* magazine. It was an appeal to members disillusioned with commu-

nism to step forward and help in the fight against Soviet
tyranny. The response was encouraging. In an Eastern city a
caller said he had read the article and wanted to give information about Party activities. Another person told our agents,
"It's never easy to tell such a story . . . Then I saw an appeal
by J. Edgar Hoover in a recent magazine article and after
reading it several times felt that I should make a special effort
to remember and pull what I could into order."

I want to set forth again the salient portions of this article.
It seems to sum up what we have been trying to say on this
most important subject:

> The individual contributions of former members of the Com-
> munist Party to the security of our way of life are shining ex-
> amples of people who have recognized their mistakes and are
> doing all within their power to rectify them.

* * * *

> If, having knowledge of persons and activities detrimental
> to his country, he breaks from the Party, yet maintains silence,
> he is still aiding the enemy. The moral obligation involved
> cannot be met by silence. The choice is simple: *help the
> United States.* The man who does this is preserving freedom
> under law. He is protecting the American way of life for free
> men and women—including his family and himself.

* * * *

> These people deserve the nation's respect, and their neigh-
> bors' fair-minded forgiveness for their past devotion to Com-
> munism. Their means of livelihood must be protected, and
> loyal Americans must accept their sincere repentance as a re-
> turn to the full scope of citizenship. All great religions teach
> that the sinner can always redeem himself. Who, then, shall
> sit in judgment on the ex-Communist? Who dare deny him
> the promise held out to those who repent of the evil they have
> done and who try to make amends?

For our part, at the FBI, we have always sought to recognize the very real human and personal problems facing the ex-Communists who have come to our offices to make such amends . . .

In discussing the ex-Communist, those who piously say that the leopard never changes its spots forget that they are speaking of human beings—mortal creatures with immortal souls. And those who say "Once a Communist, always a Communist" are simply advertising their ignorance. To deny that men can change is to deny the truths which have eternally guided civilized man.

Part IV

LIFE IN THE PARTY

10.

How the Party Is Organized

LOOK IN FOR A MINUTE on a typical secret meeting of a communist "club" or cell "somewhere in the United States." This particular meeting is selected because it is typical of hundreds of such meetings.

The house is frame, painted gray with green shutters. A wire fence runs around the trim yard. The owner works as a draftsman in a downtown company, his wife keeps house. They have lived in the neighborhood for many years.

It is now dark, a little after eight o'clock on a winter evening. The downstairs light is on, the blinds are drawn. A man comes to the front door, raps lightly, and is admitted. Soon another man, walking at a leisurely pace, rounds the corner and enters. He has parked his car on another street.

Ten minutes pass. A third man knocks. He has come by bus from downtown. To make certain nobody was following him, he had ridden two stops past his correct destination, then walked back. Five minutes later a fourth person, a woman in a dark coat, arrives. Everything is quiet: no loud voices, no cars parked in front, no reasons for the neighbors to suspect that a Communist Party meeting is in progress.

Communist Party groups like this are small, containing three, four, or five people—a security precaution. In that way fewer members know each other and detection is less likely. Meeting places are frequently changed: this evening a private home, next time a public library or an automobile. Members have been known to sit on park benches, in bus terminals, even in hospital waiting rooms, hatching their plots in casual, conversational tones.

The third man is the Party organizer, a paid official who serves as the group's leader. He sits in a chair in the corner; the others form a rough semicircle. He speaks quietly but in a commanding tone, acting the dictator that he actually is.

"Joe," he says, addressing the first man to arrive, "you remember the last time we met you were given an assignment to collect three to five thousand sheets of paper, a Mimeograph machine, and some ink. How did things go?"

"Fine," Joe replies. "I bought four thousand sheets of paper. Got them at three different stores."

"Good," says the organizer, "that's using your head."

"I also bought a Mimeograph machine and plenty of ink. Everything's safe now in the right place." (The "right place" refers to an apartment in another section of the city occupied by a concealed communist, which the Party uses as a secret hideout.)

"One thing more," Joe says. "I've made inquiries about a portable printing press. It's pretty old, but it'll work."

"Fine," the organizer says, obviously pleased. "Follow that through. You took the serial numbers off the Mimeograph, didn't you?"

"No, I didn't," stammers the comrade. "I forgot . . ."

"Forgot!" explodes the organizer. "What's wrong with you? That's just plain stupid. Joe, this is serious business. You've got to keep alert. Someday this machine may be used to print secret Party instructions. We can't afford to have it traced. Take off all identification marks at once."

Then turning to another man, the one who had parked his car around the corner, the organizer says, "Phil, how are things coming at the plant? Making any progress on getting Bill installed as shop steward?"

"No, not much. Things look pretty bad." The man shifts his legs. He is a big fellow, weighing over two hundred pounds. "Looks like we're blocked."

"Nonsense," snaps the organizer, "we've gone over that before. There's always a way. Communists never give up.

You've got things good. You're at home enjoying life. Remember Lenin, exiled from Russia, going from town to town. He didn't quit, and look what he did. He was a genius. What's the big problem, Phil?"

"It's Red, the union president. He knows Bill is a communist and he's fighting him. Red is smart, he knows the ropes. He's always been a hard worker for labor unions. He's got a clean record and he's liked by the members. As long as Red is president, we're in a bad fix."

"That's the wrong attitude, Phil. If one thing won't work, try another. Can't we accuse him of something? Have you gone over his past life? Hasn't he ever done anything wrong?"

"If he has, we can't find it. He's a straight shooter from 'way back and he really hates communists."

"Phil, this is your Number One assignment," the organizer says. "You get something on Red. He's got to be discredited. Maybe we can make up some letters, mail them in another city, accuse him of working against the union. You figure out the details."

The organizer goes around the circle to the other members. Are they carrying out their assignments? Ethel, the draftsman's wife, thinks she will soon be elected an officer in a downtown women's group.

"Wonderful," says the organizer. "Don't rush things too fast but try to get some of the women to write letters to Washington. Let them say the FBI is a Gestapo; that they're violating civil liberties by arresting Party leaders. That's good, Ethel."

"They haven't the slightest idea I'm a communist." She laughs. "I'm working hard at it." The other woman, the last one to arrive, reports her activities as secretary of a communist-front organization.

The organizer, wanting the meeting to be short, speaks a few words about "new things" in the Party: A pamphlet from national headquarters has just been received and should be bought by all; finances are not in good shape; a new Party school is going to be held next month. Ethel should attend.

Shortly after nine o'clock the meeting is over, and as quietly as they have come the members slip out into the night.

This Communist Party club is representative of many hundreds throughout the nation. Night after night, week after week, these men and women are plotting against America, working out smears, seeking to discredit free government, and planning for revolution. They form the base of a gigantic pyramid of treason, stretching from the little gray house with green shutters to the towers of the Kremlin.

The Communist Constitution (18th version, 1957)

At least in theory the Communist Party, USA, is based on a "constitution," which sets forth the group's organizational structure. That constitution, being a public document, is filled with typical Aesopian language. The Party member, for example, isn't fooled when the constitution proclaims, "The Communist Party upholds the achievements of American democracy and defends the United States Constitution and its Bill of Rights . . ." He knows better. His Marxist training enables him to recognize the Party's real aim:

> The Communist Party seeks to advance the understanding of the working class in its day-to-day struggles for its historic mission, the establishment of socialism. (Preamble)

Here is the key, *"historic mission."* What does it mean? Not something traditional, respectable, or patriotic, but the overthrow of this government by force and violence. Engels talked about the "historic mission" of "the proletariat," which "can only free itself by doing away once for all with class dominion, subjugation, and exploitation." That, in communist terminology, means revolution. The Communist International spoke of the Party's "historic mission of achieving the dictatorship of the proletariat."

Today's communists, with deceitful double talk, are attempting to camouflage the true meaning of this old and well-defined revolutionary term. Comrades in the early 1920's weren't quite so squeamish about their intentions. The Party's constitution (1921) proclaimed the communist purpose:

. . . to destroy the bourgeois state machinery; to establish the Dictatorship of the Proletariat in the form of Soviet power; to abolish the capitalist system and to introduce the Communist Society. (Article I, Section 2)

Regardless of current communist claims, "historic mission" is the Party's linguistic description of its revolutionary intent.

The National Convention, according to the constitution, is the highest authority in the Party. This convention, normally held every two years, is composed of delegates "elected" by state or district conventions. The National Convention, after hearing "discussions" of the various issues, is authorized to make decisions binding upon the entire membership.

These affairs have the trappings of big-time conventions. Various committees are chosen, resolutions adopted, and speeches given. Proceedings are secret, although communists say they have nothing to hide. Members of the legitimate press are excluded. Exploiting this blackout of news, the communists often issue slanted press releases in an effort to influence public opinion. Another tactic is to allow the attendance of selected noncommunists, persons carefully hand-picked wherever possible, who the Party hopes will later make favorable reports.

Extensive preparations are made for the National Convention. Party officials as a general rule work up a "draft program," a summary of proposed Party aims on current issues, national and international. This "draft program" is widely circulated, with members being asked to discuss indicated approaches. Then, theoretically, the convention, based on the opinions developed, adopts a final program. Actually, in practice, the draft program represents a technique whereby the leadership "sells" the membership the ideas it wants to stress. Frequently, convention reports, resolutions, and speeches, properly edited, are later published. They serve as policy guides for the membership.

Never forgotten are Soviet trimmings. Proudly read on the floor of the Sixteenth National Convention (February 9-12, 1957) were greetings from the Central Committee of the

Communist Party of the Soviet Union. Other Communist
Parties in China, Canada, Italy, Japan, and Czechoslovakia
also sent "best wishes." From these, members gain a sense of
communist solidarity, or, in Party language, *proletarian internationalism,* the feeling that they are integral parts of the
world-wide communist movement. This is one of the driving
forces of modern-day communism: the Party-promoted idea
that no member is alone, that he is part of a vast movement
which, in communist eyes, is destined to conquer the world.
Singing the "Internationale," the communist marching song,
also engenders this feeling.

The Three Levels of Power

The Party's organizational structure may be likened to
layers in a pyramid, one placed on top of the other.

1. The top level centers around national headquarters and
contains the Party's policy-making organs: (1) *National Committee;* (2) *National Executive Committee;* and (3) *National
Administrative Committee.* With ruthless hand this echelon
rules the Communist Party, USA. The designation given here
is the current arrangement, which is always subject to change.
The Party never hesitates to reshuffle its top administrative
bodies, changing their names and sizes. For many years, for
example, it had national officers: National Chairman, William
Z. Foster, and General Secretary, Earl Browder and, later,
Eugene Dennis. The power remains, however, in the hands of
a small minority.

2. The second or middle level contains the many administrative organs that implement the decisions of the inner
hierarchy: (1) *various commissions and departments;* (2)
special organizers; and (3) *front groups.*

3. The bottom or third level is broad and extensive and
contains all the subordinate regional and local units in the
Party: that is, *district organizations,* and, in turn, various *state,*

county, city, section, and *club* setups. This level encompasses
the entire nation.

National headquarters is located in a three-story, twenty-
foot-wide, brownstone building at 23 West 26th Street, New
York City, just off Broadway. A pygmy amid Manhattan's
towering skyscrapers, with iron bars shielding the bottom-floor
windows, this American Kremlin is the symbol of communist
power in our country. Here meetings are held and important
decisions made. The national office occupies the third floor and
penthouse; the New York State Communist Party is on the
first and second floors. However, the 1957 Party convention
authorized shifting national offices to Chicago.

Level 1: The High Command

The real power of the Party rests in the *National Committee*. This committee, "elected" by the national and state
conventions, is responsible for running the Party between
conventions as provided by the constitution:

> Between National Conventions, the National Committee is the
> highest authority of the Party, representing the Party as a
> whole, and as such has the authority to make decisions and
> take actions necessary and incidental to the good and welfare
> of the entire Party, and to act upon all problems and develop-
> ments occurring between Conventions. (Article V, Section 9)

This provision covers a multitude of possibilities and forms
the basis for the dictatorship of a few leaders, in typical communist style. The National Committee is America's Politburo,
a small group of some sixty individuals directing war against
noncommunist institutions.

Minority control is strengthened still more by clever manipulation. The current National Committee elected a twenty-
member National Executive Committee, which in turn selected
administrative officials. In actual practice, the latter group is
the dominant power, making day-to-day decisions. There is
no free election of the membership. With members of the

National Committee spread throughout the country, "on-the-spot" New York comrades tend to monopolize control of Party affairs.

This atmosphere of almost unlimited authority often produces a repugnant type of person. Many of the top leaders are haughty, swaggering, overbearing. They feel that they are better than "little" comrades. They are the "experts" in Marxism-Leninism. Their job is to teach the "less informed."

William Z. Foster went to Seattle, Washington, a few years ago to make a speech. "We're glad you've come," the welcoming local official commented. "Many of our comrades are looking forward to meeting you."

"Not so fast," warned Foster. "I'm not going to see any of them. I'm too busy. These little Party people just sit down and pour out their personal problems. It wears me out and you can't get rid of them."

"But," protested the local organizer, "they've been busy for weeks, working to make the meeting a success. They want . . ."

"Nonsense," snapped Foster. "You decide which ones are worth my time and I'll see them. Make appointments. I can't solve everybody's problems."

Later the local leader told Foster that the comrades wanted to give him a present, perhaps a traveling bag.

"Oh, no," Foster interrupted. "I've already looked at traveling bags, and I didn't find any costing less than seventy-five dollars which would be suitable. I don't think the members want to spend that much."

Right he was. The organizer had probably browbeaten all "volunteers" to collect twenty to thirty dollars.

"What about a watch?" inquired the local leader, intent on pleasing the high-ranking visitor.

"I already have one," replied Foster. "It cost a hundred and twenty-five dollars. I don't think it's advisable to buy a more expensive one, and I wouldn't wear a cheaper one."

That settled it. This "proletarian" leader, the "champion of the poor and downtrodden," acting like a miniature Hitler, was indeed difficult to please.

Level 2: The Special Units

The attack weapons of the Communist Party are contained in the middle layer, the *commissions* and *departments* to carry out the decisions of the inner clique.

Communist leaders view American life not as a vast, uniform whole but as a series of different segments, each, in its own way, open to the appeal of communism. There are, for instance, farmers with their special problems, trade-union members, and groups with special interests related to nationality, youth, and race. Communists realize that a single program, slanted to appeal to all groups at once, will not work. To be effective, communist propaganda must be tailored to fit specific problems. What are a group's dissatisfactions, desires, and aims? How can communism most effectively appeal to this group? The fact that programs designed for different groups are often mutually contradictory makes no difference to communists. The main point is to attract followers and stir up discontent in as many areas as possible.

This is the task of various commissions and departments, each headed by a national Party leader. Merely to list some of them will give an idea of the scope of the Communist Party's appeal: Veterans' Commission, Women's Commission, Education Department, Cultural Commission, Negro Commission, Labor Department, Nationality Groups Commission, Youth Commission.

In addition, there are related organs dealing with the internal administration of the Party. The National Organization Department, for example, handles the placement of Party officials throughout the nation, while the National Review (Control) Commission (also known as the Appeals Commission) is in charge of security and disciplinary matters.

These commissions and departments are little dynamos attempting to spark enthusiasm for the communist cause in their special fields. They prepare literature, arrange speaking tours, organize fronts. Their job is to work out the practical details of implementing the Party line.

This task is accomplished largely through the employment

of "experts," men and women trained in special fields. There are experts of all kinds, on both local and national levels: waterfront organizers specializing in seamen's groups; labor organizers interested in penetrating labor unions; organizers in virtually every other field, such as aircraft, mining, steel, agriculture, youth, nationality groups. Then there are fund raisers, recruiters, Marxist teachers, organizational experts.

If a Party district is planning, let us say, a special organizing drive, an expert from national headquarters or another district may arrive to assume charge. He may deal with top officials or descend to club levels. He may stay a few hours, a week, or even months. John Williamson for many years was considered one of the Party's top labor experts. Henry Winston was an authority on organizational problems. Both Williamson and Winston were convicted under the Smith Act; Williamson later accepted voluntary deportation to Great Britain and has since been reported to have served as liaison between the Communist Party of the Soviet Union and the United States Party.

If the visitor is a high national officer, special arrangements are usually made to receive him with "extreme cordiality." If his schedule is crowded, a rank-and-filer may be assigned as a chauffeur. Never must the Party be regarded as a "desk-type" organization, operating only through letters, telegrams, and phone calls. It is a fast, hard-hitting, mobile organization, based primarily on personal contacts, with its officials traveling thousands of miles a year by auto, train, and air to pursue subversive activities.

Level 3:   Regional and Local Units

This layer provides the broad base for the pyramid and includes the remainder of the Party structure. The United States is divided into Communist Party districts, some of which have jurisdiction over more than one state. The Ohio State Communist Party, directed principally from Cleveland, Ohio, for example, includes the states of Ohio and Kentucky and West Virginia's four northern "panhandle" counties.

Communist membership is strongest in the Northeast section of the United States. The greatest concentration of Communist Party members is in the area of New York City. Other states having large numbers of communists are California, Illinois, New Jersey, Ohio, Pennsylvania, Washington, Connecticut, Michigan, and Massachusetts. Few members, relatively speaking, reside in Southern and Rocky Mountain states.

District (or state) organizations, patterned on the national structure, hold periodic conventions, "elect" state committees, and have officers. Hence there is a Chairman, New York State Communist Party, or Secretary, Ohio State Communist Party. Sometimes state conventions are held in "split sessions": the first, before the National Convention when selected topics, such as those proposed in the "draft program," are "discussed"; the second, after the national meeting when the state convention reassembles to ratify the decisions of the national body. State leaders take no chances, they stay on the Party line.

Many states and districts have open headquarters. In recent years most were closed, but the Party realizes that an open headquarters is essential in carrying out its day-to-day agitational work. These Party offices are usually located downtown in a dingy room or suite in an old building. Battered desks, with typewriter, Mimeograph machine (the good right arm of the Party), and perhaps a literature rack are standard equipment. Here are the offices of the state chairman, state secretary, and other officers. An old-time communist, usually a woman, will "triple" as receptionist, stenographer, and Mimeograph operator. Knowing all the members, she's a good "lookout" and can answer most questions: Has Oscar come back from vacation? Where does Joyce work? Is Ruth a club chairman?

Normally, headquarters is a busy place, with people going in and out all day long. Here special state, county, and city meetings are held as well as personal conferences. The busiest items in the place are chairs; they seldom have a rest until after midnight.

The local organizational structure, under state (or district) headquarters, varies from area to area. The city (or county) sections in turn are subdivided. Intracity sections may encompass several wards, each, like the county, having its own set of officers. Each section, of course, is rigidly controlled from the top.

The basic unit, at the bottom of the whole structure, is the *club*, formerly known as the cell, like the one described at the beginning of this chapter. Clubs are of various types: *community clubs*, comprising members who live in a certain geographical area; *shop clubs*, composed of members who work at a certain company; *industrial clubs*, which include members employed in the same basic industry, such as steel, automobile, aluminum, though working for different industrial firms; and *specialized clubs*, appealing to professions or other natural groupings. In the latter category, for example, there may be a professional section (often called white-collar), comprising clubs of teachers, doctors, or lawyers. A few members, especially the deeply concealed communists, do not belong to any club but are considered as *members-at-large*, subject to control only from headquarters.

Determining which club a member should join is simple: where can he do the most good for the Party? If he is employed in the aluminum industry, for instance, he would probably be instructed to join an aluminum club (made up of members employed in the aluminum industry). If he is a union officer, he might join a shop or industrial club. Or, again, if his membership should be carefully concealed, he would be a member-at-large. The organizational structure is always in a state of flux, members being frequently shifted from club to club, while headquarters organizes and reorganizes sections and clubs, tearing down one, establishing another, always hoping to gain greater efficiency.

Each club is required to have a chairman, a financial secretary, and an educational director. A well-run club has many more officers: literature director, press chairman, dues secretary, membership chairman, and so on. The same is true of county, city, and section groups; the communists have plenty of officers. Moreover, a definite chain of command is always in effect. Everybody knows his relative position: who are his

Party "inferior" and Party "boss." Instructions are quickly carried out, and in the event of an emergency a commanding officer is always available.

Communist clubs are often named after famous American historical figures such as Tom Paine, Thomas Jefferson, Abraham Lincoln, Walt Whitman. Other clubs bear the names of communist "heroes" such as John Reed.

The Principle of "Democratic Centralism"

This is a complicated structure, you might say. How does it work? The point is: *it does work*, efficiently, effectively, and all too often to the detriment of this nation. The whole Party organization, regardless of its structural shape, is based on strict discipline, a rigid hierarchy, and a unified structure.

The cement that holds it together is a principle called *democratic centralism*. That sounds like a contradiction in terms; it is. But communists like fancy words to fool their opponents and, perhaps, to satisfy themselves. Democratic centralism is the basic principle of communist organizational structure—a term meaning, in actual practice, simple, naked, and unadulterated dictatorship.

According to communists, Party members have a right to participate in formulating policy and electing officers. That is, to them, democracy in action.

An issue has arisen. The city is planning to close a playground. What stand will the Party take? All members are encouraged to express opinions. There may be different points of view.

Then a decision is made—the communists say by an "election," but actually it is by the leader clique. The city's action will be opposed. From that moment, "centralism" takes over and "democratic" falls away. All members, regardless of their previous opinions, are required to support the Party's stand. No minority can exist.

Democratic centralism, communist leaders claim, combines the "strictest discipline with the widest initiative and independent activity of the Party membership." It is "democratic" because of the preliminary "free discussion of issues" and "right of election"; it is "centralism" because once a decision is made, the discipline of the Party enforces the decision. This is the ideal type of organizational structure, say the communists.

The tyranny and dictatorship that are part and parcel of the Communist Party are laid down by the rule: all lower Party organizations are subordinated to the higher bodies, and the highest of all are the Congresses of the Communist Party of the Soviet Union, which are run by the Kremlin.

A practical demonstration of democratic centralism at work recently occurred in New York City. As we have mentioned, a campaign was launched to circulate a petition to put Elizabeth Gurley Flynn, a member of the National Committee, on the ballot as candidate for the New York City Council. Although the 1957 National Convention of the Party emphasized that Party members could dissent from official Party policy, William Weinstone, another member of the National Committee, issued the order that "Those members who may not agree with this campaign should nevertheless understand that it is their duty to participate in signature getting."

We in the FBI, through confidential sources of information, know what goes on in hundreds of these meetings. We know who the speakers are, what they say (and don't say), what decisions are made. These "free discussions" would be amusing but for the deadly malady they highlight: a ruthless thought control.

Communist members learn what to think, how to vote, what to say by a process of "automatic osmosis"—the seeping of predigested thoughts along the Party line into all subordinate minds, disciplined to accept. The members become ideological sleepwalkers, drugged into complete obedience by an unconscious discipline.

Sometimes, absurd as it may seem, secret ballots are used. Members go through all the motions of argument, taking a vote, nominating and electing officers. They become excited, waving their arms, pounding desks, shaking their fists. You would think there was open opposition. But that is merely part of the show. Communist thought control, operating through Party ranks, is a terrifying spectacle, freezing into fixed rigidity the mental processes of thousands.

Seen in its true light, democratic centralism is a deceptive cloak dropped over a ruthless dictatorship.

Sometimes a member, somehow or other, does not fathom the Party line. He says something out of step. He is simply "ill-informed" and needs more "education." A Party school or a conference will probably bring him back to his "right senses."

Occasionally a stubborn member will persist in criticism. That takes courage. He is made of metal the communist thought-control machine has not yet melted. He carries the fight to higher Party bodies. But he can't win and out he goes.

In one instance a member was accused of falling down on the job. The section organizer recommended that he be removed from both his Party office and the county executive committee.

"He's irresponsible," stormed one old-time comrade, "and in the Soviet Union irresponsibles are not voted out of office— they are shot!"

That's democratic centralism, the organizational principle that has welded the Communist Party, USA, into a terrible instrument poised and eager to destroy this country if given the opportunity.

11.

This Is the Party!

WHAT ABOUT LIFE in the Party, how members live, who they are, how they earn their money, what they do with their time, and how they get their orders? The following are accounts of day-to-day activities of Party life.

Eleanor is washing the dishes. Her husband, Henry, has just gone to work. The two children are scurrying around the house, ready to leave for school.

Suddenly there is a knock on the door. It is Ruth, who lives across the street. Ruth is chairman of the East Side Communist Club. Her husband, Robert, is state secretary of the Communist Party and a full-time paid functionary.

"Starting the day out just right," smiles Ruth. "The kitchen is all cleaned up. You can come and help us."

Ruth outlines her plans. The state office needs some typing done this morning. Eleanor was a stenographer before she married and often helps on a part-time basis at headquarters. She is a trusted member. But that is not all. In the afternoon Eleanor is to make "some calls"; that is, visit some comrades. She must pass out word that the next meeting of the county executive committee will be held on Friday evening. This message cannot be given over the telephone. Then tonight will be the regular meeting of the East Side Club. Eleanor probably won't get home in time to fix supper. If she doesn't, Henry and the kids can make some cold meat sandwiches. Besides, Henry is scheduled to meet with the state education secretary tonight and he won't have time to eat supper anyway.

Life in the Party! For good members nothing is left for life outside the Party. The housewife is doing typing, running errands, Mimeographing, arranging meetings, collecting dues; her husband, even while working at the grocery store, in the shoe factory, or at the service station, is thinking of his Party assignment that night, distributing literature, soliciting money, serving as a courier. The Party is the most important force in their lives.

If anybody joins the Communist Party expecting to lead an easy life, perhaps read Marx and Engels, buy some literature, and not exert much effort, he is completely misguided. Party work is hard, tough work, and the Party is a ruthless task-master. The member is always on the run, doing this and doing that. He has no spare time, energy, or money for himself. His whole life becomes dominated. The Party is his school, source of friends, and recreation, his substitute for God. Communism wants the *total* man, hence it is *total*itarian. That is part of its indoctrination policy: by concentrating everything on the Party, all other interests are squeezed out.

Day and night the Party structure is buzzing with action: fund drives, registration of members, collection of dues, sale of literature. Leaflets must be passed out on Olive Street, a picket line formed at city hall, a meeting attended. Workers, not playboys, are wanted; or as one Party spokesman expressed it, we must rid ourselves of the member who "makes noises like an eager beaver but accomplishes little." A major characteristic of the Communist Party is perpetual motion.

The man who keeps this subversive beehive of activity going is the paid Party functionary. He is the key to the whole apparatus. Working on national, state, and local levels, he pumps in energy, gives orders, coaxes, cajoles, threatens, smiles, scowls, pleads, anything to keep the Party bustling.

Most communist functionaries are old-timers with ten, fifteen, or twenty years of service. Some have been trained abroad, possibly in the Lenin School in Moscow. They are transferred at frequent intervals, depending on the needs of the Party. One may serve as an organizer in California, as a section secretary in Rhode Island, or as a fund-raiser in

Florida. Their full-time job is to advance the communist cause. The Party employs women functionaries, especially on the lower levels. During World War II, when many male comrades were drafted, a number of Party offices were run by women.

Salaries vary, depending on the size and location of assignment, but they average fifty to seventy dollars weekly. As a general rule, officials are paid by the local organization, although the national office, in case of a deficit, may step in with cash. Some functionaries operate on an expense account, especially if they travel.

The communist official will probably live in a modest neighborhood. His wife will patronize the corner grocery store, his children attend the local school. If a shoe store or a butcher shop is operated by a Party member, the official will probably get a discount on his purchases.

Most Party officials drive cars, usually older models. They are generally out late at night attending meetings. A car is essential for transportation and carrying literature. Except for special affairs, communist activity is slight early in the morning. The organizer, coming in around midnight or one o'clock, will sleep late. But that doesn't mean all day. One Southern official was severely censured for sleeping too late; to solve the problem the Party bought him an electric alarm clock.

Functionaries eat away from home a great deal. They generally are well versed on "cozy" places where they can talk with a minimum of observation. Much Party business is conducted at luncheon appointments. Their wives are also engaged in Party work, and often both are away from home night after night. "Home," to the communist organizer, is more a place to sleep than to enjoy restful relaxation.

If a Party convention is to be held, and many out-of-town delegates are coming in, the organizer may turn his apartment into a temporary hotel. He will pull out all the spare cots, beds, and blankets and "put up" a half-dozen visitors.

The paid official's job is to keep the Party going, to see that everybody has something to do, that meetings are scheduled, that money is collected, that the Party's program is carried out. He may start his day around ten-thirty or eleven o'clock with a "staff" conference at headquarters. There he will discuss the day's agenda with other officials, give or receive orders, and get squared away for the day's work.

The organizer must be a fairly intelligent man with an ability to get along with people. He is always asking for something: Can you deliver papers, how about attending this class, making a speech? He must know how to overcome fears, suspicions, and laziness, and encourage members to work. He may, for example, approach a member for a donation: "We need five hundred dollars. Sell your car and donate the money." Communists come up with all kinds of schemes. The organizer must go out and "sell" the idea.

He also spends a great deal of time smoothing out personal problems. In one case a communist "love triangle" erupted. A young Party member, even though married, decided that she loved another member's husband. The man's wife, however, was determined to fight. The problem reached such bitterness that the trio's Party work began to suffer. There was little hope of solving it by themselves. So the state chairman stepped in.

He talked to them personally. They poured out their inner feelings. The young woman and her "lover" requested Party approval for a divorce. A few days later the wife, with fire in her eyes, told the state chairman she wanted three months' leave of absence from the Party to regain the love of her husband. A regular free-for-all was brewing. The Party, however, exerted pressure and the situation was settled. No divorce was approved. The organizer must be ready at any hour to settle everything, from a hair-pulling contest to the distribution of an estate.

For most members the Party is their whole life. If any problems arise, changing jobs, adopting a child, lawsuits, etc., they solve them with the Party's advice. If a member has a case of ulcers, the organizer will recommend a "Party doctor"; if somebody is threatening suit, he will suggest a "Party lawyer"; if one has lost his job, he might know somebody in the Party, perhaps the owner of a store, a union-shop steward, or an industrial executive, who will help out.

The Party, in many respects, is a vast paternalistic system. Not that it is humanitarian, full of mercy, or interested in the members' welfare. Nothing like that. The Party's interests come first. If a member is sick, tied up with a lawsuit, or unemployed, his Party work will suffer. Each member should be in top working shape at all times. The Party functionary's job is to seek out and solve these problems. He is an administrator, expediter, and nursemaid.

Also, any activity that might injure the Party must be prevented. The discipline of the Party, exercised through the functionary, extends to the most intimate details of personal life. Here are a few actual cases:

A member in Ohio desired to adopt a child whose parents were members of the Catholic Church, and the member had taken steps to join the Church. The state chairman was furious and said no. Finally the member asserted his independence and left the Party.

❖   ❖   ❖   ❖

Another member, in the Party's eyes, manifested "bourgeois" tendencies. He spent too much time working on his house! He was removed from his Party position.

❖   ❖   ❖   ❖

One member in the state of Washington went to Alaska, without permission, to secure a job. He was suspended on the ground that he would attract the FBI's attention in Alaska.

❖   ❖   ❖   ❖

A member in New York City, age thirty-five, was dropped from the rolls. Why? In the Party's eyes he was too much dominated by his mother.

Sometimes the functionary will order the member to take an affirmative step:

A strawberry farmer was visited in Everett, Washington, by a Party fund-raiser who demanded one hundred dollars, which the farmer did not have. The farmer was ordered to mortgage his house. He refused and was expelled for failure to abide by Communist Party discipline.

*   *   *   *

In Philadelphia the district organizer called at the residence of a couple with a long record of devoted Party activity. The organizer announced that the wife was being dropped from the Party because she was anticommunist. When pressed for an explanation, the organizer stated he had concluded that the wife had written critical letters regarding the Party leaders, which she vigorously denied. The organizer then advanced a further reason. A news account had appeared in the papers recounting that her brother, an Air Force Reservist, had been killed in a plane crash and she had failed to advise the Party that he had been called to active duty. The wife then made the futile complaint that, since she was being dropped from the Party and not expelled, she had no way to appeal the decision or to defend herself. Then the organizer told the husband that he had to either leave his wife and children or be dropped from the Party. When he elected to remain with his wife, he was ousted from the Party, as was a former Party organizer who continued to associate with the wife.

*   *   *   *

A promising young communist was attending a Communist Party training school in New York. He was called out of class and advised that the Party had decided that he was to marry a young lady who had just arrived from Hungary on a student visa. The Party felt the girl was promising Party material. The communist went to City Hall accompanied by a fellow student, the bride-to-be, and her sister. The ceremony was performed, which enabled the girl to stay in the United States since she was now married to an American citizen. The marriage was in form only, and three years later the girl secured a divorce. In the meantime the young communist was sent to West Virginia as a functionary and started living with another girl. She also had a citizenship problem. This was met when the two were called to New York for a meeting. In passing through Elkton, Maryland, they secured a marriage license and returned after the New York meeting for the ceremony. The girl then went on to Chicago. When the communist finally met the lady of his choice, he went to a communist lawyer who arranged for an annulment of the second marriage on the ground that a prenuptial agreement to join the church had been violated.

The Party functionary can order members to resign from one job and accept another, to move from one town to another, to stop seeing their families and friends, to lie, cheat, or steal.

Then there is the problem of money. The functionary is always prodding. First, members must pay dues. They are collected monthly from each member and give the Party a substantial source of revenue. Payments of dues are based on regular schedules, depending on a member's income. Here is a sample schedule:

Income Per Week	Dues Per Month
Housewives	.50
Students	.50
Unemployed	.50
To $80	$1.00
To $110	$2.50
Over $110	$5.00

Dues also serve another purpose: to control the member. The Party official can keep track of him, see if his interest is waning (if he doesn't want to pay), and also, if possible, determine how much money he actually has (which the Party can later extract). If he falls behind in payments, the financial secretary will be right after him.

Another related obligation is to donate money (besides paying dues). Every member *must* pay, and pay until it hurts. The Party conducts an annual fund drive, involving the whole membership. Goals are set for clubs, sections, regions, and on a national basis. A big celebration, perhaps a dance or a dinner, marks the "kick-off," and a definite conclusion date is established. During this period, say September 1 to October

15, a white heat of intensity is reached. The theme: "Money, money, money." No member, regardless of excuse, is spared. If the amount isn't reached, the campaign is extended.

How much should a member give? Usually a week's wages is the accepted minimum. If a comrade has extra sources of income, the amount will be higher.

The Party raises money, lots of it. In one fund drive alone, for example, national headquarters announced a collection of over 165,000 dollars. And the campaign was still not complete. The nickels and dimes (although communists say they like "folding money" best) soon add up. With the effectiveness of a vacuum cleaner, the Party pulls money from everywhere.

Laggards, renegers, and backsliders are pushed hard. "That's not enough. You're a piker," the Party organizer will scoff. Sections and clubs vie for "collection honors." The first state or district to reach its quota is enthusiastically hailed.

But that is not the end of "donations." Time after time there are assessments or special fund drives. They come like snowflakes in a winter storm. Party leaders have been arrested, they need help! (Defense Fund). The *Daily Worker* needs money—urgently! (Press Fund). The Party must have 100,000 dollars in thirty days! (Emergency Fund). An "emergency" is always stalking the Communist Party. The best way to solve it is money. The only thing better is more money. The cost to members: at least a day's pay for each special fund.

Fund drives do not exhaust the financial wizardry of the communists. Money is obtained in still other ways, such as Hallowe'en parties, dances, waffle parties, going-away affairs, testimonial dinners, anniversaries (such as of the October Revolution in Russia or the birthday of Lenin). In most instances tickets are sold and, in addition, a collection may be taken up. Everything you have belongs to the Party. That's the philosophy.

One top leader explained how to obtain contributions. Visit the prospective victim. Take along an out-of-town comrade (he's the high-pressure expert) and a local member. The latter should have plenty of money with him. The prospective victim might say, "Yes, I'd like to contribute, but I haven't any money now"—the easy way out. If so, the local comrade would interrupt and say, "Fine, I'll lend you the money. Would a hundred dollars be enough?" This squeeze always works, the leader said. Blank checks are also carried.

To show how far money-raising can go, one member dreamed up the idea that bodies of deceased comrades should be sold for medical experimentation. The Party would gain doubly: first it demanded the fee for the cadaver and then the money ordinarily spent for the burial. Another member suggested that gifts no longer be given at "stork" showers for expectant mothers. This money should be donated to the Party.

Then there are extra revenue sources. At the end of World War II, Party officials requested comrades returning from military service to donate part of their bonus money. In many instances they set the actual amount. If the member didn't comply, he might be disciplined.

Estates are also juicy morsels. If members, or maybe sympathizers, have any extra money, the Party urges that wills be executed naming the Party or certain functionaries as beneficiaries. Large sums are thus often gained.

Some years ago a former Episcopal bishop died in Ohio. Years before, during an illness, he had started reading Marx and other communist books. Then he turned author and wrote a book entitled *Communism and Christianism,* wherein he expressed doubt that Christ had ever lived, and asserted that he had "found Christ via Karl Marx." The bishop was given a trial by his church and deposed. Following his death, his will provided that the residue of his estate, valued at between 300,000 and 400,000 dollars, was to go to a corporation whose trustees were to devote all or any part of it to the cause of communism as "propagated by Karl Marx."

Another communist sympathizer in Oregon a few years ago received more than 100,000 dollars upon the death of a son. A communist friend persuaded the sympathizer to bequeath a part of his estate to two West Coast communists.

A Party member died in Massachusetts in 1953, leaving a

14,000-dollar bank account and real estate to the Party, naming three Party officials as executors of his will.

Over the years the Party has been blessed by angels and foundations whose money was made through the American free enterprise system and is then used in an attempt to destroy the system that made wealth and affluence possible.

In years past, each member was given a membership card or book (which was numbered) on which he could paste his "dues stamps," showing that he was current on this obligation. But today, for security reasons, this practice is no longer followed. Membership records, if kept, are carefully concealed, and only a trusted few know their whereabouts. Sometimes elaborate code, color, and tab combinations are used on such records to indicate the name, occupation, sex, length of Party service, etc., of the members.

To join the Communist Party does not automatically mean life tenure. Memberships must be renewed every year or, in communist language, members are "reregistered." This represents another means of control. If a member is delinquent in dues or donations, he'll have to pay a penalty, perhaps contribute ten dollars, or be disciplined. These annual registration drives are important events in Party life. Each member is personally contacted. Clubs and sections compete for speed and percentage of successful registration. The drives usually start in October and often extend well past the December 31 deadline.

A member moves. His district organization will send details concerning him to his new area: name, Party history, whether dues are paid, along with any other remarks. A member may be given half of a dollar bill and the other half forwarded to the new district. When the member arrives, the halves are matched. Identity is thus established.

So it goes, a constant round of rushing, driving, pushing, paying, never time to stop. The member is regimented from life to death. His chief obligation: to follow instructions eagerly, energetically, obediently. He is a mere wisp of living matter, born, as a *Daily Worker* birth announcement proclaimed, "for swelling our ranks."

This complete absorption in the Party creates an exhilaration that warps judgment. One comrade became so wrought up over the supposed superiority of communist culture that he cited statistics that the Soviet soldier in World War II was an inch taller and had a chest one and a half inches larger than his Czarist counterpart!

Such fervor sounds laughable, but it is symptomatic of paranoiac behavior. To an individual like this, any communist achievement surpasses anything American. This bigoted communist fanaticism drives members to mortgage their homes, spend years in underground shelters, and betray their native land.

Even in death a member may become a pawn to enhance the Party. The passing of a prominent comrade invariably is the occasion for a "state funeral." The departed member is now a valuable showpiece and his passing is exploited to the fullest extent. On such occasions the deceased lies in state on the day of the funeral, with "mourners" passing the bier. A large, blown-up photograph of the deceased, draped in black, hangs at the rear of the stage. An honor guard of from two to four comrades stands at attention wearing red armbands.

There is seldom a religious quality to the music, eulogies, or the "mourners'" conduct. At the "state funeral" of Mother Ella Reeve Bloor in 1951 the "mourners" talked, laughed, and smoked.

The eulogies are numerous and recount the contributions made by the deceased to the Communist Party, to the advancement of socialism, and state how the Party can learn from the life of the departed. At Mother Bloor's funeral in New York City, for example, Pettis Perry, a member of the National Committee, said:

> This is not farewell to you, Mother Bloor. We pledge to follow in your footsteps . . . We will build your Party and our Party and some day we will have a nation and a society built on the brotherhood of man . . .

At the funeral of Peter V. Cacchione, an elected member of the New York City Council, nineteen speakers delivered eulogies. Gilbert Green, then chairman of the Party in Illinois, speaking for the National Committee, observed that the deceased fell in the struggle as "a soldier in the cause of human freedom," and vowed that the remaining comrades would take "the banner from his hands."

After such services a cortege of automobiles laden with mourners journeys from the funeral hall to the cemetery. As Mother Bloor was lowered into her grave at Harleigh Cemetery in Camden, New Jersey, Walter Lowenfels, then the Philadelphia correspondent of the *Daily Worker,* read Walt Whitman's poem, "The Mystic Trumpeter."

At the Cacchione interment Henry Winston, a member of the National Committee, delivered these parting words, "We are confident, as you were, dear Pete, in ultimate victory . . . We will carry out your heritage."

Through it all runs the hope, not of life everlasting, but of communism everlasting—if the members can be stirred up to work harder.

12.

Making Communist Man

IN THE LAST CHAPTER we examined life in the Party—the constant hustle, collecting of dues, registration of members, holding of conferences, issuing of instructions.

These activities, however, have a meaning more sinister than just keeping the Party going, a meaning that we overlook at our peril. It is this: the Party is a vast workshop where the member is polished and shined, his impurities melted out, his loyalty to communism strengthened. He is made into *communist man.*

The revolution requires, as Lenin taught, that the fanatical believer be a man who, if so instructed, will give his life to the cause. He's the paid functionary we met in the last chapter, the agitator and propaganda agent we'll see in future pages. Without him communism would be just another "ism."

This type of man doesn't just grow; he must be created. To understand fully how this happens, we must now briefly examine the Party's educational, press, literature, and cultural programs, its chief weapons of indoctrination.

Suppose one joined the Party. How would these techniques of regimentation affect the new member? We can best consider this question under several headings.

Back to School

One of the first things a new member does is to go to a school. He'll receive his instructions soon after joining, probably from his club chairman. And as long as he stays in the Party, he'll continue to go to school. Even the grizzled veterans go. There's a diabolical reason behind this, which we'll soon see.

Most people don't think of the Communist Party as an educational institution. Yet year after year the Party operates a school system of vast proportions: theory schools; orientation schools; specialized schools in current events, history, economics, social problems; schools in Party techniques: how to collect dues, recruit new members, serve as a club chairman, be a better public speaker; and, of course, schools on revolutionary tactics and procedure. In recent years the Party has been extremely subtle in teaching its doctrines of revolution, always remembering federal laws such as the Smith Act, which prohibits advocating the overthrow of the United States government by force and violence.

Education, in the communist scheme, means indoctrination, imbuing the member with qualities desired by the Party. The pertinent question always is: How can the member be trained to serve the Party better?

Classes are held on all levels—local, state, regional, and

national, varying in length from an hour to several weeks. For security reasons members meet in an isolated building, a home, or even in an automobile or a public park. The teacher is usually a paid functionary or someone from the county or state educational commission. Class consists of an extended lecture, perhaps for an hour or so, followed by discussion. As a general rule, no note-taking is allowed. The class over, each student leaves, careful not to attract attention.

After the beginning, or orientation, school (where members are soaked with Aesopian double talk) is over, the member is ready for a more advanced class. Never is he told at the outset that he is being changed into a Bolshevik, that his loyalty is being shifted to Soviet Russia, and that the American government must be overthrown. That would scare him away. The Party's indoctrination process is slow and gradual. The member himself seldom realizes that bit by bit his precommunist training is being extracted and replaced by Party ideology.

Most important, he is grounded in love of the Party. This is a cardinal duty of the communist teacher.

> . . . the cause of Communism is the greatest and most arduous cause in the history of mankind.

❖   ❖   ❖   ❖

> To sacrifice one's personal interests and even one's life without the slightest hesitation and even with a feeling of happiness, for the cause of the Party . . . is the highest manifestation of Communist ethics.

❖   ❖   ❖   ❖

> The true Communist . . . must feel that the Party does not owe him a thing; it is he who owes everything . . . to the Party.

Party schools make extensive use of study outlines and lesson aids supplied by national, state, and local educational commissions. They are written in a simple style and slanted to the average reader. Many contain suggested readings, illustrative examples, and review questions. Usually Mimeographed, they deal with all phases of the Party's program. Sample titles are "Lenin and Our Party," "World Significance of the Events in China," "New Members Session and Introduction in the Communist Party," and "Farmers in the Coalition."

Amazing attention is shown to detail. In advanced classes members will have homework and examinations. As part of the instruction, classes often are given practical "field work." Students in one Midwestern school were dismissed, divided into teams, and sent to industrial plants to distribute Party literature. That evening they reassembled to discuss their experiences and receive ideas on how better to do the job.

The longer one stays in the Party, the more specialized are the classes he attends. The goal, of course, is to be selected to attend a national leadership school. This means going to New York City or a Party camp and staying several weeks. Students probably will not know the true names of their fellow students; they'll remember them as Sam (an alias), the man with the crooked arm, the redheaded girl who talked so much, the old man with the green shirt. That's part of the Party's security program.

The communist educational system is extremely practical: training members to do what the Party needs. Perhaps more Mimeograph operators are needed; then there'll be a Mimeograph school. Maybe more dues secretaries are needed; then there'll be a dues secretaries' school. All the time, through training, the member is being pulled more closely under Party discipline.

Home Study

Another indoctrination technique is self- or home study. Going to school is important, but at best it can be for only an hour a day or several weeks a year. More study is needed to bind the member to the Party.

One Party directive puts it this way:

Every Communist must read and study the classics of our

literature, past and present. Everyone must rigorously enforce the slogan, "One night a week for Marxist study."

Communists may be busy or deeply involved in other Party work. But they must also carry on self-study or, as the communists call it, *ideological self-cultivation* or *raising the ideological level of the member*. This means daily readings in the communist bible—the works of Marx, Engels, and Lenin. (Following Khrushchev's denunciation of Stalin, the late dictator's works were appreciably de-emphasized in Party study programs.) This is not something optional; it is an absolute requirement. To study the communist "masters," says the Party, is to be made "perfect" as they were "perfect"—and incidentally to make members work harder selling papers, collecting dues, and handing out leaflets.

In the final analysis this communist education, like all phases of the Party's program, is geared to *revolutionary action*. "It is for the Party and for the victory of the revolution that we study." The Party isn't training its members just for fun. Each one must be steeled, hardened, and purified of his capitalist "scum," "filth," and "dirt." The new member was born and reared under capitalism and, in communist eyes, therefore he is infected with "selfishness," "intrigue," "class attitudes." "Is it anything strange," one communist writer asks, "that there are muddy stains on a person who crawls out of the mud . . . ?"

These stains must be washed off. It's a lifetime job. Non-Party or "capitalist" attitudes keep cropping out. Some have been inherited, others newly acquired from capitalist contamination. That's why even old-time members keep attending school. It's like cleaning a skillet that tarnishes. Constant scrubbing (more indoctrination) is needed to make and keep the member ideologically pure.

Communist education is constantly seeking to destroy the "remnants of bourgeois ideology," the undigested lumps of independence not yet crushed by communist thought control. That is the gnawing fear of all communist regimes: that an undigested lump will be missed, that somewhere lying undetected is a member who has not been completely indoctrinated. This individual is a potential enemy who may someday rise against his masters.

The Party has a term, *political maturity*, to signify the member who has been so indoctrinated that, as a matter of sixth sense, he will always know the Party line.

Party Literature

The Party's literature program (comprising newspapers, magazines, pamphlets, and books) is a companion to Party schools and self-study in helping to create communist man.

These publications, regardless of their form, tell but one story, the Party's story. The member must believe no other. For this purpose the Party is operating a multihundred-thousand-dollar propaganda machine.

Inside the Party the refrain is constantly heard: Buy our literature. "Got a nickel, mister? Try this pamphlet." "You don't want to miss our paper." "Here, subscribe to *Political Affairs*" (the Party's monthly theoretical magazine). The pressure is terrific. Party-operated bookstores and newspaper carrier routes distribute a steady stream of Party literature, as do the clubs themselves.

"We probably circulate more literature per member of our organization by ten times," one former Party leader said, "than any other organization in existence."

The Party's chief newspaper is the *Daily Worker* (and its week-end edition, *The Worker*), published in New York City. On the West Coast it's the *People's World* (a weekly published in San Francisco).

Don't think of the *Daily Worker* in terms of your own daily newspaper. It is strictly a propaganda organ. A tabloid with bold, black headlines, its "news" stories, editorials, book reviews, even its sports columns, are slanted to promote the Party's views.

For example, *Daily Worker* sports writer Lester Rodney, in his column "On the Scoreboard," praises "the phenomenal and growing successes of the Soviet Union in the world of sports."

He says, ". . . the answer is socialism. If Russians were just so all-fired hot as Russians, where were all their champion teams and athletes under the Czar?"

In obvious glee Rodney writes: "So fellow sports lovers, this socialism deserves a little open-minded study, at least, that's clear. (There's a fine school over on Sixth Ave. and 16th St. where you can study it if you're lucky enough to be a New Yorker.)" The Jefferson School of Social Science, a front school, was then located at this address.

And Rodney couldn't miss the chance for another propaganda plug:

> Just one more thing and really the most important for today with all the "Soviet menace" hogwash. No matter what you may or may not think of their socialism, it is self-evident that a nation which loves to play and is turning out fine athletes in increasing numbers and building more and more sports fields is a nation which is thinking about peace and not war.

The *Daily Worker* serves as a unifier of policy, an organizer of action, and a Party builder. It is a public document. Hence, don't expect to find there Party secrets, such as the identities of underground officials or decisions of confidential meetings. However, for those who understand its double talk it provides a quick means to communicate the Party line. Moreover, it does not let the membership forget the identity of the Party's enemies and sometimes its friends. Like a vast searchlight, it gives direction to members, wherever they may be.

Day after day the *Daily Worker* drills a central theme into its readers: that life in the United States is terrible; that only in communist countries, especially in the Soviet Union, is life worth living at all.

The day's news is scanned for some incident to distort and use to browbeat the United States. Any action of the American government is always, somehow or other, part of a conspiracy to engulf the world in World War III. One rat in a tenement house becomes an army of rats devouring thousands of people. Pick out every weakness, real or imaginary. Stir up dissension. Try to weaken morale.

After Khrushchev's denunciation of Stalin, the *Daily Worker* carried some criticism of Soviet Russia, for the most part pertaining to anti-Semitism and illegal arrests. Certain aspects of Russia's intervention in Hungary were also criticized. Highly novel for the *Daily Worker*, this criticism apparently reflected the personal views of John Gates, the editor. Gates, of all the top Party leaders, appeared to have been most affected by Khrushchev's revelations. He was severely attacked, however, by other Party officials, including William Z. Foster, and his resignation was demanded. Nevertheless, despite this limited criticism, the *Daily Worker* remained loyal to the over-all aims of Soviet Russia and continues to belittle, mock, and criticize American life.

This loyalty to things Russian has caused the *Daily Worker* to perform some interesting gymnastics. A good example was the famous "Doctors' Plot," early in 1953, just before Stalin's death. Moscow reported the arrest of nine doctors charged with plotting to kill high-ranking Soviet officials. "Moscow Nips Plot to Kill Army Chiefs," headlined *The Worker* (January 18, 1953), obviously happy. Then the doctors were suddenly released. Back-flipped *The Worker* with the greatest of ease: "The Case of the Soviet Doctors, How a Socialist State Protects Its Citizens" (April 12, 1953).

In March, 1953, *The Worker* reported Stalin's death. "STALIN: Man of Peace," "The Cobbler's Son Who Built a New World," " 'His Name and His Work Will Endure Through the Ages,' " "Stalin—Architect of a Working People's World." In 1956 the headlines shifted: "Lenin's Principles Abandoned by Stalin," "Minorities Were Exiled and Mistreated," "Says Stalin Unleashed Mass Terror 1936-1937." One writer headed his column: "Stalin Wasn't God—And We Weren't Angels."

Communists regard themselves as "apostles" of a new order living in "enemy-controlled" territory. Communists claim that the *Daily Worker* cuts through the "capitalist press" and its smog of "lies," "distortions," and "fakes," bringing "truthful information." This is the highest principle of a "free press."

The communist press, with its bigoted, perverted, single point of view, is a disturbing reality. It seeks the definite, systematic, and mass indoctrination of the minds of men to trust only the Party. Truth becomes what a group of men say it is.

Here's an example of how "freedom of the press" works for the communists:

A Party leader hurried toward the building where a convention was being held. Just outside the door he paused. An individual was handing out leaflets urging the election of a slate opposed by the Party.

"That guy ought to be thrown out," the Party boss remarked to a companion. "He's nothing but a Trotskyite. He shouldn't be allowed around here."

Some time later the same two men were again attending a meeting. This time the *Daily Worker* was being sold outside. The companion objected, saying this wasn't a communist meeting.

"Uh," retorted the Party member. "This is a free country. You can't stop him from passing it out."

No wonder communism can operate only in the glow of book burnings. No opposite view can be tolerated. "Down with non-party writers!" Lenin demanded.

As an example, after Browder's "fall from power" in 1945, many of his books were burned. Shifts in the Party line also cause book burnings. One New England headquarters, caught in a Party shift, destroyed three barrels of literature. What is "true" today in the Party may not be "true" tomorrow.

Modern-day techniques of literature dissemination extend the tyranny of communist indoctrination. The Party wants mass readership. Always remember that the communists are practical, everyday agitators. Why publish something at a high price that few will buy? There are few fancy bindings, engravings, or pictures. Communist publishing firms have exploited the publication of pamphlet-form editions and paperbacked volumes, anything to gain circulation and spread the communist message.

Prices are now higher, but communist literature is today being sold for five, ten, twenty, twenty-five, and thirty-five cents. Even these prices are considered too high. "I do not consider a five-cent pamphlet mass literature. We have to go back to mass penny literature . . . ," one Party leader commented. Amazing circulations have been achieved. Editions of Lenin's *Imperialism* and *State and Revolution,* totaling 100,000 copies each and costing ten cents a copy, were issued. Other pamphlets were printed in editions totaling 307,000; 275,000; 350,000; 440,000.

Everything possible has been done to make available in English the works of Marx, Engels, Lenin, and Stalin. A twelve-volume series of Lenin's *Selected Works,* over 6000 pages, sells for twenty-five dollars. Marx's *The Civil War in France* is offered for a dollar and fifty cents (cloth); paperbound, twenty-five cents. The most important writings of Lenin are made available in the "Little Lenin Library" (for Marx it's the "Little Marx Library"), with prices ranging from five to ninety cents. Many foreign communist writings are also printed. During the period 1948-55, according to a report of the United Nations Educational, Scientific and Cultural Organization, the writings of Lenin were more widely translated than the Bible, with Stalin's writings ranking third. Mention should also be made of communist-shop leaflets, neighborhood papers, and throwaways that are placed on doorsteps, thrown into parked cars, or scattered in buildings. Generally Mimeographed, they represent an easy, cheap, and effective method of stirring up trouble.

The pressure is terrific—buy, buy, buy. Widely publicized campaigns to sell the *Daily Worker* are regular features of Party life. The more communist material a member reads, the less time he has for reading "capitalist propaganda."

Cultural Indoctrination

Even if a member faithfully went to school, studied at home, and read Party literature, he would still have spare time during which non-Party thoughts might seep in. That would never do.

Every facet of the member's life, even when he plays the piano, sings, goes to a movie, sees a painting, or reads a book, must be saturated with communism. Art doesn't exist for art's sake. Art, as Lenin taught, is a weapon of the class struggle. "Culture" becomes an indoctrinal spray seeking to control every part of the member's heart, mind, and soul.

The member is subjected to a barrage of Russian, satellite, and native communist "cultural" propaganda. There are art exhibits, folk dances, theater groups, nationality bazaars. Many of these are carried on through front groups and hence not labeled as communist. The *Daily Worker* advertises Soviet movies, which are often shipped to Party units across the country. Short stories, novels, and poetry come in steady streams. Forums extol the virtue of Soviet life. Here, the communists say, is the new "people's culture," bringing the "real truth."

The theme is always the same: Russia and communism represent a new world of "hope," "promise," and "achievement," creating "communist man" in all his "remarkable spiritual qualities." The United States is a "weak," "decadent," and "sick" country, dominated by vulgar tastes, thievery, and debauched living. No wonder, according to the *Daily Worker*, the Soviet soldier in World War II spent his time reading Shakespeare and Tolstoy while the "uncultured" GI read assorted inferior trash!

The member is urged to read Soviet literature and see the "glorious" communist "hero" working his heart out for the regime. This "hero"—usually just an ordinary, plain fellow (like the member)—can repair a blast furnace in one day instead of the usual six to eight weeks. Why? For the glory of communism. Another "hero" is sad and disheartened. He has bungled his factory job. He wasn't doing his share. But a strong arm is around his shoulders, the arm of an experienced worker. He'll show the worker "hero" how to break production records, for communism—when in real life he might be headed for a slave labor camp.

Day after day this propaganda is dinned into the member. Children are included. The Party feels that the basic responsibility of indoctrinating the child lies with the communist parents. A member in Buffalo announced, for instance, that a class for children, aged five to seven, would be held in the basement of her home. Ironically, it was called "Sunday school" because it was held on Sunday. But, the member added, this school was not to teach "the word of God or in any way teach religion." The instruction obviously would be directed to the fundamentals of Marxism.

Books are published for children. One, *Our Lenin,* is a story of Lenin's life, translated and adapted "for American children." In this an American worker is quoted: " 'It [the Soviet Union] will last forever, and we here will follow its example.' " It's a steady diet of propaganda.

Suppose the member wants to write, paint, or compose music? He, too, must follow the Party line. His work must promote communism.

Some of the writings are very crude, but they get across the Party line. Here's a poem that appeared in the *Daily Worker* shortly after Stalin's death, eulogizing the Soviet dictator:

> He was melted in the open hearth of feudal czarist oppression
> He was forged in the fire of revolution
> His chemistry was the chemistry of struggle
> And left him as pure as the hope of liberation
>   of the working class
> He was alloyed with large masses of the Soviet
>   peoples and heaping shovelfuls of inter-
>   national brotherhood with just the right
>   amount of love for humanity to finally make—
> A man of steel. . . .

An artist wants to paint a flock of birds in a tree. That's silly, the Party says. There's no communist message. Here's how his idea can be improved.

Make one bird a white dove and, presto, you're right in line with the communist "peace" offensive. Another improvement: Put a mean-looking capitalist "warmonger" under the tree taking aim at the peaceful dove.

Just the name of the picture often gives a communist twist. A drawing of a sleeping child, cuddling her baby bear, couldn't be labeled "Slumber." No propaganda there. "Too Hungry to Stay Awake" would be better, to show how people are starving in the United States. A young lady walking down the street smiling and confident isn't "Girl on a Stroll" but "Battler for Peace." The beauty and power of any work of art must be measured by "the degree to which it is permeated with the ideas of Communism." This is the way, the communists say, that the masses can be directed.

The Party, in the final analysis, has an interpretation for the whole of human life. Nothing is untouched: science, psychology, sex, love, care of children, literature, history, the origin and end of life. Everything must be absorbed. Communism is a unitary, all-embracing, and absolute system.

Not only the present but also the past must be controlled. Communist writers have already reinterpreted American history, claiming that the Party is today the true inheritor of the traditions of 1776. They seek to associate themselves with such men as Paine, Jefferson, and Lincoln, whom they identify as "advanced fighters" for the ideals that the communists claim they now represent. For example, the *Daily Worker* on Lincoln's Birthday in 1953 said, "Lincoln's heritage is carried forward mainly by the working class and its Marxist party."

In literature they seek to pervert such writers as Walt Whitman and Mark Twain, claiming, for instance, that Whitman's love of freedom is the story of their own aims. ". . . poet and prophet of a people's democracy" was the *Daily Worker's* salute.

The Party conducts an annual pilgrimage to Whitman's tomb in Harleigh Cemetery, Camden, New Jersey. Mother Bloor, the "old mother" of communism, made a fetish of her alleged friendship with Whitman.

Twain's life, a *Worker* article asserted, was an inspiration to fight against "imperialism and war."

Carried to its logical conclusion, this attitude creates different holidays, customs, and habits for the communists. Christmas, for example, is exploited for propaganda purposes; it is a time to send out cards for "peace," to urge amnesty for communists in jail, to appeal for funds. It holds no religious significance for Party members. A communist America would celebrate the birth of Karl Marx rather than the birth of Christendom.

This constant saturation with communism, through Party education, literature, the press, and "culture," has had its effect in shaping communist man. A comrade writing in *Party Voice,* organ of the New York State Communist Party, frankly admitted what is happening:

> I have no doubt that there are comrades in our movement who have not read a single American book outside of progressive literature in many moons but who can discuss in detail the latest Soviet book or periodical from China.
> . . . we have many comrades who have been brought up on Soviet culture and who are not familiar with the cultural life of our own people.

*   *   *   *

> There are some comrades who never see an American film but confine their movie-going to nothing but foreign films. There are others who see only the decline and fall of American culture but fail to see what is new and growing.

So far has the creation of communist man gone that, in some instances, Party members are embarrassed to salute the American flag. The *Party Voice* comrade tells how embarrassed he felt as he hesitantly saluted the flag at a Memorial Day parade. "At times I looked up and down the street and hoped, inwardly, that none of my 'left' friends were looking at me." So great is the erosion of patriotism that the author even poses this question: "Should Communists know the verses of the Star-Spangled Banner?"

This is how communism is working to promote an alien way of life in America. The whole story, however, is still not told. How are all these facets of Party life held together? What gives a ruthless uniformity to Party actions? We must now turn to a study of Party discipline, a system of terror that holds Party members in the grip of an unbelievable tyranny.

13.

Communist Discipline

IN COMMUNIST EYES the processes of education, the press, and "culture," which we considered in the last chapter, are not enough for molding the revolutionary. Important as they are, they must be supplemented by *communist discipline*, a discipline that enforces uniformity, ensures Party supremacy, and files fanaticism to a sharp cutting edge.

Modern-day communism, in all its many ramifications, simply cannot be understood without a knowledge of communist discipline: how it is engendered, how it operates, how it tears out man's soul and makes him a tool of the Party. The very core of communism is discipline. Without it communism would lose much of its momentum, terror, and striking power.

The Party's constitution provides for disciplinary action. An elaborate "appeals" framework is provided whereby a series of "courts" is available to hear "charges," with the National Convention being the "court" of final resort. Generally speaking, disciplinary problems are handled, on all levels of the Party, by Review and Control Commissions (often called Security Commissions). They serve as the "courts" to discipline any member who might be hostile to the Party.

These "courts" must not be confused with courts as we know them in the American judicial system. Run by hardened, old-time comrades, they are weapons of Party discipline. "Sentences" are meted out on the basis of expediency, not justice.

Rules of evidence, the fair balancing of opinions, and the seeking of truth play no role. Communist discipline is a repugnant totalitarianism.

Here is the account of one victim of communist discipline. John Lautner had been a member of the Communist Party for more than twenty years. He had risen through the ranks until he was a member of the National Review Commission of the Communist Party; he headed the New York Review Commission, was security officer for the Party headquarters building, then at 35 East 12th Street, New York City. He considered himself a dedicated member of the Party.

One day in January, 1950, he was told to proceed to Cleveland, Ohio, to help in perfecting plans for the communist underground in Ohio. Upon arrival he was taken ostensibly to a Party meeting in the basement of a residence. There he was ordered to remove his clothes and for a period of several hours was subjected to the basest of indignities. He was told that he would not leave alive as six other communists, who Lautner said had "butcher knives," "revolvers," "rubber hoses," and a "recording machine," started questioning him about his knowledge of the underground, his army record, his relationship with Hungarian defectees, and his reports to federal agencies. He was accused of being an enemy agent, a spy, of hiring unreliable people to work in the Communist Party defense office, and protecting government "spies" in the Party. Actually, Lautner was innocent of these charges, and the Party's injustice inured to the government's benefit. Finally Lautner had the presence of mind to state that he had left at his hotel the name of one of the communist officials conducting the star-chamber proceedings. He was released and returned to New York, where he read in the *Daily Worker* that he had been expelled from the Party as an enemy agent.

Lautner even filed an appeal of this expulsion order but never received an answer. Several months later he came to the FBI with his story for the first time and since has testified in several legal proceedings. Such is the way communist "justice" is dispensed in the United States.

In this connection we must distinguish between the discipline that communism can exact when it is in state control, as in Russia, Hungary, and China, and when it is not. Communists in the United States cannot exact the death penalty; they cannot operate slave labor camps; they cannot deport families to isolated areas. Yet the disciplinary actions of the Communist Party, USA, as we shall see in the "purge" of Earl Browder in 1945, show unmistakably that communists in this country think and would like to act in disciplinary matters precisely as do communists behind the Iron Curtain. Moreover, the stronger the Party in this country, the more able it has been to enforce its discipline. Every Party member should realize that, by working to strengthen the Communist Party, he is thereby giving the Party greater power to discipline him in the future. Today, at most he can be expelled and vilified, unless he is subjected to the treatment given John Lautner. We can readily conjecture, however, recalling the purge trials under Stalin, what could happen here if communism ever controlled our government.

Communist discipline is a part of the everyday life of the Party. It is not something that can be developed overnight or learned exclusively from a book. It comes gradually from attending schools, reading, and doing Party work. A "conscience of responsibility," as one old-time member explained it, is created; a feeling that, whatever your personal desires and responsibilities, *the Party's orders come first;* that every task is surrounded by a Party "halo of sanctity," thereby becoming an emergency urgently demanding instant handling; that a "guilty" feeling arises if the member relaxes for a moment or doesn't do the job assigned by the Party "boss."

In the communist system, discipline means *conscious* and *voluntary* submission to the will of the Party. To obey Party instructions is regarded as a high ethical duty, to be undertaken joyously and willingly as an honor and privilege, never as bondage. Not to obey is unthinkable and a matter of personal shame and Party irresponsibility. This is the terrifying danger of communist discipline—that in the name of freedom, by appealing to the most noble qualities in man, the human being is pushed into deepest tyranny.

Communist "courts" seek out those who do not "knuckle under" to communist discipline. If a mistake is made from bad judgment, a lapse of memory, or lack of knowledge, that is one thing. This can be corrected by more "education." But if the member persists in error, that is, doesn't follow undeviatingly the Party line, he must be "flayed without mercy." ". . . an organization of real revolutionaries," says Lenin, "will stop at nothing to rid itself of an undesirable member."

Members may be disciplined for many reasons. One of the most serious is being a *deviationist*, that is, differing from the Party line. This charge has led to wholesale purges in the past, including the ousting of such leaders as Lovestone, Gitlow, Browder, and literally hundreds of lesser members.

The Party claims to be an "advanced" element, teaching the noncommunist masses the "glories" of socialism. As leaders, communists must be "in front" of the less informed yet not too far ahead to be out of sight. Just where to be at any given time is decided by the Party inner clique. Anyone disagreeing is a deviationist, guilty of either *left-wing sectarianism* or *right-wing opportunism.*

Some individuals, the communists say, may stray too far to the left. They want the Party to be more militant, to hurry up the revolution. They rush on ahead, forgetting to guide the noncommunists. That's wrong, says the Party. Such an attitude would isolate the Party, make it an ineffectual sect. These individuals are guilty of left-wing sectarianism. They must turn around and come back.

On the other hand, many members lag behind the correct position. They disregard the Party's role as an "advanced teacher" and allow it to work too closely with capitalism. They are right-wing opportunists, equally as guilty as left-wing sectarians. They had better rid themselves of this "capitalist complex" and catch up.

These terms sound massive. To communists, however, they are everyday expressions. Time after time in Party meetings the charge will be heard, "He's an opportunist," or, "He's a left-wing sectarian." To the communists that's like calling a man a thief or coward.

You can well imagine how these "errors" are corrected. Disciplinary scythes can cut down anyone disliked by the leadership. If you want to get rid of a comrade, accuse him of left-wing sectarianism or right-wing opportunism. He'll probably then be hauled into Party "court." Disciplinary vogues sweep the Party: for a while, left-wing sectarianism becomes popular, then right-wing opportunism. After Browder's removal in 1945 as a right-wing opportunist (also called *revisionist*), the style was to criticize opportunism. Since the Geneva Conference of 1955 the fashion has been to attack left-wing sectarianism.

Another serious error is *chauvinism*, applied to a member who supposedly thinks himself superior to others.

Any member can bring charges, no matter how silly, trivial, and stupid. That's a communist technique: always keep members in fear. Never must a comrade become secure, complacent, or unconcerned. He must constantly be worrying about "what's coming next." This prevents the entrenchment of Party bureaucrats and the formation of cliques; it makes discipline easier to impose.

Perhaps, in his Party work or in his personal affairs, a member has given more attention to Mr. A than to Mr. B. If Mr. B's feelings have been hurt, he may bring formal charges. In one instance, a group of Party comrades made plans to hold a picnic, then invited two additional comrades. The two declined, saying that by being asked at the last minute they had been slighted. Result: they planned to bring charges of chauvinism.

There are different types of chauvinism. *White chauvinism,* for example, means that a white comrade, through word or deed, has "slighted" or shown that he feels himself better than a Negro comrade. If the reverse is true—that a Negro member considers himself superior to a white comrade—this leads to the error of *inverted white chauvinism* or *Negro nationalism.* Then there is *male chauvinism,* also called *male supremacism,* when men comrades "look down on" the position of women. In one instance a man was accused of disapproving of his wife's smoking. He was a male supremacist. If a woman thinks she is superior to a man, that's *commandism.*

Still another cause for disciplinary action is the charge of being an *informer.* Ever since 1949, when FBI informants testified at the first New York Smith Act trial, communists have been <u>terrified of informers</u>. They go all-out to catch "spies." Member after member, completely innocent of the Party's charges, has been expelled. "If you have to kick ten guys out to get the right one," a comrade explained, "that's the way to do it." In one instance Party officials without any authority searched the home of a member "under suspicion." In another instance an anonymous letter was received at national headquarters charging, among other things, that a high Party official was "a big bag of wind." The Party instantly collected typewriting samples, hoping to catch the culprit.

The Party, as part of its disciplinary program, encourages what is called self-criticism. The communists point to this technique as proof of the democratic nature of their Party. Actually, however, self-criticism plays into the hands of the ruling clique, enabling it to detect discontent and criticism of its leadership. It becomes an effective disciplinary technique to keep the membership in submission.

Members are encouraged to criticize themselves and others. A well-established Party admonition is: "Test your work against Marxist-Leninist principles. Is anything wrong? Why did the registration program fall short? Are the officers of the club doing their duties properly? Why weren't more pamphlets sold?" The membership is expected to bewail its errors, to say, "We were wrong. Have mercy on us. We will do better." They prostrate themselves before Party bosses. For those who don't "confess," there are others to point out their errors. What else could be asked?

When a comrade confesses, the communist custom is for other members to heap abuse on him, often in the most sarcastic and sneering manner. "You're a deviationist." "You're a chauvinist!" The idea is to drive the member to the lowest depths of humiliation.

When Earl Browder was deposed in 1945, a national officer

suggested that he be given a job scrubbing floors at national headquarters. Browder later told the Yonkers, New York, communist club, "If there had been any evidence that there existed a real need for my services in this capacity, I would gladly have given them."

Members often work themselves into a state of frenzy, tearing apart their best friends. Sometimes self-criticism becomes contagious, with Party sections and committees confessing en masse.

Tongues are sharp, but comrades soon learn whom to criticize. To attack a fellow comrade, especially one you don't like, is the thing to do. In attacking the club chairman the comrade had better take things a little slowly. If he is a friend of the chairman's superior and thinks he can get the chairman's job, then it's proper. If not, he should be content with self-criticism. Good Party manners would say "no" to disparaging a state or national leader, unless one was assigned as a "hatchet man" for another top official. Communist criticism flows more safely downward than upward.

Criticism is encouraged—but it must be of the right kind. An organizer isn't doing his job. To criticize him is proper; that's *constructive criticism*, designed to make the Party stronger. "But this criticism," one high official said, "must never depart from the line of the Party. . . ."

That's the crux: Criticism must be limited to how the Party line can best be advanced. Anything else is *destructive criticism*. It's like a house full of furniture. A comrade is permitted to discuss how the furniture can be arranged, whether the blue chair should be in the front room or the bedroom. But as soon as he questions the size of the house, whether a new room should be added, or the entire house destroyed and rebuilt, well, that's just too much. The Party line must not be questioned.

Some members learn the hard way. They push criticism too far and are quickly put in place.

John was highly regarded as a club chairman. He was aggressive and a hard worker. Promotion was his reward. He was sent by the National Committee to another city as a section organizer. Soon things began to hum. He reorganized some clubs. He shifted other Party activities. He was putting his ideas to work.

Then he went one step too far. He suggested that the state organization, headed by his superior, could be improved. John should have known better. An organizer can work out new schemes to sell the *Daily Worker,* to recruit members, and to reshuffle clubs; in fact, that is Party initiative. But he doesn't criticize state chairmen and, as John did in this instance, threaten to take up the matter directly with national headquarters.

John quickly became the fellow who "went up fast, down faster." State headquarters, in a special report, severely criticized him and recommended additional Party training. The result: He was recalled and assigned to an insignificant desk job. He had to learn his lesson.

Destructive criticism may lead to *factionalism,* which, in Party eyes, is open rebellion. A member holds a critical opinion. Others agree and soon a faction, or group hostile to the Party line, is formed. Every resource of the Party is mobilized to destroy it.

For a show of democracy, the Party's constitution says:

> Every officer and member shall have the right to express a dissenting opinion on any matter of Party policy with respect to which a decision has been made by majority vote of the appropriate Party committee or convention, *provided that such dissenting officer or member does not engage in factional or other activity which hinders or impedes the execution of such policy.* [Emphasis supplied.]

In other words, in practice any criticism that "hinders" the Party line is called factionalism and is forbidden.

Often, factionalism becomes so pronounced that an entire group is expelled. The Communist Party, with its unreasonable discipline and rigid structure, is peculiarly susceptible to factionalism. There are in America today a number of Marxist factions (called *splinters*), each small in number and with varying degrees of hostility to the Communist Party.

Noncommunists will have difficulty in understanding the utter inhumanity of communist discipline. It is a discipline that pervades every facet of life, drives wedges between husband and wife, and separates families. The best friends today, because of a Party action, may become the bitterest enemies tomorrow.

A Party member heard that her husband, a high-ranking functionary, had just been expelled. The shock was terrific.

He claimed that he was innocent. "I didn't do anything," he stated. And he was right. The charges were completely false. But she refused to believe. She double-checked with Party headquarters. They said he was guilty. The more she thought about it, the angrier she became. Her eyes grew bitter and her mouth curled with scorn. Finally her decision was made.

"Get out of this house," she ordered. "I don't want you around. You're a traitor. Now, OUT!"

Without hesitation she accepted the Party's version, refusing to believe her own husband. The wedge of Party discipline had conquered. The husband was driven away from his own home and his own child. Loyalty to the Party supersedes all emotions of love and mercy and justice.

In California the parents of a young lady were Party members. Both had held high offices in their section. They objected to their daughter's staying out with another Party member until four and five o'clock in the morning, and claimed it was injuring her health and her progress in school. The daughter's boy friend complained to a Party functionary that he was being discriminated against because he was a Negro. The girl's mother, a former section chairman, defended her action. The daughter then took the floor and charged her parents with chauvinism. They were expelled and the daughter then married the complainant.

The Party's constitution provides a number of specific penalties of increasing severity, including expulsion.

The mildest Party penalty is *reprimand,* usually designed to assist Party members in correcting their mistakes. This may take the form of *private censure,* such as, "You had better be on time in the future," or, "Your work wasn't well organized." Somewhat more severe is *public censure,* whereby through written notice or public announcement a comrade is reprimanded. In this way others know of the Party's disapproval.

Then there is *probation.* This may involve a shift from one type of work to another or an assignment to special tasks. If the offender is a paid Party official, he may be demoted (for example, from a state office to a minor position) or transferred to another city. Next is *suspension,* usually for a specific length of time. This amounts to a temporary relief of assignments. The most severe penalty, next to expulsion, is *removal from office.* In such instances the comrade may be stripped of all Party assignments and demoted to being a mere rank-and-filer. This is a hard jolt, especially with the whole Party watching. These acts are object lessons to the membership. "Comrade, be careful. Don't you do the same." Fear plays an important role in communist discipline.

The most drastic penalty, of course, is *expulsion,* and thousands of case examples, even of the highest leaders, form mute evidence.

Once the communists turn on a comrade, the treatment is complete. For example:

Earl Browder, onetime General Secretary, was expelled in February, 1946, for

> . . . developing factional activity and for betraying the principles of Marxism-Leninism and deserting to the side of the class enemy—American monopoly capital.

Sam Donchin, Associate Editor, *Daily Worker,* until shifted to leadership position on the Party's Education Commission, was also expelled. The *Daily Worker* on March 12, 1951, in announcing his expulsion, said, "Donchin was expelled for factionalism, anti-Party activities, hostility to the line of the Party and to the Party leadership, and white chauvinism."

The announcement continued: "Donchin tried to cover up his factionalism in the name of criticism and self-criticism in the Party. He demagogically tried to identify criticism and self-criticism in the ranks of the Party with a right to carry on factional conduct in the Party."

Once a former member breaks with the Party and testifies or makes a public statement, he can expect a merciless campaign of vilification. On April 10, 1952, the well-known stage and screen director, Elia Kazan, appeared before the House Committee on Un-American Activities and testified that he had been in the Party for a year and a half in the 1930's and quit because of the regimentation and thought control that had been directed at him. Two days later he took a paid advertisement in the New York *Times* explaining his reasons. *Daily Worker* writer Samuel Sillen on April 17, 1952, gave Mr. Kazan the full treatment with such vitriolic words as:

> We have seen a lot of belly-crawling in this time of the toad, but nothing has quite equaled last week's command-performance by Hollywood director Elia Kazan. . . . Not even in Hitler days did renegade intellectuals sink so low. . . . Kazan is not content with being a toad. He must also be a philosopher of toadyism.

Communist discipline, however, is not blind or without a deceitful purpose. Individuals should not be expelled impulsively but should be shown the error of their ways. Only when he is deemed "unimprovable" is a member to be ousted. For this reason offenders are often compelled to perform special "disciplinary chores" to "earn their way back," to show through hard work, devotion, and acknowledging the supremacy of the Party that they should be readmitted to favor. In a Northern city, for example, an official in disfavor was placed in charge of arranging a mass meeting. He had to "prove" himself by doing the most menial tasks—running errands, selling tickets, recruiting ushers—he who used to be a keynoter himself. In most instances the more menial the task, the better. In Party eyes, a member who has gone through this self-abasement becomes a better comrade because of it. All thought of resistance is pounded out and he becomes a viable Party tool.

He can be reprimanded, criticized, treated in a brutally unfair manner, yet he'll keep on working. Lash him, and he'll clench his teeth tighter. That's the true revolutionary, in communist eyes.

The key is always acknowledging the supremacy of the Party. Hence, one of the fastest ways "back" is to acknowledge it quickly and completely.

In a Midwestern section an old-time organizer was accused of conduct detrimental to the Party. In a report read at an executive committee meeting he admitted his error. His conduct had been atrocious. Everything charged was true. He should have known better. He was ready to accept punishment. He even suggested his own removal as organizer. This attitude was exactly what the Party wanted. The state office did not relieve the organizer, though cautioning him that if his conduct were repeated, more severe action would be taken. The result: public (and mild) reprimand, not suspension or removal from office.

This explains why, in some instances, severe errors receive minor penalties, whereas small mistakes result in expulsion. The test is often not what a member did wrong but his attitude after the error was committed. If the member is willing to admit his mistake, real or fictitious, accept punishment gladly, and still maintain absolute faith in the leadership, he will probably soon be restored to favor. If he tries, however, to defend himself in the light of the evidence, he must be dealt with harshly. On one occasion a member involved in domestic difficulties replied "none of your business" to an inquiry by the Party. He wasn't long in good standing. In Party language, he showed no "political capabilities," meaning he was not amenable to discipline.

The Communist Party has a systematic campaign of creating hatred against the expelled member. It is not enough just to expel him; he must be vilified, blackened, and made to appear the scum of the earth.

These individuals become "spies," "stool pigeons," "rats," "Trotskyites," "renegades," and "degenerates." To communists, ordinary curse words have no meaning. They have a vocabulary all their own. Hence, "opportunist," "deviationist," and "anti-Party" are their choicest terms of defamation, of characterizing a person as being the meanest, foulest, most black-hearted derelict imaginable.

The higher in Party leadership the ousted member has risen, the greater must be the efforts to defame him. For example, Robert Wood, the Party's onetime Eastern railroad organizer, was expelled with an explosive statement in the *Daily Worker* on March 23, 1951, which said:

> ... various violations of Party discipline, for panic in the face of the fire of the class enemy, for acts endangering the Party, for issuing instructions in the name of the Party which were unauthorized and false, for acts of white chauvinism, and for conduct unbecoming and inconsistent with his post of Party leadership.

From the campaign of vilification there arises a fantastically bitter element of communist discipline and hatred. Every man, woman, and child in the membership must be mobilized against the accused. One Party manual, written by a top leader, recommended:

1. Photograph the spy, and print his picture in the *Daily Worker* and in leaflets and stickers. . . .
2. Organize systematic agitation among the workers where the spy was discovered.
3. Mobilize the children and women in the block in the part of town where the stool pigeon lives to make his life miserable; let them picket the store where his wife purchases groceries and other necessities; let the children in the street shout after him or after any member of his family that they are spies, rats, stool pigeons.
4. Chalk his home with the slogan: "So-and-So who lives here is a spy." Let the children boycott his children or child; organize the children not to talk to his children, etc.

This represents the utter depths of depravity, hate, and

inhuman venom to which the Party will descend in order to wreak vengeance on an expelled member.

An expellee must have no association with any member of the Party—even though that member be his own father, mother, wife, or husband. "Associating with the enemy" is the usual charge. This means the splitting of families, the tearing apart of friends. In one instance a woman member was expelled. Her husband was instructed to leave her and the children. When he refused, he was expelled. Another member who remained friendly was also ousted. It becomes a dizzy merry-go-round of personal spleen.

Once a communist is expelled and there is a likelihood that he might become a government witness, then the communists go to work to compile such information as is available to discourage the witness from testifying for fear of exposure or of being discredited in cross-examination by a communist lawyer. In one case a woman rose to a prominent position in the Party. When she later left the Party, the communists reportedly compiled a large file of her early indiscretions and weaknesses. Consequently, she has always been most reluctant to testify.

Communist discipline has another facet often difficult for noncommunists to understand. In some instances penalties, expulsions, and exposure are not enough; the culprit must pay with his life. Nothing less is satisfactory. The world has witnessed, both in Russia and in the satellites, highly publicized "purge" trials.

The "crime" was not opposition to the Party, lack of loyalty, or unwillingness to sacrifice everything for communism. Rather, these victims were renowned for their devotion, often having spent their entire lives in the movement. Suddenly, within days, their whole position was overturned. They were accused of trying to destroy the very thing they had labored so long to create. How does this make sense?

Communism is cannibalistic. Its servants are periodically offered as sacrifices on the communist altar. If something goes wrong, the trouble lies, in communist eyes, not in the policy decreed on high but in its human instruments. Whenever the "infallible science" of Marxism-Leninism has been incorrectly applied, disciplinary action must follow.

The purge is characteristic of the communist movement everywhere. Lenin was a firm advocate of purges and urged: "If we really succeed . . . in purging our Party from top to bottom, 'without respect for persons,' the gains for the revolution will really be enormous."

William Z. Foster, then Chairman of the Communist Party in the United States, said:

> Communist parties, in line with Lenin's teachings, also constantly strengthen the fiber of their organization by cleansing their ranks of elements that have become confused, corrupted, worn-out, or defeated in the hard and complex struggle to build the forces of socialism in the face of a still powerful and militant capitalism.

A stocky, mustached man stood before the convention of the Communist Political Association in 1945. A few days earlier he had been the undisputed leader of communists in the United States. He was now a "renegade," an "enemy" of the foulest proportions! Earl Browder was fighting for his Party life.

Browder's crime was not disloyalty to the Party but obedience to a policy that, in his opinion, was in the best interests of communism. Moscow thought otherwise. Actually, Browder was a pawn of communist tactics and had to pay the penalty.

He was stripped of Party authority, accused of every conceivable Party crime—by the very subordinates who had been his most loyal supporters. He was later expelled ignominiously, becoming a target of vilification for the entire membership.

Here was a "purge trial" grimly reminiscent, except for bodily punishment, of the infamous purges under Stalin. We need not wonder what Browder's fate might have been if communism had possessed the power of the state.

In our review of life in the Party we have seen how all communist processes are pointed to molding the revolutionary. He is the man who must carry out communist programs such as mass agitation, fronts, and infiltration, to which we now turn. If anywhere he falters, from the Party's point of view, the communist drive for mastery is weakened.

The ousted member in most instances frees himself from the communist thought-control machine. In him lies hope for regeneration. The deepest tragedy lies in the conscious and voluntary submission, day after day, of thousands of Party members. These fanatical devotees, giving their all for the Party, represent a real danger to our way of life.

Part V

THE COMMUNIST
TROJAN HORSE
IN ACTION

14.

Communist Strategy and Tactics

IN PRECEDING CHAPTERS I have briefly outlined the history and internal structure of the Communist Party, USA. Now we must consider the Party's attack against noncommunist society in the United States.

The Communist Party, USA, is a weapon of attack, not only for the day of revolution but for *now*. To Party leaders each day is a day of preparation and dress rehearsal for the day when they hope to come to power. Noncommunist ranks must be infiltrated, penetrated, and subverted. The success of the communist mission depends on capturing the enemy's stronghold from within.

To this end the Party employs a variety of *mass-agitation* techniques. The communist is in the market places of America: in organizations, on street corners, even at your front door. He is trying to influence and control your thoughts. Mass agitation weakens the noncommunist enemy and builds Party structure.

Communists conceive of their attack against capitalist society in terms of warfare. They see the Party as the "vanguard," leading the proletariat in battle against the bourgeoisie. Periods of offense and defense, attacks and retreats, skirmishes, even pitched battles and casualties are demanded. They realize that victory can be achieved only by force and violence.

This warlike character of communist policy is reflected in Party expressions such as "strongholds of reaction," "mobilizing the masses," "advanced detachments of the proletariat," "storming the fortress of capitalism," "seizing the initiative." Basic battle plans are conceived in terms of *strategy* and *tactics*.

The ultimate aim of the Communist Party is the establishment of a Soviet America. For more than a generation, never for a moment have American communists forgotten their allegiance to the Soviet Union. This is the ultimate strategy of the Communist Party, USA.

Party leaders realize, however, that they are a minority. They simply cannot march straight to victory. For that reason the approach (tactics) must be varied, flexible, and constantly subject to change.

To communists, strategy means the determining and carrying out of long-range goals (such as winning a war), whereas tactics are the working out of strategy on a day-to-day basis (winning particular battles and engagements). "Tactics," Stalin said, "are a part of strategy, subordinate and subservient to it."

To achieve the long-range goal, retreats and maneuvers sometimes are necessary. Is it not like climbing an unexplored mountain? asks Lenin. How can we "renounce beforehand the idea that at times we might have to go in zigzags, sometimes retracing our steps, sometimes abandoning the course once selected and trying various others?"

That explains the communist phrase, "strategic retreat." It means: Don't be afraid to take two steps backward today if it will help to achieve three steps forward tomorrow.

Keep the goal always in mind, teach the communists; remember that the enemy is superior in numbers, better armed, more experienced. Moreover, communists must be willing to endure hardships. Lenin urged: ". . . if you are not inclined to crawl in the mud on your belly, you are not a revolutionary but a chatterbox. . . ." Fight hard and be disciplined, "carefully, attentively and skilfully taking advantage of every, even the smallest 'fissure' among the enemies. . . ." Seize "every, even the smallest opportunity of gaining a mass ally, even though this ally be temporary, vacillating, unstable, unreliable and conditional." And "Those who do not understand this fail to understand even a grain of Marxism. . . ."

Use anything to advance the ultimate goal: offensive and defensive tactics, legal and illegal, long- and short-range policies. All are part of the over-all battle plan.

Don't allow the Party to advance too rapidly. Stop, consolidate, maintain contact with the masses. ". . . an advance *without consolidating* the positions already captured is an advance doomed to failure." Likewise, never make a permanent truce with the enemy. Don't be trapped by his lures, bribes, and promises. Cooperation or collaboration with noncommunists must never be more than a "tactic." It must have as its actual long-range goal the weakening and discrediting of democracy and its eventual destruction. The task of the revolutionary leader is to gauge the comparative strength of the proletariat and the bourgeoisie and decide what particular tactics are then most likely to promote revolution.

Communists employ various tactics in devising methods to inject themselves into various phases of American life. Their obligation to defend the interests of the Soviet Union dictates their tactics in seeking to obstruct and undermine public confidence in our foreign policy. Thus, seizing upon the inherent desire of all Americans to reduce taxes, the *Daily Worker* editorializes that foreign aid should be curtailed and billions should not be taken "out of our pockets for a new phony 'emergency'. . . . The huge seventy-billion a year 'defense' budget is rushing America to inflation, and economic crisis." Actually, communists would like to develop an economic crisis.

Then they urge the development of a peacetime economy by advocating trade between the United States and Russia because Russia would benefit. *Political Affairs* thus urges, "The only remaining untapped market for U. S. goods is the Soviet Union, China and the Peoples' Democracies, in which the threat of crises of overproduction has been removed forever. . . ."

In seeking to curry favor with labor, communists employ tactics of calling for immediate demands such as higher wages, a shorter work week, increased vacations, and an abolition of the high cost of living. To that end a communist labor tactician calls for putting ". . . ideological differences aside in order to work together in behalf of a *single immediate objective* or a *number of immediate objectives.* . . . the unions must work together. . . ."

The immediate demand tactics are also employed by the communists to find favor with Negroes by urging the abolition of "Jim Crow Laws," "full representation," and "the fight for Negro rights." The controversy on integration has given the communists a field day.

They also have a program ". . . to stimulate broad united-front actions in the rural communities in defense of the economic interests of the farming masses"; "to weld youth unity"; and to "work still harder" for mothers.

A primary tactic of the Communist Party is to preserve the legal status of the Party. Thus, any organization which has the duty to investigate or expose communist activity is singled out for attack. For years the Party has campaigned against the House Committee on Un-American Activities, the Senate Internal Security Sub-Committee, and the Senate Investigating Committee. The Department of Justice and the FBI have not been spared, and we have come to judge our effectiveness by the intensity of communist attacks.

The Red Fascists have long followed the practice of making full use of democratic liberties: elections, lawful agitation and propaganda, and free speech, press, and assembly. Their basic premise: Reap every advantage possible. However, if it will help, don't hesitate to use illegal methods, such as underground operations, terrorism, espionage, sabotage, lying, cheating. "We have never rejected terror on principle, nor can we do so. Terror is a form of military operation that may be usefully applied. . . ." wrote Lenin. Morality is strictly a bourgeois device. To the communists everything that promotes the revolution is moral, legal, and beautiful.

Many people are confused by the Party's abrupt twists and turns, such as denouncing the United States as an "imperialist" nation from 1939 to 1941, then overnight, after Russia's entrance into the war, hailing America as a great ally. Communists often look like frightened rabbits chasing back and forth. But in reality these "changes in the Party line" are merely shifting tactics, all designed to promote the ultimate goal of world revolution. They are not changes in heart.

The Communist Party, USA, has been and is engaged in an all-out war against American freedom. Its tactics of confusion, retreat, advance, infiltration, and hypocrisy are in full play. The attack is both legal and illegal, offensive and defensive, open and concealed.

Above the surface a gigantic propaganda and agitation campaign is in progress, a campaign that depends for success upon the support of noncommunists. Basic communist strategy dictates that noncommunist hands, knowingly or unknowingly, under communist guidance, must further the influence of the communist world.

To understand communist strategy and tactics, as designed to destroy American democracy, we must first observe *above-ground* communist operations: mass-agitation campaigns, infiltration techniques, and Party fronts; then in Part VI we will consider the *underground* organization.

15.

Mass Agitation

As STATED IN CHAPTER 10, the Party's attack is geared to the wide variety of American life. Communism has something to sell to everybody. And, following this principle, it is the function of mass agitation to exploit all the grievances, hopes, aspirations, prejudices, fears, and ideals of all the special groups that make up our society, social, religious, economic, racial, political. Stir them up. Set one against the other. Divide and conquer. That's the way to soften up a democracy.

Here is the advice of a top leader giving instruction on how to spread the Party's influence:

Study your friends. See what they spontaneously talk about. What problems interest them?

—is he an unemployed worker, skilled in his craft but without work?;
—a storekeeper? Maybe business isn't so good;
—a trade-union man or a dairy farmer? What are their problems?;
—a young man just out of school? Looking for a job?;
—a member of a minority group?;
—a young mother worrying about sending her child to kindergarten?

". . . unless each one of us grasps the meaning of this individual approach to every one of our friends and acquaintances, we are in danger" of being ineffective.

Agitation must be carried on in specialized fields: among women, among youth, among veterans, among racial and nationality groups, farmers, trade unions. That's the responsibility of the Party commissions.

Consider youth, a prime target of communist attack. Communists start out with this major premise: American imperialism aims to create a corrupt, completely militarized youth—a "gagged," "scared" generation. This theme is expounded by word of mouth, in forums, in literature, in cartoons, hoping to exploit the lofty dreams of youth.

The approach always has two sides: (1) *the deceptive line designed for public consumption,* and (2) *the real Party line designed to advance communism.* Consider this *deceptive line* for youth:

1. Increase trade with all countries, including the communist bloc, to provide "hundreds of thousands of new jobs for young people."
2. Outlaw all mass destruction weapons (atomic bomb).
3. Promote universal disarmament and peace.
4. Reduce military expenditures and repeal the draft.

5. Repeal all "repressive legislation" and "restore the Bill of Rights."
6. "Restore full academic freedom for students and faculties."
7. Promote world-wide "youth friendship for peace and democracy," drop all bars to the travel of youth.
8. Appropriate more money for schools, community centers, etc.

That is the line designed for public consumption. Sounds acceptable, doesn't it? But the communists are not genuinely interested in improving the status of American youth.

For window-dressing, they always support items desired by most of the people: lower taxes, higher wages, better housing, old-age security, higher farm income. These are thoroughly legitimate interests. To support these aims, and many others, is not to be a communist. The Party is simply attempting to exploit such interests for its own selfish aims. They become Party "talking points."

Behind this front, as in the call for world-wide youth friendship, more education, academic freedom, and so on, lurks the ulterior motive, the real Party line. The attractive "come along" points are merely bait. Look closely to see how the adoption of these demands, *as conceived by the Party,* would distort their true meanings and aid the communist cause:

"*Restore the Bill of Rights,*" in communist language, means eliminating of legal opposition to communism, stopping all prosecution of communists, and granting amnesty to those presently in jail. "*Repeal the draft law*" and "*peace*" mean curtailing our national defense effort and allowing Russia to become militarily stronger than the United States. "*Increase trade with the Soviet Bloc*" means selling materials that could be used by the communist nations for armaments. "*Restore academic freedom*" means to communists that we should permit the official teaching of communist doctrine in all schools and that we should allow communists to infiltrate teaching staffs. If the communists had their way, America would be rendered helpless to protect herself. Incidentally, notice the communist use of the word "restore," indicating that freedom is already gone and that the Party stands for its return.

Now substitute "veterans" for "youth." The approach is the same: Increased trade with all countries, including the communist bloc, would mean thousands of new jobs for *veterans*. "Restore" academic freedom so *veterans* can think as they want. Promote world-wide *veteran* friendship. Drop all bars to the travel of *veterans*. Also, it is good propaganda policy to add a few "come along" points appealing specifically to veterans. The technique continues: substitute "women," "trade union members," "nationality groups," etc.

The propaganda platform contains a combination of immediate "come along" demands, designed for deceptive and specialized appeal, and basic policy aimed to advance the communist cause.

Thus the Party, through its specialized and immediate demands, is able to gain entree into various groups and create favorable working conditions for future revolutionary action. Very quickly, for example:

—a veterans' meeting endorses "peace."
—a nationality festival passes a resolution for "peace."
—a youth affair favors "peace."
—a neighborhood group comes out for "peace."
—a women's rally fights for "peace."

Whatever its composition, the group, once under communist control, is switched to the Party line. The feigned interest in legitimate demands is merely a trap.

Even holidays are used to enhance the Party's aims. For example, the *Daily Worker* once headlined a story "Mother's Day to Be Marked by Peace Tables . . ." Postcards should be distributed on Mother's Day, the story continued, "declaring the deepest need of all American mothers to be a ban on A- and H-bombs. . . ."

Also planned, according to the story, were special Mother's Day leaflets and placards as well as balloons for the children reading "World-Wide Ban of A- and H-bombs."

Many people sincerely believe, for many reasons, that these

bombs should be banned. However, to communists, the true meaning of peace and banning the A- and H-bombs is weakening the United States and advancing Russian aggressive aims.

And so it goes. A discussion may start about the low price of oats, better working conditions on the second shift, equal pay for women, the death rate among Eskimos, but it will end with the endorsement of "peace"; "amnesty for the Smith Act victims"; "repeal of the Internal Security Act of 1950 and the McCarran-Walter Immigration and Nationality Act."

Scattered, variegated, and inarticulate interests, under Party guidance, are brought into a common denominator: support for the Party line.

The Party line, in fact, is the sum total of all Party demands at any given time. You must learn to see it as a whole. Some demands are always present and seem innocent enough, such as those for higher wages, lower taxes, and better housing. But, remember, communists don't really care about genuine social reforms. These immediate demands are strictly for agitational purposes. They serve to arouse people and to cause tension. William Z. Foster says very candidly: "Our Party is a revolutionary Party. It aims not simply to ease conditions a bit under capitalism for the workers but to abolish capitalism altogether."

If ever achieved, these demands will be restated in more extreme form.

Other demands in the Party line are short-term; that is, they may quickly change, depending on the current national and international situation. Consider the Party's stand that Formosa should be returned to China proper. Suppose the present communist regime in China were overthrown and a government hostile to Soviet Russia gained power. This demand would be quickly abandoned. On the other hand, certain demands never change, such as support of the Soviet Union.

The attack is primarily agitational. Propaganda, although valuable, is a long-range softener, to be handled chiefly on an intellectual level by the educational department; agitation is immediate, inflammatory, conducive to acute discontent, the specialty of the field organizer.

Lenin's distinction is decisive. A propagandist, he says, to explain unemployment must talk about the capitalist nature of the crisis, the need for building a socialist society, etc. " 'Many ideas' " must be expounded, "so many indeed that they will be understood as a whole only by a (comparatively) few persons."

But the agitator, on the other hand, selects one well-known aspect of the problem, such as "the death from starvation of the family of an unemployed worker." He will concentrate on imparting a single idea to the masses: why this family died. Or, in Lenin's words, he will show "the senseless contradiction between the increase of wealth and increase of poverty." Evoke discontent and revolt *now*. "Leave a more complete explanation . . . to the propagandist." Here is an example of how agitation works:

The communists publish a story: John Doe has been arrested, the charge is murder. Of course it is a tragic event. Crime always brings sorrow. It reflects maladjustment in society and points up abuses that genuinely need correction. But the communists aren't interested in John Doe. They do not try to discover the true facts in his case, study his background, or improve his condition. Here in the day's news is a human tragedy that can be exploited for propaganda purposes. That is enough.

The Party machinery springs into action, typical of thousands of mass-agitation campaigns.

The communist press publicizes the case with pictures, an interview with the wrongdoer, stories about his family. It carries heart-rending and sentimental accounts, without regard to truth or the suffering of the victim of the crime or the sorrow of his loved ones.

If the arrested person is a member of a minority group, or a veteran, the father of ten children, a union member or unemployed, the agitational appeal is broadened. "Union Member Framed on Murder Charge." "Unemployed Veteran Railroaded to Jail." "Father of 10 Arrested on False Charges." Almost always the charge of "police brutality" is thrown in too.

In a few days a decision must be made. Should the campaign continue? Maybe the case is quickly over, no special interest having been aroused. Or the "victim" himself announces that he's been treated fairly and has no personal ill feelings. That's the end. The Party drops it.

Such campaigns are sometimes carried on for months or years, with varying degrees of intensity. The Party is a self-appointed collector of "victims" of "framed evidence," "lynch justice," "Gestapo brutality," "academic witchhunts." These "martyrs of injustice" include old-timers like Sacco and Vanzetti and the Scottsboro Case, now remembered only in "memorials"; and recent ones, such as the "Martinsville Seven," the "Trenton Six" or the Rosenbergs; or hot-off-the-griddle varieties, such as those appearing in the current Party press. All are trotted out at the slightest twist of tongue or pencil as exhibits of capitalist "terror" and communist "benevolence."

Certain exploitation standards determine whether the campaign is to continue: Can large numbers of people be influenced? Is a public official involved—the more prominent the better—who can be undermined and smeared? Will other communist ventures be aided? Can the Party gain recruits? (Mass agitation is always linked to Party building.) Can financial gains be secured for the Party?

The Party searches American life for agitational points: the eviction of a family, the arrest of a Negro, a proposed rise in transit fares, a bill to increase taxes, a miscarriage of justice, the underpayment of a worker, the dismissal of a teacher, a shooting by law-enforcement officers. Some of the cases, unfortunately, do reflect mistakes or blemishes in American society. Others are twisted by the Party into agitational items.

Once the decision has been made to continue the campaign, the next step is probably the formation of the XYZ Committee to Save John Doe: a communist front, born at 9:00 A.M., full grown by 10:30 A.M., mailing out letters by noon. This gives the illusion of organized interest, focuses attention, and masks communist participation. Purpose (deceptive) is to gain "justice" for the defendant; purpose (real): to advance communism.

Attract attention by building up a bonfire of agitation. Suddenly, almost like magic, a "women's" group in Oregon, a "farmers'" meeting in Oklahoma, a "consumers'" conference in West Virginia pass resolutions: "Save John Doe!" Literature is scattered, other groups contacted. The Party becomes the agitational base. Who is John Doe? The members don't know, except that he's the newest twist in the Party line. That's enough!

The Party has now started a mass-agitation campaign. Its success depends on securing noncommunist support. Members contact community leaders, such as judges, members of the city council, doctors, lawyers, clergymen, educators, social workers, trying to obtain statements or testimonials.

The communist is no longer a shadowy figure deep underground or meeting secretly at night. He is knocking on doors, seeing prominent people, attending city council meetings.

> I feel that John Doe has been wrongly arrested [or convicted, as the case may be]. I am compelled in the interests of justice to demand that he be released.

That is a typical testimonial to be sent to authorities and the press.

The technique of obtaining testimonials is always to start with a sympathizer, the kind who will authorize his name for any communist campaign. Some are so "controlled" that headquarters uses their names without consultation, even preparing their statements. Others are contacted on each occasion.

They next reach out for other prominent sympathizers. Officers of communist fronts make good signers. They usually have imposing "titles." Next, branch out to the lukewarm, those who are on the fence; sometimes they will sign, other times they will not. If not, they must be sold. Finally come the unsuspecting noncommunists, with contact being made either in person or on the telephone.

"Mr. X, I'm So-and-So from the XYZ Committee to Save

John Doe. I was just over at Mr. Y's office. You know him, don't you?"

"Yes," will come the reply. That gets the interview off to a good start.

"This is a case I am sure will interest you. You are a lawyer and here is an individual who is the victim of injustice. . . . Have you heard about it?"

"No." That's good, the field is clear.

On and on. "Dr. F, Rev. O, etc., have given statements . . ."

The man signs. Another "innocent victim." Did he know the communist identity of the solicitor? No. Did he know that the XYZ Committee to Save John Doe was a communist front? No. Did he realize that by making the statement he was aiding the communist movement? No.

For sincere, honest reasons of their own, entirely unrelated to communism, many individuals may support John Doe. This, of course, does not make them communists. To call them communists is an injustice, but it is not unjust to point out that the Party always seeks to exploit such personal convictions for partisan propaganda.

The cause of communism must be linked with as many elements in society as possible. Our fight for John Doe is your fight, the communists say to labor unions, Negro, professional, cultural, and nationality groups. Today he's being "persecuted." Tomorrow it'll be your turn. Join with us and we'll fight together.

> . . . we Communists join with every other democratic-minded American, irrespective of views, in the common fight to preserve a common democratic heritage.

Deceptive: the communists are fighting for our "common democratic heritage"; *real:* to gain the support of noncommunist groups (even ". . . those who do not accept Socialism as a final aim"). As Lenin instructed, seize allies everywhere. Use them for the advantage of furthering communism.

Mass agitation is most effective in capturing the support of noncommunists. By securing even the temporary allegiance of an individual, as in a testimonial, the Party gains. In this way communist propaganda enters the orbit of that individual's personal influence. "Why," a friend will say after reading the testimonial, "if So-and-So endorses that organization [or issue], it must be OK." The dupe becomes a communist thought-control relay station. That's why communists are always eager to secure the support of doctors, clergymen, teachers, and other persons highly respected in their communities. The more widely known the person, the better.

Circulating petitions is another favorite communist technique for capturing noncommunist support.

A young woman stands on the sidewalk. A housewife, carrying a package, comes out of the grocery store.

"Pardon me," the young woman says, approaching her. "Wouldn't you like to help a young man win his freedom?"

The appeal is attractive. The housewife stops. "We have a petition to the governor asking for the release of John Doe. He's sentenced to die. . . ." The housewife looks at the petition. It contains nothing communist. There is no hammer or sickle or mention of Russia. It is just a statement that we the undersigned believe that John Doe should be released. "You can help a lot by signing. . . ."

She signs and so do thousands of others. Party teams are everywhere, on street corners, at factory gates, in bus terminals. Sign here, please. Won't you send a telegram or write a letter? Here's a sample all fixed up. Just sign it. Would you like a leaflet? Won't you call the governor's office? Come to our rally tonight. Write a letter to the newspaper. Is your club meeting soon? Have it pass a resolution. Your pastor can help. Have him call a protest meeting.

The pressure is tabulated in thousands of letters, resolutions, and telegrams, ten, a hundred times the number of all Party members in the United States.

Agitation campaigns are of all types, local, state, and national:

—dealing with the high cost of living;
—against a rise in transit fares;

—opposing a bill in Congress or a state legislature;

—protesting the showing of a "Fascist" movie;

—urging amnesty for convicted Smith Act "victims";

—demanding "peace"; "repeal the draft"; "more aid to schools";

—protesting the arrival in town of some celebrity not liked by the Party.

Campaigns involving court cases as a general rule provide the most sustained agitation. These can be divided into various *exploitation stages.*

1. *The arrest stage:* the "victim" has been illegally arrested. The charges are "trumped up."

2. *The trial stage:* "false evidence" is being used, the jury is "packed," a fair trial is "impossible."

3. *The appeal stage* (assuming that the defendant is found guilty): in most cases a guilty verdict serves the communist purpose best. Otherwise, little propaganda is left, except for a few self-congratulatory articles. The communists use every device, inside and outside the courtroom, to break down the American judicial system.

4. *The clemency stage:* this is probably best suited to agitation. The Party operates a whole series of tactics. Here are a few:

Mass meetings. Rallies. Demonstrations. Picket lines. These, also used in other exploitation stages, now become imbued with "gravity." "John Doe Will Die in 2 Weeks. Wire the Governor. Demand His Release." "Save My Boy, Please. He's Innocent." "Where's America's Conscience? This Man Has Been Framed."

Sojourns. Treks. Pilgrimages. Motorcades. Encampments. The convergence on a selected spot, the state capital or Washington, D.C., of members and sympathizers from all over the country.

They arrive by train, battered old trucks, rented buses,

hitchhiking. Get your tickets, meet at the station, don't miss the Clemency Train. Day after day the *Daily Worker* pounds this theme. An operational headquarters is set up, usually under a fancy Aesopian name such as "Liberty House" or "Inspiration Center."

This tactic—concentrated pressure—is reserved only for special occasions. Teams visit offices of legislators, officials of the government, and demand to see the governor or President. Make everyone think that "millions" are demanding clemency. A cascade of telegrams, letters, petitions, resolutions pours in, promoted by comrades back home. "The city was stirred today by the *nation's* demand for clemency for John Doe. . . ." writes the Party's press agent. Probably 250 communists and their sympathizers were in town.

The hour of judicial decision or execution nears. The drama is heightened. "Prayer meetings" are held by communists, who do not believe in prayer. Then the super climax: a "vigil." The comrades start a marching line, twenty-four hours around the clock, demanding "mercy," "clemency." One day, two days, five days, twelve days, the line moves back and forth in front of the governor's mansion, or more dramatic, the White House. Placards read: "Mercy for John Doe." "Mr. Governor, Don't You Have a Heart?" Any testimonials secured from prominent individuals bob and weave in the marching line. Leaflets are handed out.

In two hours comes a new shift. Paraders walk silently, sometimes in single file, at other times two abreast, usually six to eight feet apart. This isn't supposed to be a flamboyant affair, but sad and mournful, designed to capture the emotions. Death is near! "Clemency *Now*—Only 12 Hours Left." "Can America Allow an Innocent Man to Die?"

The shift is over. The members whisk back to "Liberty House," grab a bite to eat, hear a pep talk, then return for another "tour of duty." Cots are available for sleep. In this way a few fanatical comrades can attract the attention of thousands. Over the week end other comrades, off from work, "flood" into a city and, in the flaming words of the Party press, march by the "thousands"—meaning probably 250 to 300.

"There's Still Time to Act. Send Telegrams, Letters to the Governor." Mount the pressure. So long as John Doe is alive he must be exploited.

5. *The imprisonment stage:* the defendant becomes a show-piece. He is visited by his wife (called a "prison wife") and his family, and delegations go to see him. Sentimental and heart-tearing accounts are written: ". . . as the train sped me northward, my eyes ached with unwept tears of loneliness." "I heard [his] quiet voice. I looked into his calm eyes. But I noted too the tight lines of controlled grimness about his mouth and the narrowed tightness about his eyes."

Birthday-card campaigns are initiated. Send John Doe a Christmas greeting. His picture is published. His "speeches" become "quotable scripture." A nine-year-old son visits him . . . the child is shocked by the "watchtowers," "gigantic searchlights," "locked iron doors" . . . the visit is over . . . the little boy tells his mother, "After all, if Daddy didn't have such good political ideas he wouldn't be there in the first place." (He is a Smith Act "victim.")

The communist press will invariably superimpose its judgment on that of a jury and judge with a trumped-up charge that the homicide was justifiable, the evidence framed, or the witness had committed perjury. It will have a defense for the crime that would cause the person not familiar with the facts or the record of the trial to wonder. And the longer the lapse of time, the more real the trumped-up defense will sound to the uninformed. This might go on for years. For example, the Women's Committee for Equal Justice was not disbanded until seven years after Rosa Lee Ingram and her two sons had been convicted and sentenced in a Georgia court for the slaying of a neighbor.

6. *The post-imprisonment stage:* most of the propaganda value is generally gone when this stage is reached. If the "victim" is dead, "memorial" services may occasionally be held or articles written.

The cycle has run. The campaign may be dropped at any

moment, shifted to a new tack, used to buttress another approach. Another purpose, especially in espionage cases, is to make the "victim" think he is a "martyr" and believe that any cooperation with the American government, such as implicating others or giving vital information, would be a betrayal. Better to have him executed by the government for his crimes than to expose other communists.

These campaigns are designed to dramatize communists and their front representatives as "champions" of the masses. They foster the illusion that these individuals are progressive, enlightened, and humanitarian, acting in the best interests of the American people. "We stand for freedom when everybody else is not interested." That is the illusion.

The real motive is to prepare both the Party and noncommunist society for revolutionary action. Members gain experience in mass work: the art of propaganda and agitation, organizing social discontent, guiding large numbers. Leadership, discipline, and organizational structure can be tested. Moreover, communists hope to make workers and the masses class-conscious, accepting the Party as their leader (in Party terms called *radicalizing* the masses). Sow seeds of discontent; weaken, divide, and neutralize anticommunist opposition; above all, undermine the American judicial process.

Law enforcement has long been a target of communist attack. As legal opposition crystallized, these Party attacks, especially on the FBI, prosecutive officials, and police, have mounted in intensity.

Lenin taught that it was essential for every "real people's revolution" to destroy the "ready-made state machinery." Wherever communists have been able to exercise any measure of control, their first step has been to hamstring and incapacitate law enforcement.

The communist performance in the Indian state of Kerala is a good illustration. Within a few months after a procommunist government came into control, "people's action committees" were formed which began to usurp the functions of the law courts. Then the state police were handcuffed by orders to stand on the sidelines except when crimes such as murder, rape, arson, and assault occurred. Many communists were freed from jail, and public statements were issued that many penal institutions would be closed and their grounds turned into flower gardens. A noncommunist official of the Indian government reported a "complete breakdown of law and order."

Experience over the years has demonstrated that every time communists are able to avert justice through technicalities, there is not only jubilation in Party circles but also increased urgings for more brazen Party action.

Day-to-day struggles are battle-hardening dress rehearsals for revolution. William Z. Foster boasted, ". . . capitalism will die sword in hand, fighting in vain to beat back the oncoming revolutionary proletariat."

Often communists find it effective to carry out their agitation campaigns through organizations not generally recognized as procommunist. These can be either (1) old-time organizations which have been "infiltrated," or (2) newly established communist fronts. The next two chapters will discuss these forms of communist campaigning.

16.

Infiltration

INFILTRATION IS THE METHOD whereby Party members move into noncommunist organizations for the purpose of exercising influence for communism. If control is secured, the organization becomes a communist front. This chapter shows how infiltration works and what you can do about it.

Infiltration is one of the oldest of communist tactics, advocated by Lenin and Stalin. For instance, listen to this exhortation by Georgi Dimitroff, General Secretary, before the Seventh World Congress of the Communist International:

> Comrades, you remember the ancient tale of the capture of Troy. Troy was inaccessible to the armies attacking her, thanks to her impregnable walls. And the attacking army, after suffering many sacrifices, was unable to achieve victory until with the aid of the famous Trojan horse it managed to penetrate to the very heart of the enemy's camp.

Homer's famous story, Dimitroff said, must be applied to the twentieth century. "We . . . should not be shy about using the same tactics . . ." The Trojan horse has enabled the Party to wield an influence far in excess of its actual numbers.

For example, a community emergency occurred and assistance was badly needed in a stricken area. A labor union in Cleveland, Ohio, raised money to purchase food for distribution to the victims of this adversity in a small West Virginia town where families actually were in want for the necessities of life. The Communist Party organizer in Cleveland instructed a concealed Party member of the union that the truck driver was to deliver the food to a specified address in the stricken area in West Virginia where it would do the most "good."

Here a noncommunist organization was paying the bill, thinking that it was doing a generous act of charity. Yet concealed communists within its ranks were subverting the generosity to communist ends. Since the Party had actual control over the distribution, who do you think got credit for the generosity?

Such incidents are frequent. Strikes have been called or settlements influenced by Party penetration within labor unions. Party manipulation has controlled the conventions of noncommunist organizations and determined the selection of officers. An idea originated in a Party office can, through this technique, be translated within days or hours into interviews with high government officials, into intensive agitation campaigns, or even, as has happened, into disruption of industrial production.

No wonder the Party desperately seeks to infiltrate labor unions, the government, civic and community groups, religious, professional, economic, and social organizations. It desires to make these organizations, in various ways, serve Party interests.

Party leaders spend much time and effort in studying infiltration strategy and tactics. A hasty, ill-advised, or poorly timed move might wipe out months of preparation. Should the objective be complete capture of the organization or the placing of a few key members? If the latter, where should the initial attack be delivered? Would it be better to place a member on the midnight or on the swing shift? Where can the greatest and most immediate gains be secured? A flexible strategy, adapted to current conditions, must be employed.

Communists have probably worked harder to infiltrate American labor unions than any other group. Since the days of Lenin, labor has been a favorite target. The Russian dictator was explicit:

> It is necessary to . . . agree to any and every sacrifice, and even —if need be—to resort to all sorts of stratagems, manoeuvres and illegal methods, to evasion and subterfuges in order to penetrate the trade unions, to remain in them, and to carry on Communist work in them at all costs.

The statement is frank: Communists are not interested in the laboring man, higher wages, better working conditions, shorter hours. They want to get inside unions in order to agitate for communism.

An overwhelming majority of American labor-union members are honest, hard-working, loyal citizens. They detest communism. This has been proven time after time. Alerted to the presence of communists, they will cast them out. Most of the Party's gains achieved prior to and during World War II in the labor movement have now been destroyed.

These defeats, however, have not halted the danger. "At least 90 per cent of all of our efforts," one Party writer asserted, must be devoted to industrial workers. Drawing on years of experience, the Party is today attacking labor unions with renewed vigor. The best way to defeat this assault is to know communist tactics of action.

The first thing in labor-union infiltration tactics is to secure a foothold inside a union, through a single comrade or, better yet, two or three. Comrades then do everything possible to build up strength inside the organization, creating a shop club.

Members of shop clubs are expected to promote Party influence in all possible ways. Very important is the recruitment of new members. The Party's influence depends on members, especially on their strategic placement in the union and in industry.

"How-to-recruit" suggestions, for example, are often supplied to shop comrades. One Party manual urges that members mix with the workers and cultivate friendships.

> Especially must the Communist mingle with his fellow workers at noon time and participate in the general discussions and conversations that take place.

Always try to steer these discussions, the manual says, into "economic and political channels"—so as to provide the chance to insert communist propaganda. And don't use technical Party terms. Learn to express "our Marxian line" in good "American slang." Communism can best be sold in the every-day language of the prospect.

If the worker shows "interest" (the communists say if "he's more advanced"), give him a *Daily Worker* or pamphlet to read. Then invite him to a meeting or "study group."

Try to stay with him after working hours. "The majority of our Party members become Communists only after working hours, around 6 P.M." For communists there is no such thing as an eight-hour day.

The over-all work of infiltration, especially of shop clubs, is coordinated by Party strategy caucuses; that is, Party-called meetings where the problems of infiltration are studied. They are generally held on an industry basis, such as the automobile, steel, railroad, mining, and electrical industries, with members employed in these fields attending.

Party caucuses operate on different levels. There will be, for example, local caucuses of Party members employed in a certain industry in a given area, such as the automobile or electrical industry in Detroit or Cleveland. Then there are state and national caucuses, with Party leaders being drawn from wider areas. Party labor directors are usually in charge. In the past, for instance, national "auto" caucuses were often held in Cleveland or Detroit, "steel" in Youngstown, "electrical" in Buffalo, and "mining" in Pittsburgh. Sometimes Party leaders in related unions, such as automobile and steel, are brought together in a general communist labor conference.

These caucuses are literally strategy-devising meetings, where problems and procedures are analyzed with X-ray precision. Noncommunists probably do not realize how carefully communists study "capitalist" companies, wage policies, personnel, etc. The objective always is: How can the company and the union be used to implement the Party line, as support for "peace," the Smith Act "victims," or some current Party "martyr"?

For an answer let's look in on one Party caucus.

Leslie, from the northwestern part of the state, was reporting on what his shop club was doing, that is, soliciting signatures to a "peace" petition.

"We got seven hundred and four signatures in a little over three days last week."

"Keep at it," the organizer responded. "Get more signature campaigns going. Contact those people who have already signed. See if they are friendly and understand our position. If so, go a third time. (Maybe a recruit could be secured.) Encourage them to circulate a petition themselves."

"At our plant," another Party leader commented, "we started a committee to protect freedom of speech. It's a good issue and we've had some fine response. I think we ought to soon rally some support for the Smith Act victims. I hope we can get some contributions too."

"Fine," the organizer added, "but always remember that we

must stress our united-front campaign. We've got to show the workers in these right-wing [that is, anticommunist] unions that the Party stands for peace, higher wages, and better working conditions.

"What if most of the workers don't agree with communism?" the organizer continued. "That doesn't keep them from working with us. We've got to convince them that we must all work together, that we have common aims. Besides, it will help us organize the rank and file against the reactionary [anticommunist] leadership."

The caucuses give guidance. This is how to agitate on Party issues: Issue petitions and resolutions, set up a "peace" stand outside the shop gate, start a front. Ideas are exchanged, weaknesses analyzed, tactical shifts worked out, all under supervision of Party headquarters.

Sometimes the caucuses manipulate special "deals" to enhance Party influence. The following case, which occurred in Cleveland, Ohio, is revealing:

"Howard," the organizer said, addressing one of the older members, "you've got to give up your job as editor of the union's newspaper."

"Give up . . . ," the member said, surprised.

"Your time's running out. You're just about pegged as a communist. If you try to stay on another year, you'll be thrown out. That'll cause a rumpus and we'll lose ground. Step out now."

"OK," the member replied, accepting the instruction. "I think I can get Elmer elected in my place. Dick may want it, but we've got to stop him."

"Right you are," the organizer said. "Dick is a vicious Red baiter. He's a faker and reactionary. I'd rather have the paper discontinued than have him as editor."

"Elmer isn't known as a communist," the member added. "Of course, if I support him it'll tag him somewhat, but . . ."

"That's our best approach, Howard," the organizer said. "Submit your resignation tomorrow. You'll catch Dick and his cronies off guard. Then push all you can for Elmer."

What follows now is a case history which reveals the whole

sinister process of infiltration. It concerns an organization that we shall call The 123 Group, typical of many trade-union, fraternal, civic, community, and nationality groups. It covers a six-year struggle for control between the Communist Party—working through a group of open and concealed members, sympathizers, and dupes—and a noncommunist opposition, at first unorganized, hitting wildly, but later to become all-powerful.

The 123 Group was an influential and respected noncommunist organization. Even partly to control its actions would be of great value to the Party.

The problem for communist headquarters was how best to attack. The obvious target, as in most organizations, was the officers. To control one officer, such as a president, secretary, or treasurer, is often worth ten, twenty, or fifty rank-and-file members. Everything must be done to prepare for the next elections in an effort to oust as many anticommunists as possible and replace them with pro-Party people or at least neutrals.

All officers of The 123 Group were bitterly anticommunist except one, the secretary. He would have loudly protested if called a Party member, and he wasn't; but for many years he had maintained cordial contacts with Party officials. He was, in every respect, a sympathizer. He was popular and had a large personal following among the rank and file. For this reason the anticommunists had not been able to defeat him. Here was the obvious weak point.

"We've got to draw up an entire slate of candidates," the Party organizer emphasized. "Let's call it the 'Reform Ticket.' We must include a few reactionaries. That'll hide our interest." Then the frank admission: "We must not show our hand. We'll run on a program acceptable to the right wing as much as possible. After we get in we'll take control."

The communist Trojan horse was jockeying for position. Maneuver often compensates for lack of numbers and organizational position. Deals, stratagems, and hypocrisy must be given free play.

The secretary-sympathizer agreed to run on the Reform

Ticket. His name would lend prestige and give the ticket a capable career officer. Here was the first breakthrough. More deals, however, were necessary.

The chief problem now was the presidency. Whom to run? A known procommunist could not win. To support another anticommunist was unthinkable. The answer: an opportunist.

The right man was at hand, a noncommunist, personally ambitious, who disliked the current president. Lacking a dynamic personality, a "little backward," as one Party official called him, he could be "guided." He was just the man to head the ticket.

He was contacted. Run for president and you'll receive "our" support. The communists, of course, didn't openly identify themselves. The opportunist, however, probably suspected, but he didn't care. That is the mark of an opportunist: his personal ambition is so great that it overrides every other consideration.

Now the other noncommunist candidates on the Reform Ticket must be chosen.

To communists there are different degrees of "foes." A "60 per cent" foe is better "working material" than a "100 per cent" foe. Another may be appraised as a 40 or even 10 percenter. In drawing up the slate, find as many "low percenters" as possible. Also there is the practical factor, always to be remembered, of selecting candidates who can "pull" votes to the ticket.

These deals were made.

Then there was the task, after selection of the slate (which contained concealed communists along with noncommunists), of getting it elected.

This meant more strategy, manipulation, and deals. The communists could count on only a small minority of the vote —their own members and a few sympathizers. Their tactic lay in exploiting existing jealousies, conflicts, and dissatisfactions among the majority noncommunists. To catch the secret of communist infiltration tactics, we must understand how the Party, with great skill, is able to exploit, guide, and capitalize on the splits and lack of interest in noncommunist ranks.

That's how the Party is able to wield an influence far out of proportion to its numbers.

There was, of course, the usual share of communist deals. One technique, often used, is a deal with a noncommunist member of the group who is running for office in another organization in which the communists also have members. "Support our candidates here," the deal goes, "and we'll help you next week." Then there is the communist who is a union official or company foreman who says to a noncommunist member of the group, "Maybe we can consider a promotion for you at the plant if . . ."

Another technique is to urge "benevolent neutrality" upon those noncommunists who are wavering and might vote for the current officers; that's a good day for them to stay home or go fishing!

Result: The Reform Ticket won a complete victory. Now one-third of the officers, five Party members, were controlled by Party headquarters. The rest were virtual prisoners.

To infiltrate an organization is only a first step. It must be made to serve Party interests. There are many ways:

1. A proposal, promoted by the communists, was made that Henry G., both a member of The 123 Group and a secret communist, be sent as an official delegate to the National Convention of a communist-front organization. This group was painted in glowing terms as a fighter for human rights. No mention was made of communist control. Opponents objected, labeled it as a communist "outfit." The vote was taken: motion passed, and the communist member went, expenses paid.

2. A concealed communist was running for public office. Motion was made that his candidacy be endorsed. Again another outcry from the opponents, but the motion passed.

3. "John Doe is a victim of injustice. We should pass a resolution to be sent to the governor demanding his freedom. . . ." An anticommunist protested, "It's not our business to be passing resolutions about such matters." "A reactionary,"

replies the spokesman for the communist line. "Aren't you interested in justice?" Label your opponents as "Fascists," "reactionaries," "hardhearted." The vote was taken: motion passed.

4. The communists had established a Party "front school." Money was needed for expansion. One source: The 123 Group. Motion was made that a contribution be sent to the "school." Passed. A tactic the communists like to use: Make noncommunists "share" the Party's expenses.

5. Other ways: seize, if possible, the group's bulletin or newspaper. Make it a Party mouthpiece, or at least attempt to silence or weaken its criticism. The instructions flow steadily from Party headquarters: start a letter-writing campaign, pass this foreign-policy resolution, contact a public official. The 123 Group becomes a masquerade for communist attack.

In one instance an official of The 123 Group (who was also a secret communist) was invited to testify before a congressional investigating committee about a certain economic development. What did he do? He went to the Party and asked for copies of the *Daily Worker* and other communist background material. Now he had the Party line!

Such victories are not always easily won. One requirement is a well-planned floor strategy for all club meetings. That's the secret of many Party successes. First, as one Party leader expressed it, "we want our mob present." No absences are allowed. Every Party vote is needed. If a motion is to be made, who will present it? When? Early in the evening while the crowd is large? Or much later when many of the delegates, but not the communists, have gone home? How should objections be handled? If concessions must be made, which ones?

Every move is planned.

If a communist is chairman, the task is easier. He can use many parliamentary devices such as not recognizing an opposition speaker, rushing votes, ruling opponents out of order. The communists, one member remarked, always had the meetings "so well in hand" in his organization that an "outsider" had no chance of even voicing opposition.

Numerous tricks can be used; for example the diamond formation, seating members in a diamond pattern. This gives the impression, during debate, that Party supporters are more numerous than they actually are. Another is the false opposition. Selected members make foolish, silly, and stupid objections to communist proposals. The purpose: to make the communists look even better.

Communist infighting is vicious and utterly devoid of moral principle.

For several years the Party controlled The 123 Group. Time after time, the organization consisting of hundreds of members was subverted for Party purposes.

Then troubles began to appear. Some sympathizers and opportunists grew restive. Noncommunist opposition increased.

Party counterattacks were launched.

The first problem was to hold the opportunist-president in line. Vanity is a weapon in the early stages. Do everything you can to "blow up" his ego. Raise his salary (the organization pays for it, not the Party). Give him a testimonial dinner. Send him as a delegate to a convention, preferably as far away as possible. The communist vice-president will run affairs until he returns.

Frequently, as time passes, opportunists and sympathizers become "big-headed." They don't do what they are told. "Jack J. is feeling the effects of power," one Party leader complained. "He's forgetting his old factional allies." Now stronger measures must be applied. Remind him forcefully that it is communist support which keeps him in office. "Encircle the guy," as one Party member recommended, meaning to make him even more dependent on the Party. Perhaps cut his salary. A little "smear" campaign might be effective.

If new alignments can be made, he might be dropped. If not, he'll be subjected to even stronger pressure. Blackmail and threats are often part of communist tactics at this stage.

Finally, six years later, The 123 Group eliminated the com-

munist infiltration after a long, tiring battle. Here were some
of the basic points the noncommunist opposition had to keep
everlastingly in mind: *Keep in mind —*
our democratic responsibile

1. *Rally the majority noncommunist strength.* The communists, usually a minority, capitalize on the lack of interest of
noncommunists. One communist member was elected to office
with only 3 per cent of the total eligible vote.

2. *Remember that communism is always an evil, never a
temporary good.* Often communists give the impression of
working for the best interests of the group. "What do you care
whether we are communists?" one Party leader asked. "We're
trying to help you." Another quipped: "Politics don't matter.
It's the issues that count." That's wrong. Any conciliation,
friendship, or trust placed in communism will sooner or later
be exploited against democratic society.

3. *Don't underestimate communist ability.* Many communists are extremely intelligent. One Party leader was described
by an opponent as very capable, well versed in parliamentary
procedure, and possessing an excellent command of English.
To think of communists as mere rabble rousers and nuisances
is to risk defeat.

4. *Understand communist tactics.* Learn how they, though
numerically few, are able to exert a maximum influence. Deceit is one of their strongest weapons.

5. *Stand up and be counted.* Many noncommunists hesitate
to speak up in meetings. They fear to be attacked by an acid-
tongued Party spokesman. They may remember Mr. So-and-
So. He opposed a communist proposal several weeks ago. Now
look at him. He hasn't slept a full night for weeks. Somebody
is constantly calling him on the telephone. His relatives are
pestered. It's best, they think, just to stay away from meetings
or, if there, remain silent. Others, irritated, bored, or simply
"fed up" with communist tactics, walk out. Just what the

communists want. They have a clear field. Speak your mind. Stand your ground. Don't be afraid to defend American liberty.

6. *Wage the fight in a democratic manner.* Emotion should never replace reason as a weapon. To pursue extralegal methods is simply to injure your cause. Fight hard, but fight according to the rules.

When communists speak of their desire to advance the cause of labor, the question should always be asked: What is their objective? In August, 1957, streetcar and bus workers went on strike in Lodz, Poland. The workers were using this means to protest against the unfulfilled promises of the leaders of the Polish Communist government. The strike was soon brought to a halt through the use of some 3000 troops with fixed bayonets and police who fired tear gas into the milling mob.

While the communists were demonstrating their brutality and terroristic tactics against labor in Poland, American communists were giving another demonstration of how they habitually ignore the truth. William Z. Foster, as the elder statesman of the Communist Party in the United States, was saying:

> One of the most striking phenomena of the capitalist world in recent years has been the enormous extension of the workers' fight for democracy—among other phases, to defend their right to organize and strike. . . . World Socialism has enormously stimulated this struggle.

The answer is a simple one. The communists, once in control, crush every opponent, while, in coming to power, they promise everything to soften the opposition. This opposition will be "softened," however, only if we allow infiltration to take place before our very eyes without knowing it for what it is.

17.

The Communist Front

THE AUDITORIUM was packed. More than 1000 delegates and observers waved their arms enthusiastically, along with some 200 others who did not fill out registration forms to avoid leaving a record of their attendance. (The *Daily Worker* said they were in ". . . fear of intimidation.") This was the founding convention of the National Negro Labor Council, a new organization dedicated to "equality," "social progress," and the upholding of "civil rights." Speeches, resolutions, election of officers, everything ran smoothly. Two days later came adjournment. A new communist front had been born.

Delegates had come from all over the United States. They would now return to their home cities, start local chapters, enroll members, issue literature.

A master organizing hand was at work. One thousand individuals just didn't arrive by accident.

The convention call was communist-inspired. For weeks in advance, local Party members had been arranging housing, running errands, securing finances.

The Council claimed that its purpose was to aid the Negro; however, the House Committee on Un-American Activities concluded that, "rather than helping the Negro worker, it has been a deterrent to him."

The founding of the National Negro Labor Council was typical of many Party fronts created over the past generation.

Fronts probably represent the Party's most successful tactic in capturing noncommunist support. Like mass agitation and infiltration, fronts espouse the deceptive Party line (hence the term "front") while actually advancing the real Party line.

In this way the Party is able to influence thousands of non-communists, collect large sums of money, and reach the minds, pens, and tongues of many high-ranking and distinguished individuals. Moreover, fronts are excellent fields for Party recruitment.

A front is an organization which the communists openly or secretly control. The communists realize that they are not welcome in American society. Party influence, therefore, is transmitted, time after time, by a belt of concealed members, sympathizers, and dupes. Fronts become transmission belts between the Party and the noncommunist world. Earl Browder, when head of the Party, gave this definition: "Transmission belts mean having Communists work among the masses in the various organizations."

Some may be newly created, or, as often happens, they may be old-line organizations captured by infiltration, like The 123 Group mentioned in the preceding chapter. They may operate nationally, regionally, or locally. Some are permanent organizations; others exist for only a day, a week, or a month.

The Party has operated hundreds of major fronts in practically every field of Party agitation: "peace," civil rights, protection of the foreign-born, support for Smith Act "victims," abolition of H-bomb tests, exploitation of nationality and minority groups. Some are based on specific appeal, to teachers, writers, lawyers, labor, women, youth. Many have national officers, local chapters, and substantial assets.

In addition, literally hundreds of minor fronts of all shapes, sizes, and types appear each year in everyday Party life. They serve a specific short-time purpose, then disappear. A few handbills, a rally, or a picket line, and a front has gone to work.

We must not think of fronts in terms of legitimate organizations. A few fronts collect dues, issue a newspaper, or sponsor organized activities, such as a sports program or cultural affairs. Most, however, exist only on paper. Their assets usually consist of a few office supplies, a secondhand Mimeograph machine, and a mailing list. The danger of a Party front rests not on its physical appearance or size but on its ability to deceive.

A few fronts may maintain separate headquarters, usually in a small room in an old building. Some operate from Party headquarters, a basement, or somebody's home. Often they are found in clusters, one office serving as the headquarters for two, three, or a half-dozen fronts. The only difference is the wording of their names.

"Front schools," where Marxist and related subjects were available for noncommunist students, have been most important to the communists over the years. In one such school it is estimated that over 100,000 individuals received instruction; in another, 75,000.

Every front, in its own way, is fighting the Party's battles:

—sponsoring agitation campaigns;
—collecting money (fronts are one of the Party's chief sources of income);
—supplying speakers for noncommunist organizations (it's surprising the number of requests received by front groups, especially those sponsoring "peace" and "civil rights," for speakers. A sympathizer or dupe who has prominence in the community, such as a lawyer or professor, will often be sent);
—issuing literature;
—sponsoring mass rallies;
—lobbying for or against legislative bills;
—influencing key individuals whom the Party could not otherwise reach;
—teaching Marxist doctrines.

During the recent period when most Party headquarters were closed because of a tactical shift to underground operations, fronts performed many functions for the Party. In Chapter 20, we shall see this aspect of fronts.

A single front can generate terrific communist pressure. Take this case, for example:

Time: shortly after lunch. Agnes G, executive secretary of the DEF Committee to Fight the High Cost of Living, is reading a letter.

Dan H enters the office. "It's happened. The legislature just passed the Anticommunist Bill."

This bill must be stopped.

As a first step Agnes dictates a letter to Professor Frank Y, a "good friend" at the university. "Issue a statement right away. This bill threatens freedom of speech. It must be vetoed."

Then more letters are sent to teachers, clergymen, several lawyers. Contact is made with key Party members and sympathizers.

"The Anticommunist Bill has passed. Send telegrams to the governor, urging a veto. Start a petition circulating."

Next, a bold step: Agnes places a telephone call to the governor.

"Mr. Governor, I'm speaking for the DEF Committee to Fight the High Cost of Living. We are disturbed about the passage of the Anticommunist Bill. We feel you should veto it. Would it be possible to have our representatives meet with you?"

The governor agrees. He wants to hear all points of view. The DEF Committee sounds like one of many groups interested in this legislation.

An appointment is made.

Pressure was being built up. The front could enter where the Party never dreamed of going. Three ministers, an attorney, and a newspaperman were contacted. Would they see the governor as part of the delegation?

"I want Larry R to go along," Agnes says. "He's not too bright a guy, but he's easy and willing. I can tell him what to say. Besides, he's from a very respectable organization."

Nothing was said about the fact that this delegation was serving a communist purpose.

Every point had to be planned. "Be sure the right people do the talking." About one fellow the Party organizer had commented, "Better have him stay quiet." You never know, maybe a dupe will say something out of place.

How to talk to the governor? The delegation could act like

"nice, little people," but that wouldn't be very impressive. Or it could be vaguely threatening. The latter suggestion was ruled out as too dangerous.

Not everything went according to plan. One minister refused to go. Agnes became angry. "It takes this kind of work," she fumed, " to see what ministers are made of—dishwater."

A wonderful guy, if you cooperate; if not, you're a "bum."

The delegation was dispatched, a delegation made up chiefly of noncommunists, yet fighting for communist aims, a delegation organized exclusively by a communist front. The DEF Committee was not interested in opposing the high cost of living. *It was fighting for communism.*

Fronts exist not in isolation but as part of a vast, interlaced front system. Communist pressure can be greatly increased by manipulating these organizations.

Take, for example, roof, or compound, fronts. Here a number of fronts, as in the nationality field, will form a super, over-all front such as the old American League Against War and Fascism, which at its peak claimed 7,500,000 members. Often the propaganda value is to show unity: all these organizations, representing many different nationalities, are working together for common aims.

Or consider the National Negro Labor Council, mentioned at the beginning of this chapter. This also was a roof, or compound, front created by already existing fronts. Let's see how this works.

First, "delegates" must be "elected" to a "national founding convention." Immediately, communist fronts across the nation "elect delegates," and communist-controlled labor unions choose as their delegates those best suited for convention service.

At the convention all arrangements are made by Party leaders, including the selection of officers, the issuing of press releases, the passing of resolutions. This includes the actual running of the convention to ensure security. To illustrate, a newspaper reporter went to the convention. He had once been a Party member but had been expelled. On the first day of the convention one of the officials invited him outside and asked if he had been expelled. The reporter admitted that he had, and was ordered not to come back into the convention hall.

Hailed as representing "thousands of members," the new organization is a front created out of fronts.

Another technique of manipulation is the continuing front. Here the same front is maintained by changing the name to meet current conditions. In 1940 the American Peace Mobilization was formed, urging mobilization for peace and no aid to Britain. In 1941, after Germany's invasion of Russia, the name was changed to American People's Mobilization, and the demands to all-out aid to Britain and a second front. This was the same group with a different name.

Again, on October 16, 1943, the Young Communist League was dissolved and the very next day the American Youth for Democracy was formed. Later the group was called Labor Youth League. All were designed to recruit young people for communism.

The continuing front is well suited for "victim" agitation cases; for example, the Committee to Save John Doe. This group, so active for Doe, had lapsed into disuse. A new "victim," Richard Roe, was now at hand. Resurrect the old front!

That is exactly what happened. A communist arrived in town and contacted leaders of the old Committee to Save the Martinsville Seven. Where had it achieved the best results while agitating for the Seven? What were the problems? How could it best be used again?

A few days later the new front was already in action; the Committee to Save Albert Jackson, the same old faces under a new name. On Sunday morning its members were handing out leaflets in front of churches. In this instance Jackson was executed and the comrades turned to other fields.

Still another device is the satellite front, a cluster of minor fronts around a larger front. A new issue, like higher transit rates or the draining of a swamp, arises. The DEF Committee to Fight the High Cost of Living (the larger front) starts satellites, such as related committees in various sections of the city. Many of these satellites are paper organizations; however, they make a formidable showing to the uninformed.

These fronts are a vehicle for communist pressure. They are highly fissionable. From many comes one; from one come many. They can be cut, sliced, slivered, or compounded to fit any need. No wonder the Party makes so much use of them in mass agitation.

The campaign is launched, urging the veto of the Anticommunist Bill. Let's see how the Party's front system is brought into play.

Suddenly telegrams, letters, petitions pour in on the governor from all kinds of groups such as organizations protesting higher taxes; youth, women's, union, and veterans' organizations; free-speech groups; civil-rights organizations. To an uncritical eye it must seem that a wide stratum of population is interested in a veto of the anticommunist legislation. Then messages arrive from other countries (from international fronts), as if the whole world, "millions of people" as the communists like to say, is vitally interested in the bill.

Many noncommunists may oppose the legislation for a variety of reasons and express their opinions by letter, telegram, and petition. That, very emphatically, does not make them communists. They are only exercising their democratic privileges. What we are interested in here, however, is how the Communist Party, through its front system, can stimulate a vast and often effective propaganda barrage—a barrage which, within hours, can be turned off or shifted elsewhere.

Many times fronts appear bewildering in their variety; agitating on countless issues; based on different groups and occupations; and working in many ways. But actually their technique of formation is virtually identical.

Let's look briefly inside a communist front and see how it operates. At the center is always the Party, organizing, manipulating, seeing that the right persons are in charge. Noncommunists might well ponder this comment by a Party organizer:

> Experience has shown that most sponsors are unwilling to give of themselves sufficiently to stop the secretary from directing policy.

So true! The communists realize that if the secretary (or other key officer) is a communist (almost always a concealed member), the Party can dominate the organization. Let the letterhead glitter with noncommunist names: president, vice-president, members of the executive board. They serve as lightning rods, camouflaging the communist interest. To the sponsors, the prestige; to the communists, the power.

Around this communist core come layer after layer of noncommunists. As we have seen in Chapter 15, great emphasis is placed on attracting noncommunists, the more prominent the better, into communist propaganda work. These noncommunists, by allowing their names to be used as sponsors, giving testimonials, or appearing at front rallies, are aiding the Party. It cannot be emphasized too often how the communists attempt to exploit for strictly partisan purposes the legitimate interests of noncommunists in social and economic problems, world peace, civil rights, and so forth.

Most important to fronts are mailing lists containing the names of persons to whom literature can be sent. Perhaps you have received such propaganda in the mail and wondered whence it came. Party-front mailing lists are compiled in many ways—from telephone books, directories, membership rolls of infiltrated organizations ("loaned" by concealed members). Then the daily press is followed. Front headquarters may jot down the names of officers in noncommunist organizations. You never know. Someday they might "come in handy."

Party fronts are aggressive. To wait for the noncommunist is wrong. Seek him out. "We must get into the neighborhoods more and into the home." Through rallies, parades, picket lines, forums, debates, circulation of literature, fronts are constantly seeking public support. They operate on the main streets of America.

Another thing: The agitation is always practical. Talk about peace, jobs, and the price of milk, not Marx's ideas of revolution. Link the struggle with "the fight for pork chops."

Peace is an everyday issue and . . . should involve the housewife, the woman who has to wrestle with budgets in the hopeless struggle with taxes, high prices and a shrinking pay check.

In one instance, for example, a cookbook was issued by a front, a "dollar stretcher" containing low-priced menus. Here is the point. These recipes will help, somewhat. But, Mrs. Housewife, you can never hope for a stable economy (where prices are always low) until "peace" (Soviet style) is achieved.

That's mixing propaganda with eggs and butter, sugar and salt.

Many times, trick "come-ons" are used. Consider communist-sponsored forums, for instance. Here are some Party-suggested topics:

—Are American marriages a failure?
—How to find an apartment.
—Should the voting age be reduced to eighteen years?
—Future of youth, what is it?
—Can heart disease be cured?
—Can cancer be cured or prevented?
—How to become a cultured person.

What have these to do with communism? Nothing. But they bring listeners within talking distance.

If one thing won't work, maybe another will, such as a special celebration, in which a front sponsors an exhibit of "peace" literature or Russian photographs. Then there are round-robin letters, chain telephone calls, forums for high school science teachers. One front sold "Christmas seals." Another was planning to put out a leaflet. "Fine," commented an associate, "but be sure to add the inscription which appears on the Statue of Liberty. That'll make it sound better." Festivals and rallies, often featuring foreign "dignitaries," attract hundreds, even thousands. Don't forget to conduct polls on the street, always securing through partisan manipulation "proof" that the "people" support points advocated in the Party line.

Communist Parties around the world collaborate whenever it will advance their cause. Some years ago a women's conference was convened in Paris, France, and out of it grew the Women's International Democratic Federation.

Long before the Paris gathering the Communist Party went

to work promoting delegations of American women. One hundred telegrams were sent out from Communist Party headquarters in New York City to leaders of various women's organizations, announcing that they had been chosen as delegates and inviting them to attend a meeting at the home of the chairman of the committee. A temporary Committee on Cooperation with the International Women's Conference came into being to make arrangements. An expediter was appointed to get passports, and a special rate of 495 dollars for a round trip by plane was secured. And so the ladies went to Paris, many without the slightest idea that the affair had been promoted by the Communist Party.

Out of the Women's International Democratic Federation grew its American affiliate, the Congress of American Women. Shortly after the Congress had its first meeting, the National Committee of the Communist Party met in New York City. At this meeting one of its members discussed the importance of the Women's International Democratic Federation to the Communist Party. This high Party official then stated that the Party did not then control the newly created Congress of American Women, and that the communists needed to "infiltrate it more." The Congress has since been designated as a subversive organization by the Attorney General, the Senate Internal Security Subcommittee, and the House Committee on Un-American Activities.

Earlier in this chapter we spoke of international fronts. The following is an example:

An envelope was postmarked at Prague, Czechoslovakia, addressed to an American college. Inside was a printed letter signed by the Prorector and Secretary of Charles University, Prague, formerly renowned as a great European educational institution, now a communist propaganda front. The letter opened:

> We send you the Proclamation of the Charles University against the use [by the United States] of the bacteriological warfare in Korea and urge you to express your views on the named Proclamation.

Enclosed was the "PROCLAMATION of the Academic Community of the Charles University. . . ."

As you read the message, note the propaganda techniques employed:

1. *The appeal prostitutes the reputation of a well-known university for propaganda purposes:* "We, professors, lecturers and the other scientific workers of the Charles University in Prague, one of the oldest universities of the world. . . ."

2. *The appeal allegedly is based on humanitarian and scientific grounds:* "With full responsibility to our human and scientific consciences we have considered the danger which threatens all of humanity through the crimes that are being committed by the American imperialist army."

3. *The appeal is directed to scientific teachers in universities.* The idea is that an appeal from a member of one profession or occupation to another is more effective than random appeals. This device is often used, with Russian writers, artists, musicians addressing their "counterparts" in America: "We address ourselves to you, scientific workers of universities of all countries. . . ."

4. *The weight of scholarly backing is designed to influence opinion.* (If scientists in this university say the charges are true, they must be true.) For example:

These facts prove that the armies of the American interventionists have repeatedly used bacteriological weapons.

* * * *

From the American airplanes bombs were dropped containing different kind of insects, rats, etc., which were infected with plague, cholera and other epidemic diseases, and infected foodstuffs as well.

* * * *

. . . we are ashamed to think of those American members of

medical science who have committed themselves to the preparation of these repulsive crimes.

5. *Action is recommended:* "We urge you to refuse to place your scientific knowledge at the service of mass extermination of mankind . . . Protest not only in your activity as teachers and in your work in the scientific press, but with your governments as well!"

The proclamation is designed to make a lie believable, to paint the United States as a murderer and the Soviet Union as a protector of peace, thanks to a dignified and "respectable" front.

Most of this communist propaganda would be laughable except for its deadly seriousness. The Party is not kidding. This is live ammunition designed to capture, maim, and kill. To regard communist fronts and their propaganda as foolishness is to risk our freedom.

Examine the communist attitude toward parades, for example. Most people think of parades as a time of interest and commemoration. Not the communists. Parades are weapons of propaganda, another form of front.

Listen to these Party instructions, for example, concerning parades, issued by the old Central Committee of the Party before it was abolished:

The marchers must be well mannered. Walk in rhythm. Don't be "a line of stragglers shuffling along like a tired and discouraged army in retreat."

> The result is that the value of the demonstration as a means of impressing and winning over or neutralizing hostile people along the line of march is lost.

Here are a few things that should be remembered:

> Every two or three hundred marchers should be led by a band, a bugle or fife and drum corps. We need scores of bands, with plenty of brass instruments.

Banners and placards! Do not be "stingy with the length of sticks." Cut out the fancy lettering. It is difficult to read.

Use good English. "Some slogans are so bad grammatically, that people are amused at seeing them." The fewer the words the better. Don't just "slap" slogans on cardboard. Make sure they are "politically correct."

More advice: carry placards "on a slight angle, with wording facing the sidewalks." Scatter them through the parade; avoid bunching. Streamers: too much pulling causes ripping; not enough causes folding.

A favorite field for communist fronts is the election campaign for public office. Running communist candidates for city council, mayor, governor, even for the presidency of the United States, is an old Party habit. Never has the Party, running under its own name, been able to secure many votes. In instances where Party candidates have run under their own colors, their defeats have almost invariably been disastrous. Party candidates have run five times (1924 through 1940) for the presidency of the United States and in 1932 achieved their highest percentage of the total vote cast—a mere 0.3 per cent, or 102,991 out of almost 40,000,000 votes cast. Three times the percentage was 0.1, and once, 0.2. In instances, however, where the Party has maneuvered political alliances, it has achieved more success, as shown by the election of Benjamin J. Davis, Jr., and Peter Cacchione, both well-known communists, to the City Council of New York City in the 1940's. Yet these campaigns give training in agitation and enable the Party to smear rivals, scream its propaganda, and cause unrest.

Party candidates also frequently run in concealed capacities. Board-of-education campaigns are well suited to communist exploitation. Usually running as independents, Party candidates can conceal their true affiliations. Moreover, national and international issues that would betray their basic sentiments, such as the Russian intervention in Hungary, are not likely to arise. In such campaigns Party-sponsored candidates are invited to parent-teacher meetings, community centers, public forums, to participate in radio debates (when the time is donated), and speak in the homes of private citizens. "The Citizens (or Independent) Committee for————"

takes the candidate where, as a communist, he could never dream of going. The Party, behind the scenes, works overtime stuffing propaganda into envelopes, passing out cards, drumming up enthusiasm.

The results are often amazing. William Z. Foster in one of his books boasts that in Cleveland, Ohio, "A. Krchmarek, Communist candidate for the school board, received 64,213 votes," while in California, "the well-known Communist, Bernadette Doyle, polled the big total of 613,670 votes on a nonpartisan ticket as candidate for Superintendent of Public Schools." Krchmarek and Doyle both ran on independent, nonpartisan tickets and were not identified on the ballot as communists. In another instance a Party member, also running in a concealed capacity, failed by only a few votes to be elected a city official. He was supported by two anticommunist newspapers that had no way of knowing his Party background.

This is the communist-front movement. Its strength rests on deceit and its ability to attract the support of noncommunists.

Fronts, however, can be detected. You, as an alert citizen, can do much to weaken their influence. Here are a few tests:

1. Does the organization espouse the cause of Soviet Russia? Does it shift when the Party line shifts?

2. Does the organization feature as speakers at its meetings known communists or sympathizers?

3. Does the organization sponsor causes, campaigns, literature, petitions, or other activities sponsored by the Party or other front organizations?

4. Is the organization used as a sounding board by, or is it endorsed by, communist-controlled labor unions?

5. Does its literature follow the communist line or is it printed by the communist press?

6. Does the organization receive consistent favorable mention in communist publications?

7. Does the organization represent itself to be nonpartisan, yet engage in political activities and consistently advocate causes favored by the communists? Does it denounce both fascists and communists?

8. Does the organization denounce American foreign policy while always lauding Soviet policy?

9. Does the organization utilize communist double talk by referring to Soviet-dominated countries as democracies, complaining that the United States is imperialistic, and constantly denouncing monopoly-capital?

10. Have outstanding leaders in public life openly renounced affiliation with the organization?

11. Does the organization, if espousing liberal, progressive causes, attract well-known, honest, patriotic liberals, or does it denounce well-known liberals?

12. Does the organization consistently consider matters not directly related to its avowed purposes and objectives?

These are some ways, direct and indirect, of the aboveground Communist Party, which is working against all of us. But this is only one arm of a gigantic pincer. The other is underground.

18.

Communism and Minorities

THE COMMUNIST PARTY from its very inception has held itself out as the "vanguard of the working class," and as such has sought to assume the role of protector and champion of minorities. It directs special attention, among others, to Negroes and nationality groups. Actually the vast majority of Negroes and members of foreign-language groups have rejected communism for what it is: a heartless, totalitarian way of life which completely disregards the dignity of man.

In the case of the Negro minority the Comintern began in

1928 to lay down a specific Party line for the guidance of comrades in the United States. According to Comintern instructions, Negroes were to be considered as an "oppressed race." The Party was told to carry on a struggle "for equal rights," but "in the South . . . the main Communist slogan must be: *The Right of Self-Determination of the Negroes in the Black Belt.*"

Communist leaders, faithfully following Moscow's instructions, promptly started a campaign of agitation. In nominating James W. Ford, a Negro, to run for Vice-President of the United States on the Communist Party ticket in 1932, with presidential candidate William Z. Foster, C. A. Hathaway, then a member of the Party's Election Campaign National Committee, reiterated instructions received in a 1930 Comintern resolution:

> In the first place, our demand is that the land of the Southern white landlords . . . be confiscated and turned over to the Negroes. . . .
>
> Secondly, we propose to break up the present artificial state boundaries . . . and to establish the state unity of the territory known as the "Black Belt," where the Negroes constitute the overwhelming majority of the population.
>
> Thirdly, in this territory, we demand that the Negroes be given the complete right of self-determination; *the right to set up their own government* in this territory and the right to separate, if *they* wish, from the United States.

Hence, "equal rights" and "self-determination" in the Black Belt became the Party's chief slogans for Negroes. By "self-determination" the Party meant what Stalin had said: ". . . the right of the oppressed peoples of the dependent countries and colonies to complete secession, as the right of nations to independent existence as states."

As for the "Black Belt," or as one article termed it, the "new Negro Republic," the communists have given various descriptions. In 1948 they described the Belt as extending through twelve Southern states: "Heading down from its eastern point in Virginia's tidewater section, it cuts a strip through North

Carolina, embraces nearly all of South Carolina, cuts into Florida, passes through lower and central Georgia and Alabama, engulfs Mississippi and the Louisiana Delta, wedges into eastern Texas and Southwest Tennessee, and has its western anchor in southern Arkansas."

By 1952 the communist concept of the Black Belt had been narrowed to "at least five Southeastern states, with port outlets at Charleston on the Atlantic and Mobile on the Gulf, encompassing the bulk of Mississippi, and a good section of South Carolina, Georgia and Alabama."

As we know from cumulative evidence, the Party's position toward Negroes is determined not by concern for their welfare but obedience to Soviet foreign policy. As World War II approached, for example, the Party switched its tactics regarding "self-determination" in the Black Belt. Instead of calling for the immediate and revolutionary overthrow of white landlords, as the Comintern had originally instructed, the Party now switched these demands to a purely theoretical and propaganda level: ". . . It is clear that the Negro masses are not yet ready to carry through the revolution which would make possible the right to self-determination." Why the shift? To satisfy the Party's united-front program, which demanded that the Party work harmoniously with other groups to strengthen the Soviet Union.

The World War II period found the Party cynically abandoning any alleged struggle for Negro rights. The aim was to help not Negroes but Moscow. "When we fought for the right of Negro workers to enter industries we often fought for such jobs mainly in the interest of the war effort." Earl Browder in 1945 admitted that as early as 1942 the Party had adopted the theory that ". . . the struggle for Negro rights must be postponed until after the war. . . ." The Negro, in communist eyes, was a mere pawn, to be manipulated for the attainment of Party aims.

It became obvious that the Party, despite great efforts, had failed to win over even a significant minority of Negroes. Negroes resented the Party's severe criticism of Negro clergymen who had been vigorously denouncing communism. Earlier the Party had been unable adequately to justify Russia's aid to Italy in its invasion of Ethiopia. American Negroes had realized that the Party was a fraud and a deception and that it was willing to betray the Negro to better serve Soviet Russia.

In early 1956 the Party decided to modify its advocacy of "self-determination," realizing that Negro opposition to communism was growing. In making this change, communists said they would still consider the Negroes as constituting a national as well as a racial minority.

Eugene Dennis, resuming his old post as General Secretary of the Communist Party (in 1956) after serving a prison term for violation of the Smith Act, said:

> In re-appraising our position on self-determination in the Black Belt, our Party should emphasize, as never before, that the struggle for Negro rights and freedom, north and south of the Mason-Dixon line, has emerged as a general, national democratic task, upon the solution of which depends the democratic and social advance of the whole nation, particularly of the workers and farmers.

The Party's claim that it is working for Negro rights is a deception and a fraud. The Party's sole interest, as most American Negroes know, is to hoodwink the Negro, to exploit him and use him as a tool to build a communist America.

The Party has made vigorous efforts to infiltrate the National Association for the Advancement of Colored People (NAACP). This organization in 1950 authorized its board of directors to revoke the charter of any chapter found to be communist-controlled. Nevertheless the Party has tried various infiltration tactics:

—In Philadelphia, the Party secured NAACP applications and instructed Party members to join.
—In Louisiana, the Party's District Organizer instructed all Negro Party members to join the NAACP and urge the creation of a youth organization, and to form committees to encourage Negroes to register to vote.

—In Gary, Indiana, a Party member, also an NAACP member, promoted the signing of petitions to pass a city ordinance.

—In Cincinnati, a Party Organizer instructed that Party members call the NAACP and urge the holding of a city-wide mass meeting. When calling, they should claim to be members of the NAACP.

The NAACP's national leadership has vigorously denounced communist attempts at infiltration. In 1956, when the NAACP and other organizations sponsored a National Conference on Civil Rights in Washington, the Party attempted to "move in," and started promoting the conference. The NAACP countered by screening the delegates.

Similarly, in 1957, in the Prayer Pilgrimage for Freedom in Washington, the Party again attempted to move in and tried to exploit the pilgrimage as a rallying point for unity. NAACP leaders publicly told the communists that they were not welcome, and steps were taken to keep them off the platform. One outstanding Negro leader even tried to cancel the pilgrimage to prevent communists from propagandizing the event. Concerning Paul Robeson, who has long fronted for the communists, he stated: ". . . the boat is waiting to take him to Russia. . . ." He added that he would raise the necessary funds to defray expenses. In Philadelphia, a Negro clergyman told the Baptist Ministers Conference that the Negro people did not want the communists interfering with their problems.

One of the most effective anticommunist measures I have heard of is the following: The NAACP had a meeting in Norfolk, Virginia, presided over by a clergyman. The minister opened the meeting with the simple statement that if any members of the Communist Party were present they would be excused. Silence ensued, with no person leaving. Then the chairman, starting with the front row, asked each individual if he were a communist. All entered denials until he got to the back of the room, where the state organizer for the Communist Party was sitting with a white woman. When asked the question, he tried to evade, but the minister pinned him down. The state organizer then stated that he did not think it was proper to ask such a question. The minister calmly replied, "You are excused," and the couple left.

The Communist Party has stated: "The Negro race must understand that capitalism means racial oppression and Communism means social and racial equality." Many Negroes, however, have learned by bitter experience how fraudulent and deceitful communists are. For example, Richard Wright, the Negro novelist, tells in the book, *The God That Failed,* why he rebelled against communist thought control. In describing how at the time he left the Party he was assaulted on a Chicago street, he wrote, "I could not quite believe what had happened, even though my hands were smarting and bleeding. I had suffered a public, physical assault by two white Communists with black Communists looking on."

In Buffalo, New York, at a Party meeting, a Negro comrade stated that many Negroes felt they were joining a union when they were recruited into the Party. The comrade, however, was stopped at this point and not permitted to speak further. In many cases Negroes have been recruited by deceptive methods with the hope that once in the Party they would be converted to communism. In one New York State club the functionary learned that thirty members thought they were joining a union rather than the Communist Party. The matter was investigated, and it turned out that a Negro woman had become overly enthusiastic in a membership drive. She had not fully explained the nature of the organization being joined.

In San Francisco, Party functionaries were concerned about a club where Negro members predominated, although the club was actually controlled by white members. It was ordered that the role of the white members be decreased. The functionaries also instructed that the club be carefully watched to prevent scandals, and warned that, while scandals must be prevented, care should be exercised not to convey the impression that white girls should not mix socially with Negroes or vice versa. Some of the Negro wives were becoming suspicious, as it seemed they were being pushed into the background after their husbands joined the Party.

The Communist Party, while preaching "equality," still

differentiates between races. For example, in the 1957 convention of the Party, an accurate record of the delegates was kept. The breakdown was as follows: 209 males, 78 females; 54 Negroes, 2 Mexicans, and 1 Puerto Rican. The hypocrisy of the Party was clearly shown when it required each delegate to register his race, although for years the Party publicly has campaigned to have the blank for "race" removed from all questionnaires.

Communist leaders have been complaining bitterly about the turnover of Negro members and of the Party's inability to indoctrinate any large number of Negroes. Information we have received follows a regular pattern: Negroes are rejecting communism.

A Negro in the Midwest became interested in the Party because it claimed that Negroes were treated as equals. Later he was unjustly accused of consorting with a white non-Party member. He quit.

* * * *

A Negro in Illinois started going to Party social functions and became impressed with communist talk of "equality." But when he attended more advanced meetings and heard the United States constantly denounced, he came to the conclusion that the communists were under the domination of Russia. He left the Party.

* * * *

A Negro woman, recruited in Chicago, was rapidly promoted by the Party. Then she noticed an incident involving a Negro man who got into difficulties on his job, but the Party refused to support him. She concluded that the Party was interested in neither trade unionism nor the welfare of Negroes. She quit.

* * * *

A Negro in New York joined the Party because he felt it was championing his race. After a period of Marxist instruction, he was told to secure a job with a work gang at a pier and to recruit other Negroes into the Party. He came to the conclusion that the Party was not interested in him as a Negro but only as a tool to recruit other Negroes. He quit.

❊   ❊   ❊   ❊

A New England Negro also became interested in the Party when he learned of its alleged interest in helping his race. But upon becoming a member he discovered that the Party's interest was strictly vocal, and nothing concrete was done to help Negroes. Moreover, he disliked the Party's denunciation of God and religion. He quit.

As early as 1922 the Comintern approved a subsidy of 300,000 dollars for propaganda among American Negroes. In 1925 the Soviets requested that a group of Negroes be selected to come to Russia for training in propaganda work. A dozen were recruited. One of these, returning to the United States three years later, brought with him a draft for 75,000 dollars to help pay for propaganda work among his race.

One Negro later was designated to attend the Lenin School, and his experience there further unmasked communist hypocrisy and the Party's true feelings toward the Negro. He went to Russia with a delegation of students to enter the Lenin School. This young Negro, as he has since related, then "believed that through Communism a better and fairer world could be developed for all mankind."

He was troubled, however, by the communist position in urging Negro "self-determination" and the implications of a "buffer" state in this country being carved out of the so-called "Black Belt." Almost immediately after his arrival in Russia he "was told long stories of political persecution" by the Negroes attending the Lenin School. He was slow to give credence to these stories until he saw for himself: "I found that Negroes were special objects of political exploitation. The sacrifices and dirty work planned for the American Negro Communists as spearheads for communizing the United States made it obvious that we were considered only as pawns in a game where others would get the prize."

Becoming more outspoken and cynical about the communist program for Negroes, he became the target of a slander campaign inside the Lenin School. Finally this young American Negro was charged and tried before a court-martial. He was guilty of disaffection. A few students, sympathizing with his position, made a bold decision to report their grievances to the Communist Party of the Soviet Union. Then things began to happen. Classes in the American Section of the school were suspended. Some of the instructors were disciplined.

The young Negro explained that the Comintern ordered Earl Browder, then Secretary of the Communist Party in the United States, to Moscow immediately. Browder arrived and sought to smooth things over. Eventually the young Negro returned to the United States, working for a while as a Party functionary in Detroit. One of his last jobs was to make preparations for the founding of the National Negro Congress. Then he quit because he could no longer give aid to the communists "concentrating on their most helpless, and whom they think to be, their most gullible victims: the Negro."

The communists have created numerous fronts over the years in attempts to attract Negroes. Once a front is discredited, it is allowed to die and a new one created.

The American Negro Labor Congress came into being in 1925, and in 1930 its name was changed to the League of Struggle for Negro Rights. Within six years it had ceased to exist.

In 1935 the National Negro Congress was launched in Washington, D.C., its chief purpose being to protect Negro rights. It started out as noncommunist, and James W. Ford complained in 1936 that although "The National Negro Congress did not adopt a Communist program . . . we Communists stand one hundred per cent behind it in its efforts to unite the Negro people. . . ."

By 1940 communists had infiltrated the National Negro Congress to such an extent that when its president, A. Philip Randolph, "warned the Congress to stick to its principle and remain nonpartisan . . ." the communists staged a demonstration and walked out, leaving only a third of the audience to finish hearing Randolph. This 1940 convention of the National Negro Congress passed a resolution condemning the war as "imperialist," and drew from a communist writer the observation that the congress had "only acted in accord with the fundamental interests of the Negro people."

In 1947 the National Negro Congress merged with the Civil Rights Congress, an out-and-out communist front which has recently dissolved.

The old International Labor Defense (ILD) also tried to influence the American Negro, and came into conflict with the National Association for the Advancement of Colored People as a result of the ILD's communist tactics in converting the Scottsboro (Alabama) Case into a vehicle for communist propaganda. In this case nine Negro boys were indicted in 1931 on charges of having raped two white girls.

After the Scottsboro boys were first convicted, the NAACP charged that the defense "fell considerably short of perfection," and then retained the late famed Chicago criminal lawyer, Clarence Darrow, to represent the boys. In 1931 the late Walter White, then head of the NAACP, said the *Daily Worker* accused another defense attorney, Stephen R. Roddy, ". . . of being a member of the Ku Klux Klan, of having conspired with the prosecution to electrocute the nine boys, of having been the inmate of an insane asylum." According to White, the communists also charged the NAACP "as being 'in league with the lyncher-bosses of the South,' as plotters to 'murder the Scottsboro martyrs,' as sycophantic 'tools of the capitalists.'" The NAACP withdrew from the case, recognizing that the Communist Party was interested only in promoting "Red Fascism" in America.

George S. Schuyler, an editor of the *Pittsburgh Courier*, reflected the consensus of American Negroes when he concluded, ". . . The record shows that where and when the Communists seemed to be fighting for Negro rights, their object was simply to strengthen the hand of Russia."

In similar fashion the Communist Party has long considered foreign-language groups in the United States fertile fields for infiltration. Since many of the early comrades were foreign-born, agitation among national groups became a natural outlet for Party activity. In recent years the Nationality Groups Commission has coordinated agitation in this field.

The Party has attempted to use national groups, among other things, to exert pressure for changes in American foreign policy. Pressure campaigns are organized, petitions circulated, testimonials secured, hoping to make the government believe that a national group, such as the Italians, Hungarians, or Slovaks, supports the line desired by the Party. Party-controlled newspapers grind out accompanying propaganda.

Party fronts have been particularly active among national groups. The communists always make strenuous efforts to infiltrate and capture fraternal insurance societies serving national groups. As we have seen, such tactics give the Party a ready base, along with somebody else's money, for further agitation. The Party, moreover, always likes to pose as the "protector" of national cultures. Hence, it often sponsors nationality bazaars, picnics, and dances, where costumes from native lands are worn and native music is played. After the Soviet conquest of Eastern Europe, however, the Party had increasing difficulty trying to peddle the "glories" of communism. Too much information was received from the old homelands describing true conditions behind the Iron Curtain.

Minority groups, like other patriotic organizations, have realized that no communist-created Utopia can compete with the American way of life. The ability of the communists to propagate their false doctrines is a challenge to our educational process. We need to counter communism by making the hopes and aspirations of the American ideal a reality for all to enjoy.

19.

The Communist Attack on Judaism

THE COMMUNIST propaganda machine with its tactics of infiltration and division has long fostered the false claim of widespread influence in the Jewish communities of America. One of the most malicious myths that has developed in the United States is that persons of the Jewish faith and communists have something in common. The people who gave the world the concept of our monotheistic God and the Ten Commandments cannot remain Jews and follow the atheism of Karl Marx and the deceit of the communist movement.

It is a matter of record that numerous Communist Party leaders call themselves Jews and claim a Jewish origin. This does not, however, make them Jews, any more than William Z. Foster's Catholic background and Earl Browder's Protestant background give them any standing in present-day Catholic and Protestant communities in the United States.

One highly placed Party leader recently pointed out that it was necessary for communists working in Jewish groups to represent themselves as Jews. This, of course, is a tactical maneuver. Such a technique, the leader urged, "can be duplicated."

Typical of communist claims which have led to the false myth indicating that Jews have an affinity for communism are the remarks of Paul Novick, the editor of the *Morning Freiheit*, a communist paper published in Yiddish in New York City. Novick said: "The development of Yiddish literature in the United States went hand-in-hand with the growth of the

Socialist movement at the beginning of this century and of the Communist Party after the October Revolution." On the same occasion Novick then went on to brand the followers of Judaism for ". . . degeneration sown among the Jews by reaction . . ." and then condemned their opposition to ". . . the progressive movement, against the Soviet Union and against Communism . . ." Novick revealed his true loyalties in December, 1956, in an article in the *Morning Freiheit* after the display of Soviet brutality in Hungary with the apology that there was an anti-Semitic and fascist element in the Hungarian uprising, and insisted that, ". . . we must not only approve the Soviet actions in Hungary, but really appreciate it!"

The widely read Jewish newspaper, *Jewish Daily Forward*, on February 16, 1957, effectively identified Novick in a story captioned "Editor of Communist 'Freiheit' Is Bitter Enemy of the Jewish People." Here it was asserted that after the Hitler-Stalin pact the *Freiheit* justified and praised it, which caused writers to leave and Novick made sure that those who remained wrote without error following the pro-Hitler line. The newspaper further revealed that Novick had gone out of his way to prove that the communist dictators in Czechoslovakia were correct in arresting Rudolph Slansky (and thirteen former communist leaders, eleven of whom were Jews) and that the arrested Moscow Jewish doctors were involved in a conspiracy to poison Stalin. The *Jewish Daily Forward* article flatly said that "anti-Semitic poison just poured out" of Novick.

One Party member, after having been in the Party for twenty-five years and having held high Party offices, explained to our agents that when he joined the Party he had renounced the existence of God, that he had tried to impose on others his atheistic views, and that he was "not a religious Jew." He flatly said that most Party members he knew who claimed to be Jews did not follow their religion; they did not attend the synagogue, although they did not work on religious holidays; and the comrades who claimed to be Jews took no part in organized Jewish religious activities.

Some of the most effective opposition to communism in the United States has come from Jewish organizations such as

B'nai B'rith, the American Jewish Committee, the American Jewish League Against Communism, the Anti-Defamation League, and a host of other Jewish groups.

The reasons for the extensive activities of the Communist Party in seeking to infiltrate and make extravagant claims for its work in some Jewish organizations and those of other minority groups are readily apparent. In the Soviet Union, the proving ground for Marxism-Leninism, communists are confronted with a minority problem of staggering proportions. Only 58 per cent of the population in the Soviet Union is Russian whereas 42 per cent is non-Russian and consists of 168 national minorities.

The Bolsheviks prior to 1917 sought to win support from minorities by defending their rights and developing such propaganda come-ons as "self-determination of nations," "national cultural autonomy," and so on. Once in power, the communists soon forgot their promises but continued to pay lip service to minority rights. The Soviet Union still retains the "legal fiction" that it is a voluntary federation of union republics, each of which is free to secede if it wishes. In fact, Article 17 of the Soviet Constitution of 1936 states, "The right freely to secede from the USSR is reserved to each constituent republic." No "republic," however, has ever tried to secede, and the possibility is remote indeed, as long as the Red army responds to the will of the dictators in the Kremlin as it did in Hungary.

A more important reason for communist interest in minorities in the United States is, of course, the opportunities they provide for exploitation and propaganda. The large number of communist fronts using the word "Jewish," as well as publications that the communists dominate, is for the obvious purpose of conveying a false impression of strength among those who embrace the Jewish faith. This also accounts in part for the literary interest communists devote to the problems of Jews. Prior to issuing the *Communist Manifesto*, Karl Marx, the atheist, wrote a treatise called, "On the Jewish Question" which sets forth his views regarding Judaism and Jewish culture.

From that time to this in dealing with those of the Jewish faith, the communists invariably do so in terms of discussing "the Jewish question." In fact, by this propaganda technique the communists deliberately try to make the Jews a "problem," which is denied by the record of good citizenship and civic responsibility of adherents of Judaism in the United States. As an example: The American Jewish League Against Communism stated as early as 1948 that "Soviet Russia's million and a half Jews are the forgotten people of the world." The League lists among its proudest achievements that ". . . it was the first American organization to expose and document the communist anti-Jewish policies."

A true follower of the Jewish faith, like those of other religions, cannot embrace communism. Marxism-Leninism is irrevocably opposed to all religious beliefs and all forms of worship, whether they be Catholic, Protestant, Jewish, or Moslem. One of Lenin's basic teachings is, "We must combat religion—this is the A.B.C. of *all* materialism, and consequently of Marxism . . . The Marxist must be a materialist, i.e., an enemy of religion. . . ."

In theory and practice the communists make no distinction among any of the world's greater religions, as the leading Soviet crusader against religion, E. Yaroslavsky, makes clear:

> . . . the priests of every cult have their own way of deluding the masses: the Jewish rabbi, the Roman Catholic priest, the Russian Orthodox priest, the Mohammedan mullah, the Evangelist, Baptist and other ministers of religion, each has his own way of fooling the people. . . . As to differences between one religion and another, they are of little, if any, consequence. . . .

If there was ever any doubt that the communists were even lukewarm toward the Jewish faith, it was resolved by Yaroslavsky, onetime head of the League of Militant Atheists in the Soviet Union, who said:

> The Jewish synagogues were not granted any privileges whatsoever by the Russian state, but they were fully supported by the Jewish bourgeoisie. The Jewish rabbinate, like its sister

priestcrafts, drew close to the side of the rich because the Jewish church had also incorporated in its *credo* the justification of the existence of exploiting classes in society. . . .

Karl Marx described Judaism as "anti-social" and an expression of Jewish "egoism." Marx, better than any other communist leader, illustrates the gulf between Jewish tradition and communism. He could not be loyal to both, so in accepting the communist ideal, he was not content to reject Jewish tradition; he had to malign it and seek to destroy it with such bitterness as: "Money is the jealous God of Israel, by the side of which no other god may exist. . . . Exchange is the Jew's real God."

The unrestrained emotional outbursts of Hitler against the Jews were reminiscent of the Marxian tirades against Judaism.

The Marxian denunciation of Judaism is not limited to invective. From the earliest days when communism came to power in the Soviet Union, communists have conducted a systematic campaign to cripple and destroy organized Judaism. On January 23, 1918, the Soviets issued a sweeping decree "On the Separation of the Church from the State, and of the School from the Church." All church property was nationalized; churches were denied rights of legal recourse; the teaching of religion was banned in public and private schools; the right of people to attend religious services on workdays was revoked; and records of births, marriages, and deaths were taken from the churches and put under the exclusive control of civil authorities.

While religious services were still allowed, the clergy was reduced to the status of second-class citizenship; a campaign of terror was launched leading to the arrest and imprisonment or execution of priests, rabbis, ministers, and other church leaders on such vague charges as "counterrevolutionary activity" or "crimes against the people." Physical destruction of church property was conveniently explained as the "spontaneous" acts of "aroused" peasants and workers to conceal the real perpetrators, Soviet officialdom.

The main target, of course, was the Orthodox Church, which

had long been the state church of Russia; but all other faiths suffered, including that of the Jews. The reports of refugees as compiled by Wladyslaw Kania in the book, *Bolshevism and Religion,* published by the Polish Library in New York City in 1946, prove the hypocrisy of the Soviet claim of minority protection with accounts as follows:

> The Jews are morally persecuted, the young Jewish population is being brought up in un-religious ways. . . .

*   *   *   *

> The Jews in Russia are living only on the memories of the happy past . . .

*   *   *   *

> . . . during the Jewish feast Purim . . . the Jews, Soviet citizens, assembled for evening prayer. One of the neighbors reported them to the NKVD. The premises were raided and the host arrested and sentenced to ten years' imprisonment.

*   *   *   *

> The rabbis have been deported; "kosher" meat, etc., though promised, does not exist . . . The synagogues and houses of worship have been closed . . .

General Walter Bedell Smith, after his three years as Ambassador to the Soviet Union, reported that in June, 1948, about thirty churches were open in Moscow, which included one Jewish synagogue for an estimated 300,000 Jews. During World War II General Smith reported, "But two religions—the Jewish and the Roman Catholic—did not gain even temporary benefits from the wartime policy of greater religious tolerance; in fact, on balance, it is probably safe to say that attacks upon them have been stepped up rather than relaxed in recent years."

Communist reports on the state of Jews in the Soviet Union make little reference to Judaism as practiced. For example, the forty-seven-page communist propaganda pamphlet, written by Paul Novick and J. M. Budish, entitled *Jews in the Soviet Union,* makes only this single reference to Judaism:

> Then, there are Jewish religious activities. I visited the main synagogue in Moscow during Yom Kippur. It was over-crowded, with people outside listening to the cantor through loud speakers . . . I visited synagogues in Kiev, Vilna, Berdit-chev, Zhytomir. There are about 300 organized religious communities in the U.S.S.R. . . .

The accuracy of this report is highly questionable, bearing in mind the cold, systematic communist program of extinguishing religion. Among the tactics employed by the Communist Party of the Soviet Union has been the liquidation of the traditional Jewish school system, including the primary school (Hedder), the secondary schools (the Talmud Torah), and the rabbinical school (the Jeshiva). Thus, when the present generation of Soviet Jews passes on, there will be no more rabbis.

This attack on Judaism becomes apparent when the role of the rabbi is considered. He is not merely a preacher; he is the teacher of Jewish moral law, the ritualistic laws governing the home, family, and individual; he presides at such religious ceremonies as the marriage, sits in ritualistic courts and supervises circumcisions and the preparation of kosher meat. Hence, in abolishing the rabbinical schools, the Soviets are gradually seeking the extinction of Judaism without a pogrom. Judaism cannot exist unless Hebrew is taught so that rabbis can study the Torah and Talmud in the original language in which they were written.

Communist practice and communist theory are in direct conflict. Communism, as we have seen, is essentially an international class movement and therefore regards national loyalty, other than communist loyalty, as a potential menace. The communists use "national rights" as a propaganda device and support national movements only when it serves the interests of the Soviet regime.

The communist propaganda line directed to Jewish people follows three general themes:

1. The Soviet Union offers the Jewish people complete freedom. As one apologist put it: "There is one spot on the earth

where the Jewish people are not under increasing pressure, one spot where the Jews have full equality . . . That is the socialist Soviet Union."

2. The Soviets have created a national homeland for Russian Jews in the Jewish autonomous region of Birobidzhan (or Birobidjan), where they claim Jewish culture is flourishing.

3. In World War II the U.S.S.R. saved thousands of Jews from certain death from the Nazis.

Standing by themselves, these claims admittedly make an impressive appeal. If true, they would even justify the extravagant claim of Alexander Bittelman, who recently was released from prison upon completing a federal sentence for conspiring to advocate the overthrow of the government of the United States by force and violence. Bittelman, long one of the chief interpreters of communism to the Jewish people, has described the Soviet Union as the "saviour of the Jewish people." The record, however, demolishes this propaganda line as a collection of half-truths, exaggerations, and outright deceptions.

At best, Soviet tolerance toward Jewish culture was never anything more than a temporary political tactic. And even then the Soviet claims were contemporaneous with the 1917 revolution, when the communists were seeking support from all quarters. Stalin's *Marxism and the National Question*, the acknowledged communist classic on the subject, though consisting of 222 pages, contains only twenty pages written after 1927, with the most important single part having been written in 1913. By the late 1930's alleged concessions to the cultures of the various minority groups gave way to a policy of forcible denationalization rivaling the brutal "Russification" tactics of the Czars.

To illustrate: In 1917 there were a total of forty-nine Yiddish or Hebrew newspapers in the Soviet Union. By 1921 these had increased to sixty-two; but no less than fifty were communist-controlled, while the forty-nine not under communist control in 1917 had dwindled to twelve in 1921.

Jewish literature suffered a similar fate. From 1928 to 1933 books published in Yiddish rose from 238 to 668, but there was a marked decline in books dealing with Jewish history and tradition. In 1932 there were thirty-six books in Yiddish classified as history—of these, sixteen were memoirs chiefly of old Bolsheviks; six were studies on the Communist International; six dealt with the revolution and history of the Communist Party; five consisted of speeches of Stalin and other communist leaders; and only three actually dealt with matters pertaining to Jewish culture. These related to the labor movement and were an attempt to rewrite history to conform with Marxist-Leninist doctrine.

The Soviet purge trials of 1936-37 should have made clear to the world the communist objective mercilessly to crush the leadership of any minority groups whose cultural resurgence conflicted with the advance of Marxism-Leninism. To cite an example: of the ten representatives of minority groups who served on the draft committee for the 1936 Soviet constitution, only one was alive at the end of 1937. The other nine were branded as "spies," "enemies of the people," and were shot, committed suicide, or had disappeared.

The sad fate of the Jewish school system in the Ukraine proves the lie to the Soviet propaganda claim of furthering Jewish culture. In 1925, government reports reflected a total of 39,474 students in the Ukrainian schools where Yiddish was the language of instruction. In 1931 the number of such students reached its peak of 90,000. By 1940 this figure had declined to 50,000, and the Jewish schools were completely suppressed when the Nazis took over the Ukraine in World War II. Since the war the efforts of Jewish educators to have the Soviet government construct new schools have apparently failed.

One of the most crippling communist attacks on Jewish culture has been prohibition of the use of Hebrew, the traditional language of Judaism. As a tactic the Soviets launched a program of "compulsory Yiddishizing" to destroy the influence of Hebrew among Russian Jews. Yiddish is a jargon based on a German dialect. It is unrelated to Hebrew. Many Jews, particularly Asiatic and Mediterranean Jews, do not know it at all. A similar program of suppression of Jewish institutions shifted to the satellites after World War II, where Jewish schools were abolished, Jewish organizations banned, and even athletic clubs bearing Jewish names were forced to change their names on twenty-four-hour notice.

The second propaganda claim of the Soviets in establishing the Jewish homeland of Birobidzhan should be closely analyzed. Solomon M. Schwarz, in his exhaustive study, *The Jews in the Soviet Union*, exposes the Soviet propaganda for the falsehood that it is. The so-called Jewish homeland was set up at a time when the threat of Japanese and Chinese invasion of the U.S.S.R.'s Far Eastern frontier was not idle. Thus, the Jewish homeland was conceived as a means of populating the vast spaces in the Far East of Russia, and also provided a convenient place to settle Jews not wanted in other parts of Russia.

By 1933 the Soviets envisioned a population of 60,000 Jews in Birobidzhan. During its first six years 19,635 Jews arrived, while 11,450 left, leaving a net gain of only 8185. By 1939, after eleven years, the Soviet Jewish homeland could claim no more than 30,000 Jews and by 1951 around 40,000 which was a small community surrounded by Asiatic peoples completely separated from the mainstream of Jewish life. Furthermore, it is in the maritime provinces of Siberia, where the climate is unsuitable for those accustomed to European life.

The third communist propaganda claim, that of rescuing Jews from Nazi extinction, is also a deception. In the first place, for two years prior to the Nazi invasion of Russia, when Moscow was allied with Berlin, *there is no record of any Soviet protest against the Nazi slaughter of Jews,* so far as is known. The good-neighbor policy between the communists and the Nazis, initiated by the Stalin-Hitler pact, is clearly established by the following report sent by the German Ambassador to Moscow to the German Foreign Office, where it came to light after the war: ". . . The Soviet Government is doing everything to change the attitude of the population here toward Germany. The press is as though it had been transformed . . ."

Later the Foreign Office was advised that:

> . . . the Soviet Government has always previously been able in a masterly fashion to influence the attitude of the population in the direction which it has desired, and it is not being sparing this time either of the necessary propaganda.

Then, too, the silence of the Soviet leaders on the outbreaks of Nazi anti-Semitism completely misled Eastern European Jews as to the real character of the Nazi threat and hence, some 2,000,000 Russian and Eastern European Jews made no attempt to escape the Nazis during the early months of the German invasion of Russia. And even after the Nazi onslaught, there was a shocking failure on the part of the Soviets to reveal Nazi atrocities against the Jews.

For example, the Soviet government in 1942 condemned the "bloodthirsty, criminal plans of the fascists" aimed at exterminating Russians, Ukrainians, Byelorussians, and "other peoples" of the Soviet Union, with no direct reference to the Jews. As late as 1945 the Soviets in a report on the German concentration camp at Auschwitz (Oswiecim), where more than 4,000,000 persons were exterminated, did not even use the word "Jew," although they constituted the majority of those whose lives were so brutally taken.

Not only did the communists in the Soviet Union fail to make any special effort to save Jewish people during the war, they showed no concern over their fate.

If further evidence is necessary to prove the falsity of communist propaganda directed toward the Jewish people, it is only necessary to look at the communist campaigns against Zionism. The communist propagandist, Paul Novick, reflected the communist line both in the Soviet Union and the United States when he wrote:

> Ever since its inception Zionism has been an instrument of the Jewish bourgeoisie to hamper the struggle of the Jewish masses. . . . a means of diverting the attention of the Jewish workers from the class struggle and of keeping them separated from the progressive forces of other nationalities. . . .

In the Soviet Union, Zionism is ruthlessly suppressed. In the United States communists have a more complex problem and avoid direct public attacks on the Zionist movement, so as not to alienate that large section of Jewish people who favor Zionism. The communist attacks are more subtle and are directed essentially at individual Zionist leaders. The aim, of course, is to discredit the Zionist movement without antagonizing its rank-and-file members. The Party line changes from time to time when it is expedient, but the communist objective of eventually destroying Zionist influence among the Jewish people, without alienating its rank-and-file members, has never changed.

Khrushchev more recently reiterated the Party line against the Zionist movement when he was asked what the Soviet Union would do if the Zionists settled in Soviet territory and demanded a state of their own. He replied with communist contempt, "We have thrown them out of our country."

Communist Party leaders in the United States exhibited some concern over the Soviet campaign against Jews which was brought to light by an anti-Zionist article in *Pravda* on September 21, 1948, by Ilya Ehrenburg, which referred to the state of Israel as a "bourgeois country." This article declared that in Russia there was no artificial division between Jews and their Russian comrades but that Jews led lives in common with other peoples of Russia. The proper solution to the "Jewish problem," according to Ehrenburg's article, is the abolishment of "nationalism" among Jews and the integration of Jews into the existing society rather than their having a distinct life apart from other people.

It is known that when the information in the Ehrenburg article reached the United States, there were considerable concern and confusion in the offices of the *Morning Freiheit* as to whether the article represented a fixed Soviet policy. The fact that *Pravda* is under Soviet Communist Party control causes Party leaders in this country to give careful consideration to anything it publishes. The matter was resolved by directing an inquiry to Itzik Feffer, a friend of Stalin in Moscow, to secure the correct Soviet line on the Jewish question. The report came back to the United States that Ehrenburg merely was reflecting his own ideas, along with some of the younger communists of Jewish origin, and did not represent the correct policy of the Soviet Union. The then foreign editor of the *Morning Freiheit,* Moise Katz, in an article appearing in the January, 1949, issue of *Yiddishe Kultur* criticized the ideas appearing in the Ehrenburg article.

Events, however, were to prove the correctness of Ehrenburg's statements, which became the fixed policy of the Soviet Union, and the Jewish Anti-Fascist Committee, of which Itzik Feffer was a member, was abolished. In the meantime the National Committee of the Communist Party intervened and, according to reports, straightened out the *Morning Freiheit* on the new Soviet line. A letter of apology over the signature of Moise Katz then appeared in the *Freiheit* on March 29, 1949. This incident was discussed in communist circles and the word leaked out that three writers were discharged from the *Freiheit* for "bourgeois nationalism."

When Khrushchev denounced Stalin at the Twentieth Congress of the Communist Party of the Soviet Union in Moscow in February, 1956, news of the long-pent-up acts of oppression against Jews in the Soviet Union began to leak out. It is, of course, significant that Khrushchev made no mention of the mistreatment of the Jews in his exposure of Stalin, whom he had so loyally served over the years.

Within a few weeks, as noted in Chapter 3, the disclosures of anti-Semitism came in the Warsaw, Poland, Yiddish-language communist newspaper *Folks-Shtimme* on April 4, 1956, regarding the Soviet purges of Jewish leaders and culture under Stalin. Later, on April 13, 1956, the *Daily Worker* expressed regrets and then admitted ". . . we were too prone to accept the explanation of why Jewish culture had disappeared in the Soviet Union in the late 1940s." With the agility of "whirling dervishes" the communists then sought to develop a justification for the Soviet communist leaders' action.

World public opinion over the Soviet communist leaders' injustices mounted and as Khrushchev turned on the "smiles" and started visiting other countries, he was confronted with the accusation of anti-Semitism in Russia.

In England, Khrushchev characterized "anti-Semitism" as "nonsense" to which he would not listen. To a French delegation he protested that he was not anti-Semitic but that the Yiddish language is fading away in Russia as the Jews in the Soviet Union are learning to speak Russian. A new low in deception was reached when Khrushchev claimed that, in the early years of the revolution, "Jews occupied a disproportionately large number of high Soviet positions because the country had few trained people." He then asserted that the Kremlin had received protests from "the various Soviet Republics that too many Jews held desirable positions." The New York *Times* story on June 10, 1956, then reported that Khrushchev ". . . reportedly pressed Lazar M. Kaganovich, only high-ranking Soviet leader of Jewish origin, to confirm his statements, which Mr. Kaganovich finally did, saying one word, 'correct'. . . ." And now there are no top communist leaders in the Kremlin of Jewish origin since Khrushchev ousted and denounced Kaganovich last summer.

The president of B'nai B'rith, Philip M. Klutznick, answered the communist propaganda claims when he made the factual observation that only in Soviet Russia and its satellites is "Jewish life languishing and approaching extinction."

The Communist Party of the United States at its February, 1957, convention sought to hoodwink the American public by a series of statements to the press of how it had declared its independence from Moscow. This deceit was established in no unmistakable terms by the handling of a resolution dealing with anti-Semitism in Russia. The resolution was submitted by Professor Morris U. Schappes in typical communist language: "Resolution: On Jewish question, some aspects."

The resolution stated: "This matter concerns us as Communists in a country which includes 5,000,000 Jews." It then points out,

> Since the Jewish question is international in scope, we communists must be alert to the problem and its world-wide

aspects. The Jewish question is a specific question that requires specific attention. . . . The liquidation of the outstanding Yiddish writers and Jewish communal and political leaders, and the snuffing out of organized Jewish cultural life have been known for some time. . . .

He, of course, was referring to anti-Semitism in Russia.

The resolution called for the creation of a Jewish Commission, a return to Leninist policy, and a request ". . . to make this subject one for fraternal discussion with the Communist Party in the Soviet Union," which, of course, negates the view of independence of the communists in the United States.

The resolution was soft-pedaled and disposed of, as was a similar resolution dealing with Soviet terrorism in Hungary, by being referred to the National Committee of the Party. *Pravda,* on February 16, 1957, had this to say: "The 16th Convention of the Communist Party, USA, confirmed the loyalty of the American communists to the principles of Marxism-Leninism. . . ."

Party leaders, however, in the face of the overwhelming evidence of communist hate for the followers of Moses, still are attempting to deceive unsuspecting persons of Jewish origin and, as this is being written, communist tacticians are at work on a program of infiltrating Jewish groups by seeking for the answers to such questions as:

—How to avoid the extremes of negating Israel and of accepting its actions uncritically.
—How to work in religious groups while keeping ourselves and our children free of the religious doctrine of these groups.
—How to avoid the extremes of taking on all issues and avoiding all issues.
—How to balance Jewish work with our interests as Marxists in general trade union, minorities and people's movements.

The vigilant and patriotic members of Jewish organizations have demonstrated their alertness to counteract the infiltration tactics in Jewish institutions by communists who were born Jews. Where communist infiltration tactics have succeeded in

Jewish organizations, it has been because of a failure on the part of leaders and members alike to be vigilant and thwart the communist tactic of infiltration into the Jewish community just as it has sought to infiltrate every other organization.

A *Pravda* editorial on July 6, 1956, should remove all doubts as to the antipathy of communism to those who worship God regardless of their faith:

> As for our country the Communist Party has been and will be the only master of the minds, and thoughts, the spokesman, leader and organizer of the people in their entire struggle for communism.

Part VI

THE COMMUNIST
UNDERGROUND

20.

How the Underground Works

THE COMMUNIST above-ground, as we have seen, constantly seeks to represent itself as a legitimate political organization working for the best interests of America. When large segments of the people are hoodwinked into believing this fraudulent claim, it becomes easier for the Party to carry on its revolutionary propaganda through mass agitation, infiltration, and fronts. Without some degree of public acceptance, the Party is doomed to an isolated impotence.

Communist tactics require that above-ground activities be pushed as far as possible. However, when the Party begins to abuse its constitutional privileges and the government takes steps to protect itself from outright treason and subversion, more and more Party activities are shifted underground, that is, to the illegal apparatus. As Lenin taught, the Party must always have two levels, above-ground and underground. Both must exist at the same time. One without the other is incomplete.

In times of "nonprosecution"—that is, when "hostile" governments are not attacking—the Party, like a submarine, will surface, carrying on the bulk of its work above ground. But a portion (the underground) will always stay submerged, concealing the Party's illegal activities, such as aid to Soviet espionage; endeavoring to place concealed members in sensitive positions in government, education, and industry, maintaining clandestine communication networks.

In event of an emergency, this undercarriage quickly expands, providing the Party with well-prepared and extensive undercover operations. Within days, hundreds of above-ground comrades can be absorbed. The Party submerges, the above-ground shrinks.

The Party will submerge only as long and as deep as absolutely necessary, always preferring surface operations (with a supporting underground). That's why it desperately fights all legislation curtailing its activities. Only to prevent annihilation will it go completely underground. This action reduces contact with the masses, wastes energy on nonproductive security measures, and decreases effectiveness. Except for outright liquidation, it is practically impossible to drive the Party completely underground or completely above ground.

As we saw in Chapters 4 and 5, the Party experienced two periods of intensified underground activities: (1) shortly after its founding, and (2) in the mid-1951 to mid-1955 period. Both were caused primarily by prosecutive action of state and federal governments.

To understand the underground we must realize that it is a maze of undercover couriers, escape routes, hide-outs, and clandestine meetings. It's not the place for the beginner, the half-indoctrinated, or the doubtful. Only the most loyal members are selected. These men and women are carrying on the Party's deceitful work away from the watchful eye (so they hope) of the FBI and other governmental agencies.

It was early in the morning. The taxi had been summoned to a number on James Street. The driver looked. On the corner stood an attractive woman, dressed in a polka-dotted blouse and navy blue skirt. From her shoulder dangled a brown purse.

"Take me to Elm and Cherry Streets," she said, jumping into the cab.

When the taxi arrived at the destination, the woman changed her mind. "Take me to the Surplus Store," she instructed. The driver complied, now almost doubling back to where he had started. The woman, however, still wasn't satisfied. She asked to be taken to another location. There she alighted.

A few minutes later she hailed another cab and went straight to her destination, a railroad station on the east side of town, some fifteen miles away, even though she was then only a short distance from a terminal where she could have caught the same train.

This wasn't the Case of the Woman Who Changed Her Mind, but the shift of a Party underground leader to a new hide-out. Why the strange gyrations? She was endeavoring to make certain she wasn't being followed.

In a northern state a scene similar to the Girl in the Polka-dotted Blouse was being enacted. A woman with black curly hair, dressed in a smart gray herringbone suit and wearing a large-brimmed hat, boarded a southbound train. She carefully surveyed the passengers, then took a seat near the rear. She was carrying on her left arm a blue tweed suit and a hook-weave black coat. In her right hand she held a brown suitcase trimmed in light tan. It was a long ride, all afternoon and night. Upon arrival she sped to an address in an older section of town. A knock, the door opened, and she disappeared inside. The woman was a high-ranking Party leader reporting for a new underground assignment.

These two women, neatly dressed and looking like ordinary travelers, were but two of many hundreds involved in Party underground work from 1951 to 1955. Many were away from home for months, even years, living under assumed names in obscure rooms; moving under cover of darkness from one city to another; scurrying along streets late at night; eating irregular meals. Life in the underground for most is hard work, drudgery; not romance, adventure, and fun.

How are comrades chosen for underground work?

As we have seen, only the most trusted and dedicated of Party members are chosen. A study of the case histories of twenty-five top Party leaders active in the underground during 1951-55 disclosed that all had been in the communist movement for over twenty years. Their average age was somewhat over forty.

Party "loyalty" is determined by an elaborate "verification" system. A prospect is compelled to execute a questionnaire asking for detailed information about his family, former employment, education, Party history. One questionnaire, for example, requested a member to analyze the "political position" of relatives, and then asked, "Have you had any extra-marital relations since you've been married? If so, with whom and how often?" Many times, older comrades must vouch for the prospect.

To enter the underground usually means simply disappearing quickly, abruptly, without warning. Whispers float: "Where's Gordon?" The answer: "He's gone under" or merely the telltale sign, a clenched fist with the thumb pointed down.

It was a Monday morning. Everybody came to work except one, a woman who had been with the firm for many years. Nobody thought anything about it. Probably she was sick. But the next day, the next week, the next month, she didn't return, although she had almost a hundred dollars in wages coming to her. At her apartment it was the same story. She had quickly moved out. Nobody knew where she had gone.

She had entered the communist underground.

These departures are carefully planned. Above-ground comrades will handle any pending personal matters, such as storing the member's furniture, moving his family, caring for his car. Sometimes departures have been so rapid that hot meals have been left on the table.

Once underground, the member is made ready for assignment. This means, first of all, assuming a new identity; that is, being made into "another person." As a general rule this involves the securing of a new name, date, and place of birth, even changing physical appearance. One functionary, for example, lost between thirty-five and forty pounds, giving him a gaunt appearance. Others were told to gain weight. Still another grew a mustache, donned glasses, and dyed his hair black. Identification marks, such as moles and warts, have been removed by surgery. One underground official boasted that he could walk down Main Street every day and even his wife could not recognize him!

In addition, the member must be supplied with fake identification papers, Social Security cards, drivers' licenses, library cards, bank-deposit books. If he is stopped on the street he must be able to prove his "identity." Likewise, he should acquaint himself with his adopted place of birth, know something about its newspapers, streets, and stores. Does it have a baseball team? It's usually best to pick a small town, for there is less chance of meeting somebody from there.

Frequently the member, in his new pose, will attempt, at least on a temporary basis, to secure employment. His underground work will be conducted in the evenings and on week ends. Some of the comrades are on the Party's payroll, but most are not. One member became, in the words of her employer, an "efficient, affable, and able" secretary. Little did he dream that she was a communist on special underground assignment. In another instance a comrade, when hired for a job, said she was born in a Southern city, had attended a certain grade and high school, and had previously worked in another city. Later FBI investigation revealed that her story was a complete falsehood. Her job was only a front for secret communist work.

That's why the underground is a nightmare of deceit, fear, and tension, where one has to tell falsehoods, fabricate a background, adopt a new name, and live in fear of being recognized by old friends or acquaintances.

Suppose the Girl in the Polka-dotted Blouse, in order to carry out an assignment, must pose as a widow or the estranged wife of a sea captain, or as the retired owner of a ladies' dress shop? Think of the problems that would arise. What types of stories must be improvised? What kind of personal possessions must be purchased to keep up the cover?

The Party has thoroughly studied these problems. Let's look at a secret study issued for the instruction of women underground comrades, like the Girl in the Polka-dotted Blouse. Here's the advice:

1. Suppose you are posing as a widow (after having been married some twenty years) and you have now come to this city "to get away from it all and try to forget."

Answer: Well, you shouldn't come in (as to a rooming house) empty-handed, with only a handbag. You "must make some show of previous accumulation," for example, have "a few personal 'precious' things," such as "picture(s), little mementoes." Where can you get them? "In any 5-10c store."

2. Suppose you have an inquisitive landlady who has access to your apartment.

Answer: You might first say (to cover up the scarcity of your personal belongings) that, being so sad over becoming a widow, you "haven't had the heart to unpack everything yet." If you stay longer, you better buy a dustmop and some other items, "so that the story of having been a housewife for so many years will ring true." And by all means have some luggage, preferably "beat-up" luggage. "The more luggage a woman moves in with the better is she accepted on the strength of her story."

3. What if you're underground in a small town? What about social life? People are sure to become suspicious if you stay seven nights a week at home. Moreover, unlike a man, it doesn't look right to go to a late movie alone.

Answer: Take a short trip out of town. This not only takes away suspicion but gives you something to talk about.

4. Then there is the problem of extra expense incurred by women.

Answer: A woman must have more luggage (she's expected to have more clothing, etc.). Then she must use a taxi; she can't carry her own suitcases. Also there is the problem of "personal upkeep." Suppose you are a blonde and you come into town as a brunette. As the study points out, you have to keep that up, to a tune of about six dollars for each trip to the beauty parlor and two dollars extra for eyebrow dye.

Attention to detail must be exacting, even to the clothes worn on given occasions. Here's a sample of a "How I was Dressed" diary kept by the Girl in the Polka-dotted Blouse:

—wore dark grey dress, high heels, walked to the movie . . .
—wore low heels, two-piece blue suit, red tam . . .
—wore high heels, white blouse and blue hankie. Carried umbrella, looked like rain.

In meeting noncommunists she doesn't want to be a strawberry blonde one day and the next week a natural brunette. If she is representing herself as a "poor widow," she probably should wear the same dress every time, not come in a variety of outfits.

Assignments in the underground vary. A select few are engaged in highly secret disciplinary work. Security is most important. The telephone and mails are to be avoided. Never carry Party documents or names on your person. Disciplinary squads may stop members and search their purses. Woe if a compromising slip of paper is found bearing a name or telephone number.

Security precautions also affect the above-ground Party. No membership books (or cards) are issued; large clubs are broken up into small groups; records are destroyed. In a Western state a Party member was instructed to go to the post office for mail. He was to carry a brown paper sack and, upon leaving, proceed to the restroom of a nearby building. There another Party member, carrying an identical brown sack containing nothing but rubbish, would meet him. They would exchange sacks. In this way, so it was thought, the person with the mail could not be detected.

Then there are couriers who carry secret messages, often in code. In addition, they bring supplies and funds, meet Party leaders in hide-outs, contact mail drops. Couriers are of various types: (1) Party officials "just going through," (2) Party members, such as salesmen and truck drivers, whose occupations allow them to travel without suspicion, (3) "professional" couriers who are trained to operate on a full-time basis.

Some comrades are given special assignments, such as stockpiling supplies (paper, ink, printing presses, funds). Others, working with above-ground comrades, secure, for future underground use, extra drivers' licenses, birth certificates, car titles, etc. In addition, comrades operate hide-outs and escape routes or hide Party records. The underground from 1951 to 1955 actually harbored Party leaders who were criminal fugitives, having been convicted by United States courts.

Depending on local conditions, the organizational structure of the underground varies from area to area. As a general rule, because of security reasons, the leadership is rotated. The Party may feel that a member is going "stale." If so, he may be shifted to another assignment or temporarily "furloughed upstairs" (meaning allowed to reappear in the "open"). A reserve leadership is always ready, in case the functioning leaders are arrested or otherwise incapacitated. This reserve may consist of other underground comrades or members still "upstairs."

On the West Coast, for example, a clandestine communist group using the code name of "Mollie" had full responsibility for carrying through not only underground but also many above-ground functions. For security reasons underground contacts are always downward, not to a higher level. This means that top officials can contact those in lower levels, but the latter (who seldom even know the identity of their superiors) cannot contact above themselves. In event of an "enemy breakthrough," only the identity of those on the level "broken through," or lower level, will be revealed.

As we have mentioned, the closest cooperation must exist between the underground and above-ground apparatuses. The former cannot operate as a self-contained unit. It must constantly be serviced from above; otherwise it would die of suffocation. As we noticed in Chapter 17, communist fronts serve as periscopes to the "upper world" through which funds, supplies, and instructions are funneled. The deeper the Party goes underground, the greater the reliance on fronts.

The overriding consideration of the underground is security, not to be discovered by the FBI. Let's see how this affects the Party's operations.

Hide-outs

Generally speaking the underground uses three types of hide-outs: (1) *temporary*, an abode for a courier or Party member en route to another destination. This will probably be a room in the home of a "politically reliable" individual; (2) *emergency*, a home or apartment where a member, perhaps feeling he is being watched or suddenly becoming sick, can hide on an emergency basis. It is not to be used too frequently; (3) *permanent*, or "deep freeze," where one or more comrades can remain for extended periods, maybe a month, or even a year, with all necessities being provided. Farms or cabins in remote areas make excellent "deep freezes."

Here are some of the requirements demanded for a "safe" hide-out. They illustrate the Party's attention to detail.

1. The owner must be absolutely loyal to the Party.

2. If an apartment, there must be no doorman or elevator operator. A walk-up apartment of three or four stories is preferable.

3. If a family home, the members must be thoroughly reliable. There should be no children, relatives, or maids.

4. The proprietor should not be too closely identified with the Party, either as a sympathizer or member.

5. The hide-out must be located where there are no curious or talkative neighbors.

6. The quarters must be sufficiently large to accommodate extra guests. Excessive cramping attracts attention.

7. The neighborhood should be well known to the owner and one in which some trusted friends reside. In this way any inquiries in the vicinity will immediately come to their attention.

Meetings

Elaborate security must surround all underground contacts, whether between just two people or groups. Here are a few points the underground has to remember:

1. Don't use the same meeting place too frequently. It might excite suspicion.

2. If a meeting is held at a home, a member of the family (who, of course, is thoroughly reliable) should be there to answer the door in case an outsider knocks. He can handle the situation and also serve as a lookout.

3. If large numbers are involved, times of arrival and departure should be staggered. Everybody should not arrive or depart at the same time.

4. If the comrades don't know each other, a predetermined means of identification (a code word, piece of clothing, etc.) should be used.

5. Bring no more documents (books, papers, etc.) than absolutely necessary. Avoid note-taking. Make effective use of memory.

6. Upon departure, a "rear-guard" comrade should thoroughly check for any incriminating items. Have any papers been left on the floor? Is there a telephone number scratched on the wall? Has someone forgotten his coat, which might contain Party data?

In one instance six weeks allegedly were spent in bringing twenty people to a national underground conference.

If two comrades don't know each other, advance arrangements must be made, usually by notes, to effect identification for a meeting. Here is one example. The note read:

On Friday, April 6, 8 P.M. at NE corner, Oak and 9th Sts.— my courier will be standing with a *Field and Stream* magazine. Bill's courier will approach her and ask, "Mrs. Polk, what time is it?" She will reply, "I'm sorry, my watch is stopped."

Note the use of a magazine and code words for identification.

Just in case the first contact didn't work out, there were alternative instructions. The note continued:

> In case no one shows, she will be on the SW corner, Walnut and 10th, same magazine, Friday, 13, 8 P.M., same question and answer. She will wait around only ten minutes each time.

Noncommunists probably will find it difficult to understand the reckless abandon, personal risk, and sheer physical endurance displayed by communists to conceal their underground activities. Here are a few of the tactics employed by communists to determine if they are being followed:

Driving cars:

1. Driving alternately at high and low rates of speed.
2. Entering a heavily traveled intersection on a yellow light, hoping to lose any follower or cause an accident.
3. Turning corners at high rates of speed and stopping abruptly.
4. Suddenly leaving a car and walking hurriedly down a one-way street in the direction in which vehicle traffic is prohibited.
5. Entering a dark street in a residential area at night, making a sharp U-turn, cutting into a side alley, and extinguishing the car's lights.
6. Driving to a rural area, taking a long walk in a field, then having another car meet them.
7. Waiting until the last minute, then making a sharp left turn in front of oncoming traffic.
8. Stopping at every filling station on the highway, walking around the car, always looking, then going on.

On foot:

1. Leaving subways, buses, and trains at the last minute, even holding the door open and jumping off.

2. Entering hotels, bus terminals, and department stores where there are many exits.

3. Stooping over in the aisles, then suddenly rising and looking around to see if anybody is searching for them.

4. Doubling back after rounding a corner.

5. Putting a coin in a pay telephone booth, dialing a number, then rushing to the adjoining booth to see if anybody is trying to listen.

6. Leaving a taxicab, but instructing the driver to go around the block and pick them up again.

7. Using store windows as mirrors to see behind them.

8. Walking slowly to a corner, then starting to run down an alleyway.

Always there is the fear of being followed. One Party couple registered at a motel, then the husband parked the car several miles away. He walked back and climbed through a side window. Maybe in this way he could conceal his night's lodging!

A woman in a Midwestern city kept riding streetcars, buses, and taxis for thirty hours, stopping at no time except for meals. In communist language she was *"dry-cleaning"*; that is, making certain that she was not being followed.

The pressure becomes terrific. As long as a comrade feels he is "dirty" (that is, he suspects the "enemy," meaning the FBI, is near) he must keep up his "dry-cleaning." He can make his "meet" or enter a hide-out only when he's certain he is "clean."

Two dry-cleaning techniques are of special interest. One is the *switch-point* operation: The communist leader is driven to a certain location in a car (called a "drop car"). There he alights and enters another car (called a "pickup car"). Before entering the second car, however, he will walk across a parking lot, over a bridge, or through a department store—the object being to lose any pursuer. In the double switch, the pickup car drops the Party leader at a second switch, where he will be picked up by a third vehicle and then taken to his destination.

In the *scramble,* members (as on leaving meetings) enter automobiles. The drivers start the motors. Suddenly the doors of the cars will open and the comrades will get out, including the drivers. They scramble, meaning they quickly take seats in the other cars, whereupon all autos will move away in different directions. It's hard for any "pursuer" to tell who went in which car.

The underground creates intense strains on family life. The undeviating demands of the Party (its interests must come first, regardless of personal consequences) leave deep scars.

For years many families are separated. On some occasions a midnight contact or a few days of furlough are permitted. Children grow up without seeing their fathers. In one instance a child was stricken with polio. His underground father did not leave his Party work to come to the child's bedside. Mothers are often hard pressed to give answers to the question, "Where's Daddy?" Some "explain" that Daddy is away on a trip, in another town, or dead. One little boy, whose father was gone, said: "I wish my father was in jail. Then I could at least see him."

Normal family relationships are disrupted. The Party may promise financial assistance to the families of underground comrades, but many times the support is miserly or does not come at all. Heart-rending results ensue:

> During the past four years, Hank and I have been separated most of the time [one Party wife wrote]. There has never been any question about carrying out the decisions made, even when Hazel [small daughter] and I were set adrift by the Party with no financial provision and I had to go to my family so that my infant could have food and a place to live. When Hazel almost died from third-degree burns, Hank didn't even know about it since we had no way to communicate. I have been cut off from my family completely. The furniture, clothes and other things that we accumulated during our marriage we'll probably never see again. We have moved, and moved,

and moved yet again . . . dragging Hazel around from place to place, carrying out decisions made, guarding our security and that of others.

The total effect was demoralizing. The wife continues:

> I can't have an operation because it would mean six months in a cast and on my stomach—and there is no one to take care of Hazel . . . I get overtired physically, and the past four years of the kind of life we have led, with its many pressures of loneliness, financial scrounging, security measures and the sword of Damocles—that of being discovered—hanging over my head, finally took its toll.

Despite this woman's hardships the Party brought charges that her husband had been seeing her without permission. The utter fanaticism of Party discipline is shown by her reaction toward the charges: "If in spite of all this the Board feels that there has been a breach of discipline, then I am willing to abide by any decision made and accept whatever control is agreed upon."

The underground, perhaps more than any other phase of Party activity, brings out the fanaticism of communist discipline. The member becomes so entranced with his mission that his hardships, sufferings, and obstacles become challenges to overcome, not reasons for discouragement. The very thought of working on this assignment, as one Party leader stated, should make him "ooh and ah."

Some Party wives, however, did not always "ooh and ah," but bitterly resented their husbands' long absences from home and the disruption of family life. This presented the Party with a serious problem. These wives were potential weak links in communist security; they might jeopardize the husbands' location by making unauthorized contacts, might give information to the "enemy" or impair morale by their uncongenial attitude. One Party instruction, for example, urged that wives should be spoken to and the importance of the Party's policies explained. They must be indoctrinated more. For some Party wives it would certainly take a lot of explaining.

Children have been born in the communist underground, children who were not even given their true family names. In one instance a father and mother living as an underground couple *(transformed couple)* entered their child at a nearby school under the family alias. In another case a baby born to underground parents was registered with county authorities under the underground alias. Imagine the hypocrisy of such a family situation. A whole world of falsehoods must be invented to satisfy youthful curiosity. What about the parents' childhoods? What about grandparents? Every family matter discussed must be carefully weighed: Will it give away any secrets?

The very character of the underground, with its emphasis on stealth and deceit, degrades human values. While many comrades struggle in poverty, living in squalid conditions at great personal sacrifice, a few enjoy the very best—comfortable hide-outs equipped with all conveniences. For them the underground is a "good life," with others paying the bill. Moreover, Party discipline often places great power into the hands of some who, as petty dictators, do not hesitate to use it to inflict revenge and spite on their personal enemies. Many times the underground becomes a catacomb of back-stabbing and the settling of old scores.

Sexual immorality is also abetted. In one instance an organizer, leaving his wife and children, lived in Chicago with another woman. In an Eastern city, a woman whose husband was underground carried on an affair with another man. In still another instance a wife kept company with a man while her husband was forbidden by the Party's underground leaders to see her.

This is the communist underground. It may appear as a "beehive of crazy confusion." But it is not. All these shifts, midnight meetings, and escape routes find meaning in only one thing: the strengthening of the Party. The cardinal question always is, "What is best for the Party?"

As one Party leader stated, "Our best people are in this field . . . They are not in it for adventure, romance, thrills or pleasure. . . ." They "are in it because that is where the Party wants them for political reasons. . . ." ". . . it is . . . probably one of the toughest and hardest assignments for anyone."

That is why the Party, as we have seen, tries desperately to create the communist man, the individual obedient even when he is beyond the Party's immediate control. "It's not me who speaks," one leader said, "but the Party." Any allegiance outside the Party must be broken. The underground worker is the member who, even if cut off from leadership, will know what to do, will carry out the assignment, regardless of what it is. He is the man on whom all revolutionary plans depend.

Here is an example of how this fanaticism works:

Shortly before noon one day a top Party official drove east out of town. At the outskirts he doubled back, twice turning corners and coming to abrupt stops. Then, at speeds varying from forty to eighty miles an hour, he continued east for twenty-six miles. Turning around, he retraced his route at eighty miles an hour.

He was "dry-cleaning" in a most dangerous and reckless fashion. Back in town, for three hours he parked and reparked his car, darting up streets, entering and immediately leaving hotels.

At roughly 4:00 P.M. he left town again, this time driving south, again at various speeds. After five hours he cut east for fourteen miles, north for two, doubled back for twelve, southeast for forty-two, sometimes running without his lights; parking for a few minutes near buildings, then darting out at savage speed.

Late that night, after roughly twelve hours of furtive, reckless driving, often at highly dangerous speeds, he arrived at his destination and checked into a hotel. He had covered some 360 miles; the normal driving distance was 195.

This type of fanatical communist, if so instructed, would not hesitate to lead a riot, steal vital military secrets, sabotage defense industries, or perform illegal activities. Here is the true communist at work, without concern for personal risk or safety.

21.

Espionage and Sabotage

THE COMMUNIST UNDERGROUND is designed to carry forward phases of the Party's program which cannot be conducted openly and lawfully. In addition, it contains weapons of attack which must always remain hidden (the permanent part of the underground), such as aid to Soviet espionage, attempts to place members in strategic positions in industry for potential sabotage, techniques to discredit law enforcement, and endeavors to infiltrate the armed forces.

Lenin taught that the enemy must be weakened in advance. To wait for something to happen is not the way to achieve revolution. The way must be prepared. The enemy must be softened up: weaken his will to resist, nullify his capacity for counteraction, impair his morale. Then, as in November, 1917, in Russia, when the crisis comes, communists can march to power through the ranks of a demoralized enemy.

The Party's relation to Soviet espionage is one of the most potent weapons in the communist underground arsenal. As past events have proven—for instance the Harry Gold-Klaus Fuchs combination and the case of Julius and Ethel Rosenberg, executed in 1953 on espionage charges—Moscow-directed spying represents a vital danger to the integrity and safety of free government. Espionage is utilized not only to secure information but also to weaken the "enemy" from within.

The Soviets very early instituted espionage operations

against the United States with the full cooperation of the Communist Party. In 1919 the Comintern was established and, as we have seen in Chapter 4, Comintern "reps" became common figures in Party circles. In January, 1919, Ludwig C. A. K. Martens, a member of the Russian Communist Party, was appointed as the first Soviet representative to the United States. Although never recognized by the American government, he set up an office in New York City. Arthur Adams, later identified as a Soviet atom spy, was a member of Martens' staff.

In the light of today's well-organized, efficiently operated spy apparatus, the Soviets in the early days were crude and clumsy. Many of the Russians were not proficient in English. They lacked knowledge of our customs and possessed no special espionage training. Many were propaganda as well as espionage agents and could be identified by their rabid preaching of communism. Often the security of their communications was not of the best.

In late July, 1920, a seaman on the SS *Stockholm* walked up Pier 95 in New York City. Noticing customs officials searching two other seamen, he turned and ran down the pier. Later, after the seaman's apprehension, a package was found concealed in his trousers. Inside was a series of envelopes, one inside the other with the smallest containing over 200 uncut diamonds valued at 50,000 dollars. The smuggling of diamonds was one of the early Bolshevik techniques of financing operations in the United States. For whom was the package destined? Inside was a typewritten letter starting, "Comrade Martens."

Unfamiliarity with America made dependence on the Communist Party, USA, more important than ever. Without the ready base of the Communist Party, USA, with its fanatical allegiance to Moscow, Soviet espionage would have had tremendous problems in getting started. As it was, there were Party members available, able and willing to carry out Soviet instructions. Often it was difficult to distinguish between a member's work for the Party and for Moscow. Comrades traveled back and forth to Russia, were given assignments by the

Kremlin, and felt it their highest duty to gather information for the Bolsheviks.

Party officials made assistance to Moscow priority Number One. We have seen in Chapter 4 how the communist leadership, for example, promised to help Comrade Loaf (a Comintern agent) collect information on the American labor movement. In another instance the Party Secretariat actually approved the release of a Party member for Soviet intelligence duties.

What were some of the ways through which the Communist Party, USA, rendered aid to Soviet espionage?

Most important, of course, was recruitment. The Party was able, time after time, to supply recruits, both members and sympathizers, for espionage use. Suppose the Soviets needed a photographer? a source of information in a Pennsylvania steel plant? a trusted short-wave radio expert? The Party would be expected to, and did, "fill the bill."

This funneling of talent to the Soviets was often accomplished through a special Party contact who was called a "steerer." A trusted old-time member, he was able to spot recruits for espionage among the Party's ranks and to fulfill requests made by the Soviets. As espionage operations became more complex, the "steerer's" role became ever more vital. The Party was a vast recruiting ground for spy talent.

The Party provided many essential "services" to Soviet espionage. Suppose a Russian espionage agent secretly entered the United States, to operate here or while en route to another country. Most likely, as so often happened, he would need a "new identity," or, in espionage language, a "change of feathers." This probably meant a faked birth certificate, a false passport, and other identification papers. Maybe he would be placed in "deep freeze" for several months. If so, he had to be "serviced"—that is, fed and clothed. After being "re-feathered," he would be on his way.

Then there were "business covers." A Party member, perhaps with Soviet funds, would set up a business, allegedly for legitimate purposes but actually for espionage. In 1927, World Tourists was incorporated in New York, ostensibly for tourist business. Actually, this "business," under the operation of Jacob Golos, a communist "steerer," became an active espionage "cover."

The Party, in addition, helped arrange the transfer of funds, established mail drops (where espionage communications come to a third person, later to be given to the espionage network), and operated couriers. In one instance a Party member even served as an interpreter for a Soviet agent.

Even from these early days, however, evidence existed that the Soviets were aware of the dangers of too close an affiliation with the United States Party. An espionage operation might be jeopardized by a known Party member's participation. Similarly, in the event of a "blow-up," the Party, in the public's eyes, would be linked directly with a foreign power, Soviet Russia. This was one thing both the Soviets and Party officials wanted to avoid. Hence, by the early 1940's there was a definite lessening of direct Soviet dependence on the U. S. Party for espionage assistance.

The Soviet spy system, moreover, was now better able to stand on its own feet. In 1924, Amtorg Trading Corporation (a Soviet government commercial agency) was established. This gave the Soviets their first "legal" base for espionage operations. In this way persons or institutions in a country openly as representatives or agents of a foreign power have an ideal cover to fulfill their assignments of clandestine espionage. In 1933 diplomatic recognition was afforded the Soviet Union. Now trained espionage agents, operating under diplomatic immunity, could direct operations. After World War II Russians assigned to the United Nations in this country gave additional striking power to Soviet espionage. Moreover, assistance was possible through the espionage networks of Soviet satellite countries operating in the United States.

This lessening of direct Soviet dependence on the Party was a gradual development. Whereas in the early 1920's Party and espionage work were often indistinguishable, the Soviets now instructed members tapped for service to drop all connections with the Party. One old-time Party member, turned spy, told the FBI that the Soviets had instructed agents to conceal their

Party affiliations. This soon became a standard technique. If engaged in espionage, cut off all connections with the Party, even contacts with former Party friends. Ethel Rosenberg, for example, indicated that she no longer bought the *Daily Worker* at her usual newsstand. Another agent, while in the company of a Soviet superior, stopped to purchase a communist publication. He was severely reprimanded. The communist label might betray the espionage ring.

The Soviets, however, still depended on communists or sympathizers for assistance. In one major apparatus detected by the FBI, for example, twelve of seventeen participants had been Party members. Both Ethel and Julius Rosenberg, executed as Soviet spies, had communist backgrounds.

Elizabeth Bentley, moreover, has given testimony as to how she collected dues from secret members of the Party when she came to Washington as a courier of the Soviet espionage system. Among those from whom she has stated she collected dues were officials of the Office of Strategic Services (OSS), Department of Commerce, the Air Corps, the Office of the Coordinator of Inter-American Affairs, the Treasury Department, and others. In some instances one person would collect dues for a group and hand them over to Miss Bentley. One such individual was Nathan Gregory Silvermaster, who, according to Miss Bentley, headed a group. (Silvermaster denied the disclosures initially and later invoked the Fifth Amendment.) On occasions a member of a group when coming to New York would deliver the Party dues collected to Miss Bentley there. The Party also benefited, as disclosed by testimony, because, as in some instances, information collected for the Soviets was made available to the leadership of the Party for review.

In 1945 the defection of Igor Gouzenko, cipher clerk assigned to the Soviet Embassy in Canada, revealed close tie-ups between Soviet espionage and Canadian communists. Then the appearance of FBI informants at Smith Act trials shocked the Soviet Union as to the amazing extent to which the FBI had penetrated the Communist Party, USA. These, among other revelations, encouraged even more the Soviet tendency to lessen its direct dependence on the Party. Today, with some exceptions, the Soviets are attempting to operate their espionage networks independent of the Party, staying away, as much as possible, from Party assistance. This does not mean, however, that the Party is today not playing an important role in Soviet espionage. As we shall see, the Party is doing much to prepare the way for Soviet espionage and, when the need arises, will unhesitatingly supply vital assistance. The present "drawing away" from direct Party assistance is strictly a Soviet tactical maneuver, subject to instant change.

Soviet espionage is no longer a clumsy, crude affair, as it was in the days of the rollicking "reps," but a deadly efficient profession, skillfully directed from Moscow, with well-trained agents supplied with money, modern technical equipment, and experience. To the Soviets, espionage is a part of over-all state policy.

On an April night in 1951, just two minutes before seven o'clock, a tall man wearing a tweed sport coat walked through the darkness toward the Washington Monument in our nation's capital. Brilliant lights played on the famous shrine. The usually bustling place was deserted. Everything was quiet.

Suddenly the tall man stepped from the circle of darkness into the light. He stopped a moment, peered up at the 555-foot top, looked at his watch, then started to walk around the base. On his left hand he wore a glove. A band of adhesive tape circled the middle finger of his right hand, and he carried a red-covered book under his left arm. This man was an employee of our Defense Department. As part of his work he had access to highly confidential information, just what the Russians wanted.

Exactly at seven o'clock, another man clad in a dark business suit stepped from the shadows. An espionage contact set up months previously in Austria was being consummated to the minute. The second man was Yuri V. Novikov, Second Secretary of the Soviet Embassy in Washington. (Novikov was well known to the FBI, since his activities in the United States had gone far beyond those of a diplomatic official. He was audacious almost beyond description. His brazenness reached a climax when he sat with defense counsel during the espionage trial of the onetime Justice Department employee, Judith Coplon. During this trial he would write out questions and hand them to defense counsel to direct to FBI agents on the witness stand. He was particularly interested in having questions asked pertaining to our internal administration and procedures.)

When Novikov met the government employee he said, "I'm Mr. Williams," the code words of recognition, along with the glove, tape, and red book. The two shook hands, then Novikov took the military specialist by the elbow, directing him from the light. A few words, arranging another meeting, and they parted.

From that night, for an entire year, the Soviets made secretive contacts with the government employee, never realizing that he was a "double agent" of the FBI. Seldom were meetings held in the same place. Some were on lonely lanes or in dead-end streets; one on a narrow rock bridge on a deserted Maryland road after dark. One time Novikov stood in a movie line; the double agent was to pass by and, seeing him there, would know that a meeting was scheduled one hour later at a nearby school. Then there were chalk marks on trash cans and a pencil mark on page 100 of the Manhattan (New York) telephone directory in Washington's Union Station, elaborate code signals between Novikov and the man from the defense establishment.

I hasten to add that the government employee was a loyal American, and in meeting Novikov he was merely carrying out a duty imposed upon him when he was assigned in Austria with the air force. His services were solicited by Otto Verber, who came to the United States as a refugee, as did Kurt L. Ponger, who had married Verber's sister. Both Verber and Ponger were in the armed services, both had acquired American citizenship, and, after the war, both had served in Europe. Upon returning to private life, both settled in Vienna, where they took advantage of the GI bill and benefits and enrolled in the University of Vienna. In 1949 Ponger was recruited by the Soviet intelligence service, and he in turn recruited Verber. It was later learned that Ponger had been a member of a Communist Party cell in England before he came to the United States as a refugee. He also had indoctrinated Verber.

The air force representative promptly reported Verber's approach to his superiors and from that time on acted under instructions. Prior to his return to the United States, Verber and Ponger arranged for the meeting at the Washington Monument. The Treasury of the United States, of course, received the thousands of dollars of Soviet funds paid to the loyal American.

In June, 1953, after pleading guilty to an espionage indictment, Ponger was sentenced to a prison term of from five to fifteen years, while Verber received a sentence of from three years, four months, to ten years. Novikov, who was named in the indictment as a co-conspirator, was declared *persona non grata* and returned to the Soviet Union.

The Soviet spy system is a disciplined structure, composed of many networks. There are the "legal" networks; that is, espionage controlled by legal representatives of the Russian government, such as diplomats. This was the case of Novikov. Then there are illegal networks, meaning spy rings operated by Moscow independent of the legal establishments. More and more the Soviets are concentrating on building illegal networks and planting "sleeper" agents. Such was the case of Colonel Rudolf Ivanovich Abel, of Soviet intelligence, who was arrested by the Immigration and Naturalization Service in June, 1957, at the request of the FBI, after we had identified him as a concealed agent. After his indictment in August, 1957, on espionage charges, information was made public concerning him which the FBI could not previously disclose. In November, 1957, after being convicted in Federal Court, Eastern District of New York, he was sentenced to thirty years in prison and fined 3000 dollars. Subsequently, a notice of appeal was filed.

Ordinarily a network includes a principal (the boss), always a Russian national in a "legal" network. Then there are, depending on the size of the network, group leaders, couriers, sources of information. Non-Russians, such as Harry Gold, may reach as high as a group leader or may be even a principal, but at all times they are under the firm control of Soviet superiors. In espionage, as in all features of communism, native comrades exist only to serve the Russian master.

Strange as it may sound, it is difficult to become a Russian espionage agent. The Soviets are highly selective. They will not accept just anybody. Does the prospect have access to confidential data? Will he accept discipline? What is his background? The Russians want to know everything about him. Sometimes elaborate verification checks, from Soviet contacts around the world, are run. Moreover, the breaking-in period of a prospect may be very slow. At first he may be given minor assignments to test his flair for intelligence work and discernment of details, all without risk to any established espionage operation. If he "comes through," he'll be given more responsible work.

Why does an individual engage in espionage? Why do native Americans betray their country for a foreign tyranny?

The motives are many, and often intertwined: money, the temporary thrill of secretive work, personal weaknesses, blackmail, feelings of spite against America because of an imagined wrong, a hope to assist relatives in communist countries. Very important, however, is ideological motivation, an attraction to the theory of communism and/or misguided admiration for Soviet rule in Russia.

Let's examine more closely this ideological motivation since it is playing such a major role today. We can distinguish two major categories:

1. *Non-Party ideological motivation:* that is, a feeling for or acceptance of the alleged principles of communism. In prior years many thousands were hoodwinked into believing, because of propaganda, that Russia represented a new "era" in humanity, that anti-Semitism was being abolished, that injustices were being rectified, that the problems of hunger, poverty, and racial discrimination were being solved. Among the reasons Harry Gold, who was never a Party member, gave for entering Russian espionage were:

A genuine desire to help the people of the Soviet Union to be able to enjoy some of the better things of life . . . Here, too, in the person of the Soviet Union was the one bulwark against the further encroachment of that monstrosity, Fascism . . . Anything that was against anti-Semitism I was for, and so the chance to help strengthen the Soviet Union seemed like a wonderful opportunity.

2. *Party ideological motivation:* the conditioning of thousands of members and sympathizers in the tenets of Marxism-Leninism, schooling them in loyalty to Moscow. Every Party member, through his training, is a potential communist espionage or sabotage agent. Julius Rosenberg, a fanatical Party member, actually volunteered his services. David Greenglass, Rosenberg's brother-in-law, was also an ardent communist. Walking along Highway 66 in Albuquerque, New Mexico, in 1944, his wife, Ruth, who had just come from New York City, told David that Julius wanted him to furnish information about his work at Los Alamos, where the atom bomb was being prepared. (David was assigned there as an army technician.) At first David said no—but his ideological motivation as a communist reversed his decision, and he agreed. He was to do great damage to America by furnishing the Russians, through Rosenberg, with valuable information about our greatest weapon.

Then there are other methods of motivating agents:

1. *Threat of exposure and blackmail.* Agents are given money (sometimes even against their will). Usually the amount is small, but a receipt is obtained, thus compromising their independence. Or they are made to sign papers, reports, or documents. If the initial ideological enthusiasm wears off, as it probably will, the agent is trapped. Even if he so desires, he cannot break away.

2. *Use of hostages.* Once they have control over relatives and loved ones the Soviets do not hesitate to let it be known

that unless their victim does their bidding a whole family will be liquidated.

Today the Party, with its thousands of members, represents a vast reservoir of potential espionage agents. Moreover, its vast propaganda and ideological program is daily saturating their hearts, minds, and souls with a sympathetic acceptance of communism. To be a Party member does not automatically mean being an espionage agent, but it makes the member potential spy material, if the request for aid to Russia ever comes. This is a tremendous and present danger to our security.

The United States is strategic spy target Number One for the Soviets. Every effort is being made to penetrate our defenses. The Soviets are interested in literally everything. Any person who believes that espionage means securing only military information is unacquainted with the nature of twentieth-century spying. An army manual, security regulations of a government building, the "political" views of a clerk in an industrial firm, incidents in the life of a prominent person which might be used for blackmail—these and many more are prize espionage targets. Soviet espionage is both mass (seeking information at random) and specific (trying to obtain a certain blueprint or military operational plan); open (gathering public source items, such as newspapers, magazines, maps, navigational charts, patents, aerial photographs, technical journals) and undercover (use of illegal means to steal information).

Here are some major "areas of interest" of Soviet espionage in the United States:

1. Scientific research and development, with particular attention to atomic energy, missiles, radar defense, electronics, and aeronautics.

2. The strength, deployment, training methods, strategy, and tactics of the armed forces of the United States, together with ordnance, weapons, and military equipment.

3. The intelligence and counterintelligence agencies of the United States, possibilities for penetration.

4. International relations of the United States.

5. Weaknesses in American public and private life that can be exploited for intelligence and propaganda purposes.

6. Anti-Soviet political opposition groups, refugees from the Soviet Union and satellite countries, and nationality groups in the United States.

The world of Soviet espionage, like the communist underground, is bleak and dreary. An individual may work for years and know his superior only as "Bill" or "Henry." His rewards: a smile, a promise, or a token award. Harry Gold, who gave a lifetime to the Soviets, was awarded the Order of the Red Star, which, among other things, gave him the privilege of free trolley rides in Moscow. To those hoping to get money, the promise is always big, but results are meager. Here are Gold's own words:

> . . . the difficulty in raising money for . . . trips; the weary hours of waiting on street corners in strange towns where I had no business to be and the killing of time in cheap movies; and the lies I had to tell at home and to my friends to explain my supposed whereabouts (Mom was certain that I was carrying on a series of clandestine love affairs). . . . It was drudgery . . . anyone who had an idea this work was glamorous and exciting was very wrong indeed—nothing could have been more dreary.

Life is disciplined to the final detail. The individual is a cog in a vast, inhuman, demanding machine. Klaus Fuchs, for example, while committing espionage in New York, asked permission from the Soviets for his sister in Massachusetts to stay with him. A petty detail but, disciplined agent that he was, he got the necessary approval.

The pressure is terrific, with the Soviet principals always wanting more and more. "If you were in Russia," one Soviet superior barked at a sub-agent who had done something wrong, "you would suffer the same fate as the traitors in the Moscow trials," referring to the purges of the 1930's. Everything is geared to promote Russian interests. If the agent fails, there are threats of dire consequences.

Espionage's twin partner is sabotage. In 1917 and after, sabotage played an important part in the Bolshevik rise to power. Revolution for the communists is a "science," of which sabotage is an important element. Not to use it, according to communist tactics, is to hinder victory.

The Communist Party, USA, has not reached the point where preparations for sabotage are vital to its future plans. Its small numbers, fear of FBI penetration of its inner discussions, and the existence of federal laws against sabotage and insurrection militate against such plans. So far the communists have carefully refrained from any show of terrorism. Any such act, even random sorties, the communists realize, would cause more harm to the Party by counter prosecutive action than any damage achieved by violence. Moreover, basic communist revolutionary tactics dictate against any such sabotage attempts until the eve of hostilities, which we pray and hope will never come. According to communist teaching, the comrades should not "tip their hands" until the "time is ripe." At a time when the Party was more open and truthful in proclaiming its objectives and tactics, Party organizers were instructed, "To raise the slogan of an armed demonstration without any anticipation of a speedy transformation into an armed revolt, and before the preconditions for a successful revolt exist, is to be guilty of playing with revolution."

Never must we forget, however, that even though acts of sabotage are not now part of the Party's program, they may become so in the future. In fact, the communist underground provides a cover to commit sabotage when it will serve the communist cause.

As part of the Party's underground the communists are pursuing a program called *colonization,* designed to place concealed members in strategic positions in basic industries and defense facilities. Colonization is part of the Party's industrial concentration program, which aims at increasing communist influence in industry and labor. This always has a high Party priority. Basic industry is a commonly used Party term, which one communist manual has defined as those industries "upon which the whole economic system depends." Hence to have a Party member in a steel plant would be more advantageous to the communists than one in a corncob-pipe factory. This technique is also often called "A Party Rooted Among the Workers."

In event of an emergency these colonizers, because of their key positions and concealed capacities, would be able to commit sabotage. A trained communist, by a flip of a switch, the pull of a lever, or the release of death-generating germs, could disrupt the work of thousands. One publication described the Party's objective:

> In order to overthrow the capitalist system, the working class must control the key positions in the capitalist system. These are not the state and federal capitals, public buildings, or residential neighborhoods, but the heart of the capitalist system— the shops, mines, mills and factories.

Moreover, the location of communist members in key industrial facilities places the Party in a position, if it desires, to promote strikes and slowdowns, which can be used as forms of sabotage. These tactics are vital, in communist thinking, to create "revolutionary situations" preparatory to the seizure of power.

Colonizers do not participate in open Party activities. Often they come from other areas of the country, even giving up their chosen professions. Sometimes a man and wife (a colonizer couple) will be sent into this phase of underground operations. The emphasis is on young people—those in their twenties and thirties. Operating under aliases, they attempt to work their way into more strategic industrial positions. These colonizers represent a deadly communist underground weapon. They are "sleepers" who, upon Party instructions, may one day rise up against our nation.

Another potential danger arises from previous sabotage

training of Party members. Some, as we have seen, attended Moscow's Lenin School. There they learned, among other things, the techniques of guerrilla warfare, how to make sabotage devices and organize civilian resistance. Others served in the Abraham Lincoln Brigade in the Spanish Civil War. According to William Z. Foster, 15,000 Party members saw duty with American military forces during World War II. The Party realizes that the enrollment of members in the armed forces provides military experience which, in a time of revolutionary crisis, could be utilized to communist advantage—at "capitalist" expense.

All the time, while the Party is attacking free government, both above-ground and underground, it seeks complete license to pursue its schemes. Any opposition by the government is labeled "persecution," "Red baiting," or "thought control."

For this reason communists grasp every opportunity to discredit, weaken, and vilify the institutions enforcing law and order. As long as the American judicial system is strong and realistically recognizes the threat of subversion to our constitutional republic, their efforts will be hampered. They know that.

Listen to these teachings. Are they calculated to instill respect for our democratic heritage?

—*The law-enforcement officer:* ". . . a servant of the boss class . . . He is your enemy."
—*The courts:* ". . . the workers must . . . recognize the capitalist court as a class enemy—as a weapon in the bosses' hands. . . ." "The worker must also understand that courts are not impartial. . . ."

At all times communists are told to try to make "bourgeois" courts look weak and silly. If members are brought to trial, turn the courtroom into a sounding board for communism. ". . . the aim should be to turn the trial into an open tribunal for the spreading and propagating of Communist ideas and aims." "The class struggle goes on in the courtroom as well as it does on the picket line, in the shops, and in the mines."

That's why every possible tactic is used inside the court-room to obstruct the orderly operation of justice. Outside, another attack is coordinated: letter-writing campaigns, fund-raising drives, propaganda leaflets, literature, all alleging that the communists on trial are being "persecuted" and that American courts are "unfair," "partial," and "undemocratic."

Another weapon in the Party's underground arsenal is the attempted infiltration of our armed forces. "Illegal work is particularly necessary in the army, the navy and police," Lenin proclaimed. Another communist writer adds, "The capitalist class has the army, navy and police at its disposal precisely for the purpose of keeping the working class from seizing power."

Yet, in the final analysis, as the communists well know, force and violence will be needed to bring about the revolution.

In fact this is exactly what Khrushchev had in mind when he told the Twentieth Congress of the Communist Party of the Soviet Union:

> . . . Our enemies like to depict us Leninists as advocates of violence always and everywhere. True, we recognize the need for the revolutionary transformation of capitalist society into socialist society. It is this that distinguishes the revolutionary Marxists from the reformists, the opportunists. There is no doubt that in a number of capitalist countries the violent over-throw of the dictatorship of the bourgeoisie and the sharp aggravation of class struggle connected with this are inevitable. . . .

Over 100 years ago Marx and Engels made this point perfectly clear in the *Communist Manifesto*. "The Communists disdain to conceal their views and aims. They openly declare that their ends can be attained only by the forcible overthrow of all existing social conditions." Lenin was more pointed:

> As long as capitalism and socialism exist, we cannot live in peace: in the end, one or the other will triumph—a funeral dirge will be sung either over the Soviet Republic or over world capitalism.

Soviet leader Nikita S. Khrushchev reveals his own hypocrisy when, in the same breath, he boasts that the communist world has no aggressive intentions and then declares as he did in August, 1957, "We are Leninists and are for peaceful cooperation." Through the use of Aesopian language he is seeking to induce the Western world to relax its guard until the time when the communist world is ready to launch its offensive and hopes to chant the "funeral dirge" over the free world.

How can loyal Americans resist this attack? I turn to this subject in the concluding chapters.

22.

What Can You Do?

THE RESPONSIBLE PERSON who gains an understanding of communism knows that such understanding should lead to the question: "But what can I do about it?"

My answer is that we can do *a lot*.

1. First and most important is to make sure that we do not permit the communists to fool us into becoming "innocent victims." Our defense? First, to know the answers to the "Five False Claims of Communism" given in Chapter 7. Next, to know the ways to "spot" deceptive communist fronts, listed at the end of Chapter 17.

2. Members of a trade union or any civic, fraternal, or social organization can help by spotting, exposing, and opposing communist efforts to infiltrate and capture that organization. How this can be done is told in Chapter 16.

3. And, finally, there may well be occasions when everyone might have the opportunity to help expose and prevent attempts at espionage, sabotage, and other types of subversive activity.

"Yes," one might say, "but I'm just a private citizen. Isn't spy-hunting a job for the FBI?"

Of course it is a job for the FBI, one given it by Presidential directives, acts of Congress, and rulings of the Attorney General. But the FBI can't do it all alone. The FBI has jurisdiction over more than 140 violations of federal law, and in a country with over 170,000,000 inhabitants there are fewer than 6200 agents of the FBI. Hence, all of these agents are not available for the investigation of subversive activities. We need the help of *all* loyal Americans.

Furthermore, in a democracy like ours, citizenship carries with it not only *rights* but *obligations*. One of these is to do *our* part to preserve, protect, and defend the United States against all enemies, whether domestic or foreign. The President of the United States, for example, in issuing directives giving the FBI the responsibility over matters relating to espionage, sabotage, and subversive activities, specifically called upon all patriotic citizens and individuals to assist us.

Therefore, those individuals who place information they have regarding the communist conspiracy into the proper hands are making a contribution of great value to the security of their country.

"But," one may say, "what can I do? I lead an ordinary life. I don't know any communists. So how can I be of any help?"

My answer to that is: You never know! Here is a case history of another average American who thought he "didn't know any communists."

This incident might be called the Case of the Forgotten Rubbish.

It was on a Saturday. A man telephoned one of our field offices. "I've been cleaning out my garage," he said, "and I've found some old rubbish there."

"Yes," said the special agent.

"I guess I'm crazy calling about this, but I thought you

might be interested. The stuff doesn't belong to me. It was left here by some roomers who moved a month or two ago. There's a box with a lot of cards."

"What kind of cards?"

"Don't know," the man answered. "I never saw any like them before. There are no names on them. Have words like 'club' and 'section' and some different colored tabs on them. Guess I should have burned them and not . . ."

"We're certainly glad you called," the agent said. "Mind if we come to see you?"

That telephone call enabled the FBI to secure the membership records of a complete section of the Communist Party. Marked for destruction by the section membership secretary, they had, by mistake, found their way into the forgotten rubbish.

Now an alert, patriotic citizen had placed these records into the fight against communism, helping to identify many of the most dangerous subversives in his very own community.

In this way he, like many others who report information to the FBI, was helping protect his own home, family, and nation.

Don't think one must have evidence establishing the identity of a spy, the hide-out of an underground Party leader, or the location of stolen blueprints before he can report information. Many cases start with very small clues, a scrap of paper, a photograph, an abandoned passport. Then, bit by bit, the entire picture is developed by investigation.

Here are a few suggestions of what Americans can report to the FBI:

1. Any information about espionage, sabotage, and subversive activities. The FBI is as close to every person as the nearest telephone. See the front of any telephone book for the FBI's number.

2. Don't worry if the information seems incomplete or trivial. Many times a small bit of information might furnish the data we are seeking.

3. Stick to the facts. The FBI is not interested in rumor or idle gossip. Talebearing should always be avoided. The FBI is not interested in what a person thinks but what he does to undermine our national security.

4. Don't try to do any investigating yourself. Security investigations require great care and effort. The innocent must be protected as well as the guilty identified. That is the job for the professional investigator. Hysteria, witch hunts, and vigilantes weaken our internal security.

5. Be alert. America's best defense lies in the alertness of its patriotic citizens.

As we have seen, identifying communists is not easy. They are trained in deceit and trickery and use every form of camouflage and dishonesty to advance their cause.

For this reason we must be absolutely certain that our fight is waged with full regard for the historic liberties of this great nation. *This is the fundamental premise of any attack against communism.*

Too often I have seen cases where loyal and patriotic but misguided Americans have thought they were "fighting communism" by slapping the label of "Red" or "communist" on anybody who happened to be different from them or to have ideas with which they did not agree.

Smears, character assassination, and the scattering of irresponsible charges have no place in this nation. They create division, suspicion, and distrust among loyal Americans—just what the communists want—and hinder rather than aid the fight against communism.

Another thing. Time after time in this book I have mentioned that honest dissent should not be confused with disloyalty. A man has a right to think as he wishes: that's the strength of our form of government. Without free thought our society would decay. Just because a man's opinion is unpopular and represents a minority viewpoint or is different he is not necessarily disloyal. Hence, one should have the facts before accusing anyone of propagating the Party line.

One of the chief jobs of the FBI, fully as important as tracking down spies, is to protect the civil rights of individuals.

In the FBI our objective in any investigation is to secure the facts which will establish the truth or falsity of a complaint or allegation. We do not evaluate nor do we make recommendations for a course of action as to whether a man should be prosecuted, hired, or removed from a job. The FBI is strictly a fact-gathering agency, responsible, in turn, to the Attorney General, the President, the Congress, and, in the last analysis, to the American people. The investigative and adjudicatory processes simply do not belong in the same organization.

When the clouds of World War-II began to lower, large segments of our people became conscious for the first time that America was confronted with an enemy from within. One of the disgraces of our era is that it was ever necessary to question the loyalty of Americans. The record, however, is clear: There were some who, using the protective cloak of the rights of all Americans as a cover, sought to conceal traitorous and subversive activities.

In carrying out our responsibilities we soon became very conscious of the fact that each allegation and complaint had to be carefully checked. There are literally thousands of people in this country who have been the target of accusation and thousands whose loyalty could be established only by investigation. Most have been grateful. Some have been resentful that they were investigated at all; but we had a job to do, and it was done with impartiality and a zealous regard for the rights and reputation of the individuals involved. One of the happiest moments in our day-to-day activities is when we can establish the innocence of a man wrongfully accused.

Here are a few illustrations of the outcome of investigations which have given us a feeling of satisfaction:

A New York man changed his name to one that was more pronounceable. He was with the Merchant Marine and the accusation was made that he was a member of the Communist

Party; that he had been educational director of a Party section and had signed a Communist Party petition. We investigated. We found that the man in changing his name had taken the name of a Communist Party member who was an educational director of a section of the Party in New York. Beyond that, we secured handwriting specimens of the man with the changed name, and our laboratory technicians established that he had not signed the Party petition.

A scientist was seeking a job with the army. The accusation arose that he had signed a communist petition. We investigated and found that a man with the same name and initial had signed such a petition but he was not the scientist.

A government agency received a letter bearing a fictitious signature stating that a government employee was working with the Communist Party. We investigated. Our inquiry revealed that all comment concerning the employee was highly favorable, except for the statement of a seventy-two-year-old woman residing in Philadelphia who was a neighbor of the government worker. This woman advised she had overheard the employee say, "I'm working for the Communist Party" but admitted the employee said she had made the statement in jest. The neighbor said she had never written any agency of the government concerning the employee. During the investigation we secured specimens of the elderly neighbor's handwriting and determined she had written the defamatory letter out of spite.

An allegation was made that a former army officer was the nephew of a French communist leader and maintained a close relationship with him. Our investigation disclosed that the two men had the same name, but were not related. The only contact the army officer ever had with the French communist leader was when he met the Frenchman on one occasion and inquired as to his ancestry.

When a citizen thinks he has been wrongfully accused of communist activity, we, as a matter of long-standing policy, are more than happy to receive any statement he might care to make. Then, if we receive a future allegation, his statement will be on file and can be considered in connection with any investigation we are called on to make.

As I have stated, time after time FBI investigations exonerate the innocent. The latest scientific knowledge, fingerprints, new investigative techniques, careful training of our special agents in the mechanics and ethics of conducting good investigations—all these represent the assurance that the FBI is zealously protecting not only the internal security of the nation but also the rights, life, and property of the individual.

There are some who feel that a national police agency should be established to meet and handle all phases of the communist menace, since under the present structure of government many agencies have a responsibility for internal security. This, they say, would cut through the "red tape," centralize all investigations and determinations, and make for more "efficiency." I disagree. This nation has no need for a national police. Such an agency would be contrary to American tradition. The present system of cooperation among the nation's law-enforcement agencies is completely adequate to meet the needs. Weaknesses do exist. They lie not in the system itself but in its implementation. These weaknesses can be and are being overcome.

What can one do in the fight against communism?

I repeat: a lot. Always remember that this fight is something which must be carried on soberly, seriously, and, above all, *responsibly*. Our best weapons are facts and the truth. "And ye shall know the truth, and the truth shall make you free." Don Whitehead in his book, *The FBI Story*, in concluding his study of the FBI and its problems stated the case most accurately when he said:

> The top command of the FBI have no illusions that communism can be destroyed in the United States by the investigation, prosecution and conviction of Communist Party leaders who conspire to overthrow the government by force and

violence. That is merely one phase of the job to be done in a world-wide struggle.

The FBI knows that the bigger job lies with the free world's intellectuals—the philosophers, the thinkers wherever they may be, the professors and scientists and scholars and students. These people who think, the intellectuals if you please, are the ones who can and must convince men that communism is evil. The world's intellectuals themselves must see that communism is the deadliest enemy that intellectualism and liberalism ever had. They must be as willing to dedicate themselves to this cause as the Communists have been to dedicate themselves to their cause.

Part VII

CONCLUSION

23.

Communism: A False Religion

SOMETHING UTTERLY NEW has taken root in America during
the past generation, a communist mentality representing a
systematic, purposive, and conscious attempt to destroy
Western civilization and roll history back to the age of bar-
baric cruelty and despotism, all in the name of "progress."
Evil is depicted as good, terror as justice, hate as love, and
obedience to a foreign master as patriotism.

Numerically speaking, this mentality is limited to a few
men and women, the disciplined corps of the Communist
Party, USA. However, communist thought control, in all its
various capacities, has spread the infection, in varying degrees, to most phases of American life.

This mentality, imported to our land for the purpose of
eventually leading to a destruction of the American way of
life, poses a crucial problem for every one of us. It can destroy
our constitutional republic if it is permitted to corrupt our
minds and control our acts.

I have tried to make the tactics of the Communist Party
as clear as possible in this book. These tactics are part of
world-wide communism and are offered as bait to divert and
capture our minds.

In our tolerance for religious freedom, for separation of
church and state, we sometimes lose sight of the historical
fact: Western civilization has deep religious roots. Our
schools, courts, legislative bodies, social agencies, philan-
thropic organizations as well as our churches are witnesses

to the fundamental fact that life has a significance that we ourselves do not create.

It is part of our tradition and belief that each of us is obligated to give, when reality requires it, a reason for the faith that is in him. The presence of communism in the world and in our own country is a kind of stern reality which should make each of us explore our own faith as deeply as we can and then speak up for its relationship to our "American way."

The very essence of our faith in democracy and our fellow man is rooted in a belief in a Supreme Being. To my mind there are six aspects to our democratic faith:

1. A belief in the dignity and worth of the individual, a belief which today is under assault by the communist practice which regards the individual as a part of the "class," the "mass," and a pawn of the state;

2. A belief in mutual responsibility, of our obligation to "feed the hungry, clothe the naked, and care for the less fortunate," which is affronted by communist policies of calculated ruthlessness;

3. A belief that life has a meaning which transcends any manmade system, that is independent of any such system, and that outlasts any such system, a belief diametrically opposed by the materialistic dogma of communism;

4. A belief in stewardship, a feeling that a great heritage is our sacred trust for the generations yet to come, a belief that stands today as the competitor to communist loyalty to Marxism-Leninism;

5. A belief that the moral values we adhere to, support, and strive toward are grounded on a reality more enduring and satisfying than any manmade system, which is opposed by the communist claim that all morality is "class morality";

6. A belief, which has matured to a firm conviction, that in the final analysis love is the greatest force on earth and is far more enduring than hatred; this forbids our accepting the communist division of mankind that by arbitrary standards singles out those fit only for liquidation.

3/18

It is only as we thus take stock of what we mean by saying that our culture has religious roots that we become ready to make an accurate appraisal of communist ideology and tactics.

The most basic of all communist comments about religion is the statement of Karl Marx that religion is "the opium of the people." This Marxian doctrine has been restated by William Z. Foster and applied to communist action in these words, ". . . God will be banished from the laboratories as well as from the schools."

Inherited from fanatic minds abroad, this mentality poses today a crucial problem for every patriotic man and woman in America. If allowed to develop, it will destroy our way of life.

Communists have always made it clear that communism is the mortal enemy of Christianity, Judaism, Mohammedanism, and any other religion that believes in a Supreme Being.

Don't think that "the communists have changed their minds about religion," said Nikita Khrushchev. "We remain the Atheists that we have always been; we are doing as much as we can to liberate those people who are still under the spell of this religious opiate." As long as communism remains, the assault will continue.

To the communists Marxism-Leninism is the "perfect science." It accounts for everything; it has a plan for everything: it can be the source of everything man needs. Therefore, said Lenin, "We shall always preach a scientific philosophy; we must fight against the inconsistencies of the 'Christians'. . . ."

In making Marxism-Leninism the "perfect science," the communists characterize religion as a superstitious relic. "Religion, in its thousands of varieties," said William Z. Foster, "was first evolved by primitive man everywhere as the most logical explanation he could devise of the complex, mysterious and often terrifying natural phenomena with which he was surrounded, as well as to work out a plausible conception of his own and the world's existence."

Though "historically inevitable" for primitive man, Foster goes on to say, religion has now been made obsolete by science. Science, as it advanced, gave "irrefutable materialist explanations" of the phenomena which puzzled primitive man. Hence, "in the modern world . . . there is therefore no longer . . . even the possibility, of a religious interpretation of man and the world." "It has now become virtually impossible for a thoroughly modern person, even if he wants to do so, actually to believe the old legends, primitive philosophies, and imaginary history upon which all religions are founded."

This communist teaching glosses over the fact that science never has given an "irrefutable" explanation of ultimate reality, neither materialistic nor any other kind. The communists ignore the further fact that the faith of religious people is a moral necessity and a sense of personal relationship, not a completion of laboratory science.

In addition to dismissing religion as primitive, the communists claim that it is a mere instrument of exploitation: another weapon in the hands of the capitalists. As Lenin said: "Religion is a kind of spiritual intoxicant, in which the slaves of capital drown their humanity, and blunt their desire for a decent human existence."

Again: ". . . it is quite natural for the exploiters to sympathize with a religion that teaches us to bear 'uncomplainingly' the woes of hell on earth, in the hope of an alleged paradise in the skies."

William Z. Foster, who in our country emphasizes the same theme, and who has always emphasized the correct Party line, declared, ". . . the Church . . . has identified itself with political reaction." And again, ". . . the Church is one of the basic forces now fighting to preserve obsolete capitalism and its reactionary ruling classes, in the face of advancing democracy and socialism."

The followers of Marx have a way of calling *scientific* any dogma to which they intend to cling, regardless of whether it can be supported by conclusive evidence. And communism has to cling to its antireligious dogma, not for scientific reasons, but for reasons of ideology and strategy. It cannot permit man to give his allegiance to a Supreme Authority higher than Party authority, for such allegiance to a higher authority carries with it a sense of freedom, of immunity to Party edict and discipline. Neither can it afford to have its members made hesitant in acts of cruelty and deception, which are ordained parts of its revolutionary program. No communist can be permitted to set an abstract truth above an expedient lie, or to extend compassion to an enemy whom the Party intends to smear or liquidate. The communists dismiss our sentiments motivated by spiritual force as silly prattlings that reflect "bourgeois weaknesses." Therefore, they have their own morality, communist morality, as stated by Lenin:

> We repudiate all morality that is taken outside of human, class concepts. . . . We say that our morality is entirely subordinated to the interests of the class struggle. . . .

Lenin made clear the function of communist morality: "At the root of Communist morality, there lies the continuation and completion of Communism." In practice this has simply meant that the end justifies the means. That is why a communist can commit murder, pillage, destruction, and terror, and feel proud; lie and feel no compunction; seek to destroy the American form of government and feel justified. Communism has turned the values of Western civilization upside down.

Hatred of all gods was Karl Marx's credo. Yet communism is, in effect, a secular religion with its own roster of gods, its own Messianic zeal, and its own fanatical devotees who are willing to accept any personal sacrifice that furthers the cause.

It would seem that communists, in view of the above, would make clear, always and at every point, their opposition to religion. Often, however, tactics have made it necessary to play down or to conceal entirely the Party's intentions in line with Lenin's advice: ". . . but this does not mean that the religious question must be pushed into the foreground where it does not belong." The communists realize that the vast majority of noncommunists believe in God. Too bold an approach might antagonize them, doing the Party more harm than good.

In the early days, before Party discipline was established, Lenin counseled: "The Anarchist, who preaches war against God at all costs, actually helps the . . . bourgeoisie. . . ." William Z. Foster, rebuking the extreme left, said that some of their efforts at "God killing" served only for ". . . overstress and distortion of the religious question."

By 1937 such tactical caution was beginning to be replaced by a calculated program to exploit religion. Foster called this the ". . . more recent practical approach to the religious question, on the basis long ago laid by Lenin."

This "practical approach" means attempting, through deceptive tactics, to capture support from American religious groups for an atheistic Communist Party. As Foster put it in 1937:

> In consequence, the anti-religious Communist Party is now to be found in close united front cooperation with dozens of churches and other religious organizations on questions of immediate economic and political interest to the toiling masses.

In line with these tactics, the Party is today engaged in a systematic program to infiltrate American religious groups. "The Communist Party," said the National Committee in 1954, "declares that it seeks no conflict with any church or any American's religious belief. On the contrary, we stretch out our hand in the fellowship of common struggle for our mutual goal of peace, democracy and security to all regardless of religious belief." Members are being told: "Join churches and become involved in church work."

The Party's objectives inside religious groups are several:

1. *To gain "respectability"*: ". . . a church is the best front

we can have." Comrades, by associating in church circles, secure an "acceptable" status in the community, greater credence for their opinions, and the lulling of noncommunist suspicions.

2. *To provide an opportunity for the subtle dissemination of communist propaganda.* Churches are convincing places in which to identify communist programs with such genuine religious values as "peace," "brotherhood," "justice." One member bragged how in a church talk he had "plugged" for Marx. The communists are careful, however, not to overdo it. One fellow was too ambitious. He was challenged by alert church members and relieved of his leadership duties.

3. *To make contact with youth:* through class discussions, recreational affairs, etc. The object is not necessarily to recruit (although in one church several young people did join) but to plant a seed of Marxist-Leninist thought.

4. *To exploit the church in the Party's day-to-day agitational program.* In the 1930's and 1940's the approach was chiefly through "immediate economic and political" problems, with the Party attempting to exploit the church's legitimate interest in better housing and the elimination of social injustices.

Today this tactic is overshadowed by the "peace" issue. Every possible deceptive device is being used to link the Party's "peace" program with the church. One Communist Party section issued instructions that every clergyman in the community be contacted to give a sermon on "peace." Encourage "Party church members" to organize discussion groups, perhaps showing a "peace" film. If possible, circulate "peace" literature. If you can't get inside, stand outside. One organizer said: "We are to dress up like other people and stand outside churches in our neighborhoods and use the slogan, 'Peace on earth, good will toward men.'"

5. *To enlarge the area of Party contacts.* One Party section

advocated: Join small churches (100 to 500 membership), so that one can more easily work himself into a position of leadership. Make as many personal contacts as possible. Learn where the church member works, what his hobbies are, etc. Someday he might be used. One Party member, active in youth work, learned that the parents of several young people were working in an industrial plant. Securing this information was most important, he said.

6. *To influence clergymen.* A dedicated clergyman, being a man of God, is a mortal enemy of communism. But if he can, by conversion, influence, or trickery, be made to support the communist program once or a few times or many times, the Party gains. If, for example, a clergyman can be persuaded to serve as sponsor or officer of a communist front, to issue a testimonial or to sign a clemency petition for a communist "victim of persecution," his personal prestige lends weight to the cause.

The church, in communist eyes, is an "enemy" institution to be infiltrated, subverted, and bent to serve Party aims. Any successes make the comrades diabolically happy. One member, talking to her communist friends, laughed about prayers in church. "Who wants to hear such stuff, but what can I do? That's the only way I can get in there."

We might expect, considering the importance of materialism in communist theory, that the Party's constitution would set forth atheism as a basic principle of communism. But ". . . we do not declare," said Lenin, "and must not declare in our programme that we are 'Atheists'. . . ."

The Party's aim, in addition to that of exploiting the church, is to neutralize religion as an effective counterweapon. At present virtually nothing is being said in open Party propaganda that is antireligious. Pamphlet after pamphlet is issued on civil rights, "peace," "democracy"; very few on religion. Communists in the United States, however, are on record in regard to their views on religion: for example, Earl Browder, *Communism in the United States* (1935), pages 334-49; William Z. Foster, *The Twilight of World Capitalism* (1949), pages 87-99 and "Reply to a Priest's Letter," *Political Affairs* (October, 1954). Also, a pamphlet, *Science and Religion*, by Marcel Cachin (1946), editor of *L'Humanité*, French communist newspaper, has been circulated.

If members are forced to present the Party's views, they are instructed to stress, as Lenin did, that religion is a "private matter" for the individual, and to pose as "tolerant." Doesn't the Party's constitution say that a person is eligible for membership "regardless of . . . religious belief"? The object here is to dull the vigilance of the noncommunist mind and to make religious belief appear as something minor, secondary, and inconsequential.

When tactically expedient, the communists even liken themselves to the early Christian martyrs suffering persecution for attempting to aid mankind.

One cartoon published in *The Worker* shows a sketch of Christ in the form of a wanted criminal. The caption reads: REWARD *for Information Leading to the Apprehension of—*

JESUS CHRIST

WANTED—for Sedition, Criminal
Anarchy, Vagrancy, and Conspiring
to Overthrow the Established Government

Dresses poorly. *Said* to be a carpenter by trade, ill nourished, has visionary ideas, associates with common working people, the unemployed and bums . . . Alias: "Prince of Peace. Son of Man" . . . *Professional agitator.*
Red beard, marks on hands and feet the result of injuries inflicted by an angry mob led by respectable citizens and legal authorities.

A *Daily Worker* writer, reviewing a movie in which the background was laid in the early Christian era, says: "Some interesting parallels can be found between the persecution of the Christians shown in the film and the political jailings in the United States today."

Behind these deceptive tactics, however, can be seen the

real nature of communism. For the member, religion is *not* a
private affair. No tolerance is allowed. He cannot be a Marxist
and adhere to a religion. The Party is today desperately working to mold atheistic materialism as a weapon of revolution, a
revolution which, if it is to succeed, must first sap religion's
spiritual strength and then destroy it.

The Party's attack can be traced through four stages:

1. *Recruitment:* keyed to the Party's general approach toward noncommunists, the issue of religion is minimized. "Try
to win recruits on the basis of wages and the class struggle
rather than religion," and, "Go ahead and tell a fellow you believe in God to keep from getting into an argument." Likewise
it is urged, "If we approach a church-goer we do not hit him
over the head and tell him his idea is crazy. We take a tactical
approach. . . ."

Lenin's advice still holds: "We must not only admit . . . all
those workers who still retain faith in God, we must redouble
our efforts to recruit them. We are absolutely opposed to the
slightest affront to these workers' religious convictions. We
recruit them in order to educate them in the spirit of our programme. . . ."

2. *Early indoctrination:* keyed to patience if recruits continue to attend church after joining the Party. They must be
gradually "educated." If new members begin to ask questions,
they are to be made to feel, not that their fellow communists
are trying to take away their belief, but that these communists
are "advanced thinkers," that they hold a "scientific" concept
of the universe, and that religion is to them simply "old-
fashioned." Typical of what members are told are these comments made by communist leaders:

—"How silly to think there is a God."
—"Religion comes from primitive man's worship of such things
   as thunder, lightning and the sun."
—"Religion was used as an explanation of unanswerable questions, such as 'Why does it rain?' Answer: 'God willed it.'"

3. *Special indoctrination:* keyed to the real job of teaching Marxist materialism are special indoctrination classes. "Our programme thus necessarily includes the propaganda of atheism," said Lenin, directing his words, of course, to Party members.

A few statements from Party members reveal how persistent is the communist fight against God:

—"The concept of God is manmade and is based on ignorance."
—"Marxism-Leninism is a science and has solved the mysteries of religion."
—"To be a true communist you have to be an atheist."
—"Communism will supplant religion and will keep you warm and give you all the comforts of healthful living."
—"Religious people fear facts and resort to such things as prayer to end war, but prayers are actually futile and leave war to the capitalists while people sit around praying."

4. *Final goal:* the utter elimination of all religion (called "bourgeois remnants") from the heart, mind, and soul of man, and the total victory of atheistic communism. Religious attitudes keep cropping up, however, even in the trained member. One individual admitted that it had taken him a long time to give up his religion. "It was one of the hardest parts of my Party development."

Even in Soviet Russia, after a generation of the most bitter propaganda, religion is far from exterminated. "One of the most widespread traces of the past in the minds of the people," said one Soviet writer, "is religious superstition and darkness, survivals of the old, antiscientific conceptions of nature, society and of man himself." He adds, "The historic victories of atheism in our country do not mean, however, that religion is over and done with. There are still among us no few believers, i.e., people who continue to remain in the fetters of religion."

To combat these religious "remnants," says this Soviet writer, more antireligious propaganda is needed. ". . . forming an advanced, materialist outlook in the rising generation and combating every type of superstition and religious belief make up a most important sector in the fight for the communist education of youth." Another Soviet writer states, "Convincing, profoundly reasoned propaganda of atheism which does not offend the feelings of believers is the main characteristic of all antireligious work at the present moment."

Here, then, is the fight the communist leaders wage. We do not believe they can ever win it. These so-called "religious survivals" represent something far deeper in man than the communists can grant: some eternal reaching toward a creative source. But if the Party does not realize the true nature and strength of these "survivals," it does realize that religion is its most potent foe. To meet this challenge no hesitant, indifferent, half-apologetic acts on our own part can suffice. Out of the deep roots of religion flows something warm and good, the affirmation of love and justice; here is the source of strength for our land if we are to remain free. It is ours to defend and to nourish.

24.

How to Stay Free

THE COMMUNIST REVOLUTION in Russia is forty years behind us. In these four decades communism has had a chance to show what it does with power in its hands; how it treats the people who live under it; what its attitudes are toward law, education, science, and religion; how it handles its relations with the noncommunist world. It stands condemned on its own record. It has revealed basic errors in theory and practice which will eventually bring about its downfall. To turn around Karl Marx's famous comment on capitalism, communism is digging its own grave. It cannot survive because it is anti-God and anti-man.

For all too long, communism's true character has been concealed by its own propaganda, abetted by public ignorance and apathy. Soviet Russia was hailed as an "advanced democracy" and communism as "twentieth-century Americanism." Such phrases deceived free people and gave the Party a protective cloak.

Marxism-Leninism stands revealed not as a "new world" of hope and justice but as an evil conspiracy in pursuit of power. Its cost in human misery and waste of human life is almost beyond description. Every home in America today is deprived of an even higher standard of living as a result of the tax burden brought on by the utter necessity of keeping our defenses strong against the world-wide advance of communism.

Time has also erased the label of "scientific" from Marxist-Leninist ideology. The communist claim of "infallible" has proved to be all too fallible time and again. The revolution began not in a highly industrialized state but in a backward, tyranny-ridden land where communism meant the substitution of an even more vicious brand of tyranny. It was conducted not as a "dictatorship of the proletariat" but as a dictatorship by dictators who rode roughshod over the workingman. Stalin, in the middle 1930's, contended that socialism was at last fully established in Russia and that the movement from then on would be toward the second stage which Marx had foretold: true communism and the withering away of the state. Even as Stalin spoke, in terms designed to attract idealists, he was making the state ever more powerful. After his death, with the "New Look" and the Khrushchev "thaw," the trend has not been reversed.

Khrushchev gives the answer to those who still repeat the shabby, deceitful phrases of communist dogma, when he desanctifies Stalin one day and on the next day rehabilitates him as a good communist. After all, Stalin during his life was the Chief Executioner, and Khrushchev did his bidding, along with many of his associates who rule Russia today. Khrushchev's answer should never be forgotten, because by his own words the alleged "paradise of human joy" was, in fact, a world of slave labor camps, betrayed human rights, and calculated fear.

The answer also comes from Mao Tse-tung, the Chinese communist dictator who, without apparent shame, admitted that 800,000 of his fellow countrymen had been liquidated between 1949 and the beginning of 1954. The answer further comes from the Hungarian Freedom Fighters of 1956, who with bare hands attacked the steel of Soviet tanks.

The answer finally comes from those Americans who were victimized by the communist deception of claiming credit for reforms and advances which the Party did not deserve. Most informed Americans now know that the communists adopt a cause only to exploit it for their own ends. Communism does not mean better housing, improved social conditions, or a more strict observance of civil rights. The vast majority of Negro leaders have rebuffed the communists' attempts to exploit them. By forcing Party members out of positions of authority and even from union membership, true trade unionists have shown their awareness that communists seek to disrupt the legitimate mission of labor unions.

Communism, in brief, has bitterly indicted communism; communist practice has indicted communist theory; communist actions have indicated the perverted use of such lofty words as "peace," "justice," and "liberty."

But we cannot afford the luxury of waiting for communism to run its course like other oppressive dictatorships. The weapons of communism are still formidable. They become even more effective when we lower our guard and when we become lax in strengthening our democratic institutions in perfecting the American dream.

The call of the future must be a rekindled American faith, based on our priceless heritage of freedom, justice, and the religious spirit.

In our reawakening, we Americans can learn a great deal from the fight against communism. Here are five special areas:

1. The communists emphasize *ideological study*, meaning, of course, Marxism-Leninism. Such study has been the very foundation of their "monolithic unity": their power to keep people in line no matter how the "line" changes. Their study allows no deviation for free thought and independent action. Also, it provides them with a "common language" since all communists give the same meaning to words and acts. This emphasis upon study has been the means whereby they have captured the minds of some of our young people who read and think and who are lacking in proper companionship.

It is sad but true that many young people have been drawn into communist clubs or study groups. Often they are highly intellectual but lonely students and fall under a sinister influence. We know this from the experiences of hundreds of former communists and from acts of near-treason we have been called upon to investigate.

American education, of course, does not make communists; communist education does. Communism, to survive, must depend upon a constant program of education, because communism needs educated people, even though it distorts the use to which their education is put. Thus, we need to show our young people, particularly those endowed with high intellects, that we in our democracy need what they have to offer.

We, as a people, have not been sufficiently articulate and forceful in expressing pride in our traditions and ideals. In our homes and schools we need to learn how to "let freedom ring." In all the civilized world there is no story which compares with America's effort to become free and to incorporate freedom in our institutions. This story, told factually and dramatically, needs to become the basis for our American unity and for our unity with all free peoples. I am sure most Americans believe that our light of freedom is a shining light. As Americans we should stand up, speak of it, and let the world see this light, rather than conceal it. For too long we have had a tendency to keep silent while the communists, their sympathizers, and their fellow travelers have been telling the world what is wrong with democracy. Suppose every American spent a little time each day, less than the time demanded by the communists, in studying the Bible and the basic documents of American history, government, and culture? The result would be a new America, vigilant, strong, but ever humble in the service of God.

2. Then there is the training of *youth*, on whom the communists place so much emphasis. To the Party, youth is not something auxiliary but an important training ground. We must meet this challenge. America must devote the best of her efforts to make youth responsible, conscious of its obligations, and eager to be good citizens. Experience and observation point to certain facts which we need to consider in providing for youth.

First, youth gravitates toward youth. The young person who feels left out may remain a "solitary." Or he may, according to his background and make-up, join a delinquent gang. He may join a Party front or club. Or he may find some other short cut to a sense of belonging. But every American youth has a right to find some place within a group that expresses rather than contradicts the real values of society.

Second, given half a chance, youth gravitates toward companionship with competent, generous, and experienced adults. Practically all my life I have been face to face with young people becoming involved in difficulties or coming under the communist spell. Invariably I have discovered that they all had one thing in common. In their early years and in the periods of their lives when their transgressions began to take form, they could not talk things over with their parents. Their parents were either too busy, or not interested, or resented any difference of opinion. Or parents simply doled out "final" answers when the young people wanted to try to think things through.

Our youth want not only to talk to adults, they want to work with adults. It is a fine thing for them to have their own groups, but it is better if, in addition, they can participate in shared projects with adults. If the adults can show, in action, that it is possible to combine high idealism with solid practicality and patience, the results will enhance character and citizenship development manyfold.

3. The communists stress *action*. This means carrying out our responsibilities now—not tomorrow, the next day, or never. To communists the Party means continual action, not just talk, waiting for annual elections, meetings, or affairs. With us action must supplement good intentions in building the America of the future. We need to provide our youth with activity groups. To give them only a high standard of material advantages or a constant diet of recreation is not enough. Recreation must be made part of a life of responsibility, otherwise it becomes merely a preface to boredom. Our young people, as well as adults, need to be working members of our republic and citizens on duty at all times.

4. Communists accent the *positive*. In their deceptive and perverted way they are always purporting to stand for something positive. "Better," "higher," etc., are trade-marks in their language. We, too, in the true sense of the word, should strive for goals that are genuinely better, higher, and more noble, trying to improve self, community, and nation. A strictly negative attitude or the philosophy of just staying afloat—all too common today—will never meet the impact of the communist challenge.

5. Most important of all is *faith*. Let us not blind ourselves to the fact that communists do have a "faith." True, it is falsely placed, but still it inspires them to sacrifice, devotion, and a perverted idealism.

The late Mother Bloor, the Party's woman "hero," often praised Walt Whitman's "The Mystic Trumpeter" as the poem she loved best. It seemed, she said, to prophesy the coming of a "new world":

> War, sorrow, suffering gone—the rank
> earth purged—nothing but joy left!

> The ocean fill'd with joy—the atmosphere
>   all joy!
> Joy! joy! in freedom, worship, love! joy in
>   the ecstasy of life!
> Enough to merely be! enough to breathe!
>   Joy! joy! all over joy!

She is trying to identify communism with the dream of a world of joy. She is exploiting Walt Whitman. Yet her feeling shows the lure of communist "faith." If communists can be so inspired from error, falsehood, and hate, just think what we could do with truth, justice, and love! I thrill to think of the even greater wonders America could fashion from its rich, glorious, and deep tradition. All we need is faith, *real faith*.

The communist prides himself on being a revolutionary—and revolutionary he is in the sense of destruction, terror, and violence. Free man can learn here too: the truly revolutionary force of history is not material power but the spirit of religion. The world today needs a true revolution of the fruitful spirit, not the futile sword. Hypocrisy, dishonesty, hatred, all these must be destroyed and man must rule by love, charity, and mercy.

The Party's effort to create "communist man," to mold a revolutionary fighter completely subservient to the Party's desires, is destined to fail. The power of bullets, tanks, and repression will bulwark tyranny just so long. Then, as the Hungarian Freedom Fighters proved, man's innate desire for freedom will flare up stronger than ever. In communism we see what happens when freedom is extinguished. This must give us renewed zeal to work untiringly to uphold the ideals of justice and liberty which have made this nation great.

With God's help, America will remain a land where people still know how to be free and brave.

GLOSSARY

and

BIBLIOGRAPHY

Glossary

This GLOSSARY contains terms frequently used by communists. Their meanings are derived largely from communist "classics," or books written by Marx, Engels, Lenin, and Stalin. (For a more complete definition of communist "classics," see Bibliography, page 328.)

BOLSHEVIK:

1. Refers to a type of communist organization, namely, Lenin's Party, of a small, selective membership, comprised of highly trained professional revolutionaries insolubly linked to each other by the deepest revolutionary convictions and discipline. The term "bolshevik" stems from the Russian word *bolshinstvo*, meaning majority. In the 1903 Congress of the Russian Social Democratic Labor Party, a dispute occurred over whether membership should be tightly controlled (Lenin's idea) or be open to sympathizers also. Lenin's opinion was accepted. Hence, his supporters became known as Bolsheviks (majority); his opponents as Mensheviks (minority).

2. Refers to a certain type of Party member, namely, the model, heroic, ideal type of communist. It is a term of high praise and distinction for communists, signifying superiority and mastery of the qualities of revolutionary leadership, efficiency, courage. Hence the terms "bolshevik courage," "bolshevik culture," "bolshevik discipline." "Bolshevization of the Party" means to make the Party a model of communist perfection.

BOURGEOISIE:

Term applied to the "capitalist" class, which includes not only the wealthy but also middle-class people. Sometimes "petty bourgeoisie" is used to distinguish small businessmen, minor government officials, etc., from the more wealthy "capitalists" and high-ranking officials. To communists the bourgeoisie is a class enemy which must be destroyed. "Bourgeois" is the adjective form of bourgeoisie, hence, "bourgeois virtue." So used, the word describes anything or anybody whom communists would ridicule or hold in contempt. The term "bourgeois survivals," or "bourgeois remnants," refers to so-called "capitalist" (that is, noncommunist) attitudes and institutions not yet obliterated by communism.

CADRE:

The trusted inner circle of trained members and leaders on whom the Party can depend to carry out its policies and programs without any questions or objections. From cadres will emerge functionaries, officials, organizers. "The Party cadres constitute the commanding staff of the Party. . . ." (*Stalin*)

CAPITALISM:

To communists, capitalism is an economic system based on the private ownership of property, the private control of the means of production, and the private accumulation and use of profits. As such, communists consider capitalism to be a form of exploitation of man by man. To them, capitalism is the last economic system of exploitation in the social evolution of man. Born as the result of overthrowing feudalism, capitalism, in turn, from its own inner contradictions, will be succeeded by socialism as a transitory stage that will end in a world communist society.

CENTRISM:

A term of contempt to communists, signifying those who try to pursue a "middle-of-the-road" position, thereby denying full and undeviating obedience to the Party line. ". . . and finally, there are the 'Centrists,' those who wobble between the 'Lefts' and the Rights . . . Centrism is a political concept. Its ideology is one of adaptation, of subordination of the interests of the proletariat to the interests of the petty-bourgeoisie in the *same* party. This ideology is alien and contrary to Leninism." (*Stalin*)

CHAUVINISM:

A term of bad repute to communists signifying that one nation, race, group, or individual assumes an attitude of biased superiority. Within the Party structure chauvinism (which can occur in various forms) often results in disciplinary action and becomes a weapon whereby the ruling clique can bring charges against opponents for the purpose of weakening or destroying them.

CLASS:

By the word "class," communists mean a section of a given population that occupies a specific relation to the means of production. For example, the capitalists own land, mines, factories, and the like. The workers or laborers do not own such possessions but work on the land and in the mines and factories. Therefore, there are two main classes in society: (1) the capitalist or bourgeoisie, and (2) the wage-earners or working class or proletariat. The communists admit that in highly developed capitalist nations (as the United States) there is another group, the "middle class" or "petty bourgeoisie," composed of minor merchants, small farmers, professional people, small businessmen, etc. The communists believe the "middle class" can be influenced to support the proletariat.

CLASS STRUGGLE:

To the communists the two basic classes in capitalist society, the bourgeoisie and proletariat, are in constant and inevitable economic conflict. This struggle is a continuation of the age-old conflict, say the communists, between the exploiters and the exploited; the rulers and the ruled; those who own the means of production and the great masses of the people who possess nothing but their capacity for laboring. In the early days this class struggle was between the slave owner and the slave (slavery), later between the feudal lords and the serfs (feudalism). Eventually, the communists claim, the capitalists will be defeated through violent revolution; and by applying the dictatorship of the proletariat, communist society will be established. The communists are constantly encouraging class struggle, trying to increase social, economic, and political tensions. To them class struggle is an agency for promoting communism. "Can the capitalists be forced out and the roots of capitalism be annihilated without a bitter class struggle? No, it is impossible." (*Stalin*)

COMMUNISM (MARXIST SCIENTIFIC SOCIALISM):

A system of thought and action originated by Karl Marx and

Friedrich Engels, developed by V. I. Lenin, continued by Joseph Stalin and his successors. This system advocates, among other things: (1) a materialistic explanation of the origin of man and the universe; (2) a comprehensive economic interpretation of history centering about the class struggle; (3) abolition of the noncommunist state, which is conceived to be an instrument of exploitation; (4) a revolutionary theory, method, and a flexible course of action to overthrow the state and the capitalistic system; (5) a moral code based on utility; on nonsupernatural class concepts; (6) abolition of all religions; (7) a world-wide communist revolution; and (8) a world-wide communist society.

COMMUNISM (primitive):

A type of communal living reported to have existed in early stages of man's history. To Marxists there was no private ownership, hence, no class divisions, class exploitation, or state mechanism.

COMMUNISM (stages of development):

Marxism-Leninism says communism will develop through two basic stages: *First or lower stage* (called socialism), which is the type of society that will be formed immediately after the communist revolution. This is an "impure" communist society, freshly emerged from the violent conflict and bearing, in the words of Marx, ". . . in every respect, economic, moral and intellectual, the birthmarks of the old society from whose womb it is issuing." In this phase, organs of the state (such as police, army, etc.) are necessary and are exercised by the dictatorship of the proletariat, crushing the opposition of the bourgeoisie. During this transitory stage the main principle will be "from each according to his ability, to each according to his work." (This is the stage of the dictatorship of the proletariat, symbolized by the terrorism that now prevails in all communist countries.) However, after an unspecified period of time (just when, no communist can say), as people become indoctrinated to the principles of Marxism-Leninism, all the capitalistic characteristics will disappear and the state will slowly "wither away" as the threshold of the *higher or final stage* (communism) will be reached. This stage will be stateless, classless, godless, where all property will be held in common and human activities will conform to the principle "from each according to his abilities, to each according to his needs." The lower phase implies controlled, planned, and ordered work; the higher, free association and voluntary work. (This false appeal to a communist Utopia is one of the Party's most potent weapons for deception.)

COMPROMISE (MANEUVER, CONCESSIONS):

Tactics whereby, in order to promote the ultimate goal of communism, adjustments and temporary agreements can be made with the enemy, that is, the noncommunist world. "Concessions do not mean peace with capitalism, but war on a new plane." (*Lenin*)

DEMOCRACY:

In discussing the communist concept of democracy, distinction must be made between what the Party calls *bourgeois democracy* and *proletarian democracy*. The communists claim that "bourgeois" or "capitalist" democracy (as in the United States) is limited, repressive, and favors the minority; ". . . in capitalist society we have a democracy that is curtailed, wretched, false; a democracy only for the rich, for the minority." (*Lenin*) After seizure of power the communists then will inaugurate, they say, "proletarian" democracy (as in Hungary and Russia), which will be ". . . a million times more democratic than any bourgeois democracy." Here the dictatorship of the proletariat will be in power, utterly crushing any capitalist opposition. Eventually, however, this "proletarian" democracy will be supplanted by full communism, which, among other things, will be stateless. Basically the communists abhor democracy as practiced in the United States, believing, as they do, in dictatorship, force and violence, and the supreme authority of the Party. However, the Party seeks to utilize "capitalist" democracy and its rights (of which it falsely claims to be a protector) in order to promote its own cause.

DEMOCRATIC CENTRALISM:

The rigid principle that the decisions of the highest body in the Communist Party (even though it be dominated by one man) are binding upon all lower bodies or organizational units in the Party.

DEVIATION:

The departure from the policy and line established by the Party. It may either be to the left (known as left-wing sectarianism) or to the right (right-wing opportunism). Regardless, any deviation from a 100 per cent acceptance of the Party line is regarded as a serious situation and a matter for disciplinary action. Obviously, any original thinking or varied interpretations of Party policy are impossible.

DIALECTICAL MATERIALISM:

The philosophy and world outlook that undergirds communism. "Dialectical materialism is the world outlook of the Marxist-Leninist party. It is called dialectical materialism because its approach to the phenomena of nature, its methods of studying and apprehending them, is *dialectical*, while its interpretation of the phenomena of nature, its conception of these phenomena, its theory, is *materialistic*." *(Stalin)* See **DIALECTICS** and **MATERIALISM.**

DIALECTICS (DIALECTICAL):

One of the most frequently used terms in communist literature. The word is derived from the Greek, meaning the art of discourse, reasoning, and debate. To communists the stress in dialectics (the process of argument and counterargument to reach a higher meaning) is placed on change, the ceaseless ebb and flow of material elements. To them the world is constantly changing; nothing is eternal. All political and economic systems have within themselves the seeds of their own destruction, and as time passes they decay and give way to higher forms of existence in man's climb up the ladder of progress. This change, however, is not just for the sake of change alone, but follows a specific direction (such a type of change is called *revolutionary change*), from the lower to the higher, meaning a change from the lower stages of man's development, slavery, feudalism, and capitalism, to his highest —that is, world-wide communism. When this final stage is reached, say the communists, change will stop, since "full" communism conforms perfectly to the revolutionary nature of matter. Unlike other systems of life, communism claims not to contain within itself the seeds of destruction. It should be emphasized that even though noncommunist thinkers time after time have pointed out the inconsistencies, fallacies, and errors of this concept, communists cling to it with undying devotion.

DICTATORSHIP OF THE PROLETARIAT:

One of the most fundamental of communist concepts, meaning the forcible dictatorship of the Communist Party (conceived as the vanguard of the workers), whereby capitalist opposition is crushed after the seizure of power. It is also viewed as a transitional period between the revolution and the final goal—communism. The dictatorship of the proletariat is one of the most brutal of communist concepts, being based on naked force and violence, not law. "The revolutionary dictatorship of the proletariat is power won and maintained by the violence of the proletariat against the bourgeoisie, power that is unrestricted by any laws." (*Lenin*)

DISCIPLINE:

A cardinal feature in maintaining the monolithic unity of the Party. Discipline becomes a whip binding the membership under the authority of the Party, stifling free opinion and making for uniformity. A Communist Party without a ruthless discipline would be unthinkable.

FACTION (FACTIONALISM):

A grouping of members of the Communist Party around one or more ideas that are at variance with the Party line. Factionalism is the conflict caused by the presence of such factions. The monolithic structure and strong discipline of the Party usually result in the brutal crushing or expulsion of factions. In communist theory and practice there can be no freedom of dissent.

FORCE AND VIOLENCE:

The necessary means whereby, according to the communists, the existing or old society will be finally overthrown and the new or communist society established. "Force is the midwife of every old society pregnant with a new one." (*Marx*) "The replacement of the bourgeois by the proletarian state is impossible without a violent revolution." (*Lenin*)

HISTORIC MISSION:

To communists this means the seizure of power, the establishment of the dictatorship of the proletariat, the abolition of capitalism, and the formation of the new, communist, society. As the vanguard of the proletariat the Communist Party has as its "historic mission" the direction of the proletarian struggle toward a communist society.

IMPERIALISM:

The highest, the most developed, and last stage of a "moribund" and "decaying" capitalism. As worked out by Lenin, imperialism develops when capital and production (in a capitalist society) become concentrated in the hands of a relatively few individuals on high economic levels. This causes, according to Lenin, capitalist exploitation in colonial areas, as capital seeks an outlet for greater markets. This monopoly stage of capitalism "causes" imperialist wars, as rival capitalist systems struggle with each other (this was Lenin's diagnosis of World War I). To modern-day communists, the United States is now in this stage of imperialism.

INEVITABILITY:

To communists the final outcome of the struggle between communists and noncommunists has already been decided in favor of the communists, due to the very nature of the struggle. They consider the victory of communism to be inevitable because it is a "necessary product of historical development." They view progress to be from slavery to feudalism, to capitalism, to imperialism, to communism.

MARXISM-LENINISM: See COMMUNISM (MARXIST SCIENTIFIC SOCIALISM).

MASSES:

The ordinary people of a society who are not "educated" in the science of Marxism-Leninism and hence must be led by the proletariat and its vanguard, the Communist Party, toward the goal of a communist society. "Radicalizing the masses" signifies efforts by the Party, through agitation, to make the masses more sympathetic to communist aims.

MATERIALISM:

A view of reality which asserts that (1) matter is the basic reality and God does not exist; (2) the universe and all life on it can be explained in terms of motion and matter; (3) human values should center around material considerations, satisfactions and pleasures; and (4) the interpretation of human history must rest on material elements. Materialism is as old as man, but Marx claimed that his form of materialism (linked with dialectics) was the only complete and true form. The main premise of materialism is atheism, and hence the denial of God and all values which stem from religion. This fight against religion has been one of the Party's most basic principles. Under communism, ethics and morality become completely transformed, being based not on religion but on Party expediency. The results have been devastating —that millions of men and women have suffered and died in the name of a perverted "justice" and "goodness."

(Materialism as here defined should not be confused with the popular conception of the term denoting inordinate desire for material goods, thirst for power, undisciplined sensual appetites, or the hunger for the passing fame and glory of the world.)

OPPORTUNISM (RIGHT-WING):

Represents one type of deviation from the Party line, to the right, hence right-wing opportunism. This deviation is characterized as too much cooperation with capitalism, causing the Party to lose its identity as the "leader of the masses." This was the error of Browder.

PARTY:

Organizational concept evolved by Lenin of those trained in Marxism-Leninism who, regarding themselves as a "vanguard," are to lead the proletariat (and hence the masses) toward a communist world society. Under communism the Party becomes all-powerful, directing all phases of activity. Strict standards of membership are set, the most important being that members must be completely obedient to Party wishes.

PARTY LINE:

The sum total of the Party's decisions, aims, programs, and demands at any given time. Distinction must always be made between the "deceptive" Party line (that is, the programs designed for public consumption) and the "real" Party line (the true Party purpose designed to advance the interests of communism). The Party line often switches, sometimes very violently in various areas.

PHILISTINE:

Any person who believes in communism but is timid and shrinks from class struggle. He is a "fair-weather" soldier who supports communism when it is easy to do so but deserts when the going becomes rough. Philistinism is a term of abuse. "What is a philistine? A hollow gut, full of fear and hope, that God have mercy!" *(Lenin)* Communists would include some socialists, reformists, and liberals in this definition.

PROFESSIONAL REVOLUTIONARIES:

Those Party members, thoroughly educated in Marxism-Leninism, who dedicate their entire lives to the Party. This body (cadre) of members, in communist eyes, represents the shock troops of revolution. "Give us an organisation of revolutionaries, and we shall overturn the whole of Russia!" *(Lenin)*

PROLETARIAN INTERNATIONALISM:

The belief that communism is international in nature, that the proletariat of all nations, irrespective of race, nationality, creed, or color, constitutes a single class and must cooperate for the ultimate victory of communism. This gives a feeling of solidarity (communists always feel a part of a larger body, they don't stand alone); creates fanaticism (the feeling that as long as there are noncommunist nations, communism is in danger, hence they must be destroyed); promotes control of the international communist movement by Soviet Russia (as the big brother of all other Parties).

PROLETARIAT:

A key word in all communist literature, meaning workers

(working class) who sell their "labor" in exchange for wages. This "class" is extolled by the communists, and virtually everything done by the Party is done in the name of the "proletariat" (as "dictatorship of the proletariat").

PURGES:

A characteristic inherent in communism whereby undesirable members are expelled from the Party (or, when communism is in state power, exiled or executed). To communists, purging is a necessary technique to keep the Party "pure," thereby creating "better" members. "The Party becomes strong by purging itself of opportunist elements." (*Stalin*)

REFORMISM (REFORMS, REFORMISTS):

To communists, reforms in the social structure can have only minor and passing beneficial results. Further, they delay the revolution. Hence, "reformism" is a term of abuse, implying a "bourgeois" or non-Marxist approach. The communists, however, like to picture themselves as leaders of reform movements, not for the purpose of improving economic or social conditions in society but to exploit such movements to advance the cause of communism. To communists reforms can often be a means to an end.

REVOLUTION:

The seizure of the government, if necessary by force and violence, by the proletariat (working class) led by the Communist Party, leading to the establishment of a Soviet state; called *proletarian revolution.*

SELF-CRITICISM:

A communist technique ostensibly to detect and correct weaknesses in Party life; actually to enforce communist discipline. The Party member is encouraged to pursue a cold, relentless, realistic, and constant examination of shortcomings and failures, both in others and himself. Not to do so is regarded as "bourgeois" weakness or sentimentalism. Communists teach: "Self-criticism is the most important means for developing Communist consciousness and thereby strengthening discipline and democratic centralism."

SOCIALISM (MARXIST):

1. The so-called "scientific" variety of socialism; that is, Marxism-Leninism or Marxist scientific socialism. (See also COMMUNISM [MARXIST SCIENTIFIC SOCIALISM].)

2. In a limited meaning, "socialism" refers to the first or lower stage of communism, which is the transitory period between the seizure of power and the higher or final phase of communism. See COMMUNISM (stages of development) for further details.

SOCIALISM (NON-MARXIST):

The communists have nothing but contempt for any form of socialism except the Marxist-Leninist version. Non-Marxist socialists are regarded as "utopian," impractical, and allies of the bourgeoisie.

STATE:

Communists regard all states to be organs of force and suppression in the hands of the rulers. They bitterly denounce the noncommunist state as an instrument of suppression, and blithely assert that when full communism comes the state will "wither away." However, inside present communist states (where the dictatorship of the proletariat is in power) the state has not withered away but has become ever stronger, increasing communist power and terror.

TRANSMISSION BELTS:

Refers to disguised mass organizations, which are used by the Communist Party to spread or transmit communism to the masses of people. "It is impossible to effect the dictatorship without having a number of 'transmission belts' from the vanguard to the masses of the advanced class, and from the latter to the masses of the toilers." (*Lenin*)

UNITED FRONT:

A revolutionary tactic designed to secure the support of noncommunists for Party objectives. This generally involves Party manipulation of noncommunist groups, usually on some current issue such as "peace" or "civil rights," whereby the Party, while maintaining its independent role, cooperates with others to work for certain goals. To noncommunists the goal is advancement of the good of society; to communists, the revolution.

VANGUARD OF THE PROLETARIAT:

Term applied to the role of the Communist Party as the leader or teacher of the proletariat. Communists often talk of the Party as the "general staff" of the revolution.

WAR:

1. Communists talk much about peace but feverishly prepare for war. In Soviet Russia communist preparation takes the form of military strength—the army, navy, air force; in the United States, the organization of an active above-ground and underground apparatus designed to wage "war" against noncommunist society.

2. Communists believe that "war is a continuation of politics by other means." Marxism-Leninism divides wars into two major categories, unjust and just. "Unjust" wars, according to the communists, are wars started by the capitalists for purposes of exploitation ("reactionary wars of conquest"). These wars, they say, inevitably grow out of the "predatory" character of the capitalist system. "Just" wars, on the other hand, are wars of "national liberation"; that is, they promote the interests of the proletariat and hinder the capitalists. In other words, a war is just (moral) if the communists stand to gain; otherwise, it is unjust (immoral). The communists classify, for example, Russia's invasion of Finland (1939) and entering World War II after Germany's invasion of Russia as just wars; World War II before Russia's involvement and the United Nations' action in Korea (1950) as unjust.

3. In the final analysis, Marxism-Leninism teaches that war is absolutely necessary to bring about world-wide communism wherever the advances of communism are resisted. This makes Marxism-Leninism such a brutal concept. Lenin, in a letter to American workers, wrote: ". . . history demands that the greatest problems of humanity be solved by struggle and war."

Bibliography of Major Communist "Classics"

THE THEORY and practice of Marxism-Leninism have been developed by communist writers over a period of more than a century. The works of Marx, Engels, Lenin, and Stalin, in the Party's eyes, are regarded as communist "classics." "These books are Communist classics. They contain the fundamental principles and program of Communism. These are universal in their scope and they are accepted by all Communist Parties, including our own." (*William Z. Foster*)

These writings, it must be remembered, are propaganda for the communist movement. Written by highly partisan and prejudiced minds, they are not based on scientific truth and accurate historical research; nor are they attempts to determine truth as we in a free society understand truth. These writers are trying to hammer out the principles of violent revolution and, in the later writings of Lenin and those of Stalin, to justify communism in state power and to teach communists in other countries how to follow the Bolshevik example. These listed works, although not intended to be all-inclusive, are prime examples of how prejudice, thrown into the stream of world opinion, has warped the minds and personalities of so many millions of human beings.

KARL MARX:

Das Kapital (*Capital*) is undoubtedly Marx's best-known and most important writing. It forms, in a literal sense, the cornerstone of modern-day communism. The work is in three volumes: *Capitalist Production* (1867), *Capitalist Circulation* (1885), *Capitalist Production as a Whole* (1894). The final two volumes were completed by Engels after Marx's death. In this massive work Marx attempted, using many statistics compiled from nineteenth-century England, to prove that capitalism was doomed. To communists, *Das Kapital* is "scientific" proof of the inevitability of communist revolution. Time after time history has proved the errors, fallacious logic, and unscientific premises of the major thoughts contained in *Das Kapital;* yet to communists the book is an infallible guide to Party thought and action.

Another important work of Marx is *The Civil War in France.* This work (which actually consists of three statements drafted by Marx for the First International) was written in connection with the Paris Commune, a revolutionary government set up in Paris after the defeat of France by Prussia in 1870-71. Although lasting only a few weeks, the Commune is regarded by communists as the first working-class government in history. This "classic" sets forth Marx's view toward the existing state apparatus of a "bourgeois" state: that is, the working class cannot confine itself merely to taking over the state machinery; but the "bourgeois" state must be utterly destroyed and replaced by the dictatorship of the proletariat.

The Poverty of Philosophy (1847) represents one of Marx's earliest works on economics, while *The Eighteenth Brumaire of Louis Bonaparte* (1852) discusses, among other things, the character of the "bourgeois" revolution. The latter work was written concerning the activities of Louis Bonaparte, President of the Second French Republic, who was later to become Emperor of France. It must be noted that Marx (and also Engels and Lenin) were acute observers of contemporary political, social, and economic affairs; and their writings abound with references to current events and personalities. Other works of Marx include: *Critique of Political Economy* (1859), *Value, Price and Profit* (1865), and *Critique of the Gotha Programme* (1875). In the latter, Marx develops his idea of the dictatorship of the proletariat and the "withering away" of the state.

Marx was a prolific letter-writer, corresponding with many revolutionaries in England and abroad. The *Selected Correspondence of Karl Marx and Friedrich Engels (1846-1895)* shows how the intimate collaboration of these two perverted minds gave birth to the communist conspiracy.

FRIEDRICH ENGELS:

Engels, like Marx, was a voluminous writer. Some of his better-known works are *The Peasant War in Germany* (1850), *Germany: Revolution and Counter-Revolution* (1851-52), *The*

Housing Question (1872), and *Anti-Dühring* (1877-78). The latter work was written in reply to Eugen Dühring, a German professor who had published what, in Engels' opinion, were erroneous ideas concerning materialism and socialism. Engels not only attacks Dühring's views but goes on to sketch the communist world outlook, discussing dialectical and historical materialism, philosophy, and political economy.

In *The Origin of the Family, Private Property, and the State* (1884), Engels endeavors to show the relationship of the family, modes of production, and society. One of Engels' latest writings on materialism is *Ludwig Feuerbach and the Outcome of Classical German Philosophy* (1886). His *Dialectics of Nature*, published posthumously in 1927, is an attempt to discuss science from a Marxist viewpoint.

JOINT AUTHORSHIP OF MARX AND ENGELS:

As is well known, Marx and Engels often cooperated in writing, and sometimes it is difficult to determine exactly who wrote what. The best-known product of their collaboration, of course, is the *Communist Manifesto*. Engels, for example, wrote articles under Marx's name for the latter to send to the New York *Tribune*. On the other hand, Engels, speaking of *Anti-Dühring*, said he read the whole manuscript to Marx and that Marx himself contributed a chapter.

VLADIMIR I. LENIN:

From roughly 1900 to his death, Lenin poured out pamphlet after pamphlet justifying violent revolution and giving instructions to his followers.

In *What Is To Be Done?* (1902), Lenin outlines the principles which should determine the formation of a Leninist-type Party. This was during the period of debate among Russian communists on the type of Party organization, with Lenin favoring a restricted, disciplined membership. In 1904, in *One Step Forward, Two Steps Back*, Lenin continues his demand for a disciplined Party. In this pamphlet he attacks his opponents, the Mensheviks. This attack was continued in *Two Tactics of Social-Democracy in the Democratic Revolution* (1905). *Materialism and Empirio-Criticism*

(1909), a philosophical treatise, represents one of Lenin's major works.

In the years that followed, Lenin continued studying and writing. In 1917 *Imperialism: The Highest Stage of Capitalism* appeared, in which Lenin develops the thesis that imperialism is the final state of monopoly capitalism. He characterized World War I as imperialistic on both sides. This work was destined to leave a lasting imprint on communist thinking. The term "imperialistic" is today one of the communists' favorite terms of attack against the free world.

State and Revolution (1918), in which Lenin studies the relationship of revolutionary theory to the state, is probably his clearest blueprint for violent revolution. It has been extensively used by communists in the United States.

Another major work of Lenin, published in 1920 after the Bolshevik revolution, is *"Left-Wing" Communism, an Infantile Disorder*. Lenin here is writing from the viewpoint of communism in state power and giving advice to revolutionary movements outside Russia. He is telling other communists how "he did it in Russia," especially warning them to be careful about ineffective left-wing tendencies. This work did much to consolidate the world communist movement and the Third International.

Of special interest to the United States is Lenin's *A Letter to American Workers* (1918). In this letter Lenin reports to "the American worker" about the Russian revolution. Communists in this country have always considered this communication a symbol of the Russian dictator's interest in the American proletariat. In truth, the letter reveals how, in communist hands, America's history and struggle for freedom would be distorted by Marxist manipulation.

JOSEPH V. STALIN:

Stalin was not as prodigious a writer as Marx, Engels, and Lenin. Included in his outstanding works are *Foundations of Leninism* (1924) and *Marxism and the National Question* (1913), a study of communism in relation to nationality groups. In the former, Stalin attempted to show that Lenin did not merely rediscover and reapply Marxism to his day but also developed it further. Given as a series of lectures at Sverdlov University, Moscow, this work discusses basic communist concepts, such as the dictatorship of the proletariat, the peasant problem, strategy and tactics, and the Party.

In addition, Stalin has claimed to be the genius behind the *History of the Communist Party of the Soviet Union (Bolsheviks)* (1938). In *Joseph Stalin, A Political Biography* (issued by the Marx-Engels-Lenin Institute), it is stated that the *History* was written by Stalin and approved by a commission of the Central Committee of the Communist Party of the Soviet Union. This book was a "short-course" history of the Bolshevik movement in which the various phases of Party development were stressed. It was widely distributed in Russia and also used by the Communist Party, USA.

Very interestingly, Nikita Khrushchev made mention of this work in his famous denunciation of Stalin at the Twentieth Party Congress of the Communist Party of the Soviet Union. Khrushchev told how originally the book was described as written by a commission of the Party's Central Committee "under the direction of Comrade Stalin and with his most active personal participation. . . ." This, however, according to Khrushchev, did not satisfy Stalin, so the wording was changed to read "written by Comrade Stalin and approved by a commission of the Central Committee. . . ." "As you see," Khrushchev said, "a surprising metamorphosis changed the work created by a group into a book written by Stalin. It is not necessary to state how and why this metamorphosis took place."

APPENDICES

Appendices

I

Key Dates in Lives of Communist "Big Four"

KARL MARX

1818	May 5: Born in Treves (Trier), in the Rhine province of Prussia (Germany).
1842	Met Friedrich Engels for first time in Cologne, Germany.
1843	Married Jenny von Westphalen.
1844	Began lifelong friendship and collaboration with Engels.
1847	Marx, along with Engels, joined the Communist League.
1848	The *Communist Manifesto* published.
1848-49	Editor-in-chief, *Neue Rheinische Zeitung,* in Cologne.
1849	Banished from Germany and went to Paris, from which he was also banished.
1849-83	Lived in exile in London.
1852-61	Foreign correspondent for the New York *Tribune.*
1864	Helped in setting up International Workingmen's Association (First International) in London.
1867	Volume I of *Das Kapital (Capital)* published in Hamburg, Germany.
1872	Russian translation of *Das Kapital,* Volume I, published.
1883	March 14: Died in London.

FRIEDRICH ENGELS

1820	November 28: Born in Barmen in the Rhine province of Prussia (Germany).
1842	Settled in Manchester, England.
1870	Moved to London to work with Marx.

1885   Volume II of Marx's *Das Kapital* published as edited by Engels.

1888   Visited United States and Canada.

1894   Volume III of Marx's *Das Kapital* published as edited by Engels.

1895   August 5: Died in London.

VLADIMIR I. LENIN

1870   April 22: Born in Simbirsk (now Ulyanovsk), Russia.

1887*   May: Brother, Alexander, hanged for plotting to assassinate Czar Alexander III.

1893   Joined underground Social Democratic circle called "Elders."

1897   May: Exiled to Siberia following a prison term.

1900-05   Traveled, wrote, and conducted work of Russian Social Democratic Labor Party (forerunner of Communist Party of Soviet Union) in Germany, England, Switzerland, Belgium. Returned to Russia in November, 1905.

1905   December: Lenin and Stalin met for first time at Bolshevik Conference, Tammerfors (Tampere), Finland.

1907   Went abroad and did not return to live in Russia until 1917.

1917   April 16: Returned to Russia and arrived in capital, Petrograd (now Leningrad) from Switzerland.

1917   November 7: Directed Bolshevik uprising.

1917-24   Dictator of Soviet Russia.

1924   January 21: Died.

JOSEPH STALIN

1879   December 21: Born in Gori, Georgia, the Caucasus (Russia).

1899   Expelled from theological seminary at Tiflis.

1905   December: Delegate to Bolshevik Conference in Finland and met Lenin for first time.

1906   Participated in Fourth Congress of Russian Social Democratic Labor Party in Stockholm, Sweden.

1902-17   Engaged in revolutionary activities in Russia; arrested and exiled number of times.

1917	Participated in October Revolution of Bolsheviks.
1917-23	People's Commissar for the Affairs of the Nationalities.
1922	Became General Secretary of the Central Committee of the Russian Communist Party.
1922-29	Consolidation of personal power, leading in 1929 to expulsion of Trotsky from Russia.
1929-53	Supreme dictator of Soviet Russia.
1953	March 5: Died in the Kremlin, Moscow.
1956	Denounced at Twentieth Congress of Communist Party of the Soviet Union.

II

International Communist Organizations and Publications

COMMUNIST LEAGUE

1847	Communist League organized under Marx's influence from League of the Just.
1852	Communist League dissolved at Marx's proposal.

FIRST INTERNATIONAL

1864	The First International, or International Workingmen's Association, founded in London.
1872	First International voted to move headquarters to New York on Engels' proposal. Split over the proposal caused eventual dissolution.
1876	July 15: First International dissolved in congress at Philadelphia.

SECOND INTERNATIONAL (SOCIALIST)

1889	July 14: The Second International formed at Paris.
1914-18	Effective work of Second International, to all intents and purposes, ended during World War I. Violently attacked by Lenin as "bourgeois."

THIRD (COMMUNIST) INTERNATIONAL
Also Known As COMINTERN

1919	March 2-6: Formed in Moscow.
1920	July-August: Second Congress of Comintern in Moscow, which adopted the "twenty-one points" of admission.
1935	July 25-August 20: Seventh Congress of Comintern in Moscow, at which United Front program instituted.
1943	June 10: Comintern dissolved.

COMMUNIST INFORMATION BUREAU
Also Known As COMINFORM

1947	Formed in Poland, with headquarters to be in Belgrade, Yugoslavia.
1948	Cominform denounced Tito and threatened expulsion of Tito and his top aides for "hateful" policy toward Russia. Denunciation prepared at meeting of Cominform in Roumania. Yugoslav Communist Party defied charges.
1948	July: Headquarters of Cominform moved to Bucharest, Roumania.
1956	April: Cominform dissolved.

YOUNG COMMUNIST INTERNATIONAL

1919	Young Communist International formed in Berlin.
1943	Dissolved.

INTERNATIONAL COMMUNIST PUBLICATIONS

1919	May: First issue of *The Communist International*, organ of the Executive Committee of the Communist International.
1943	July 5: Last issue of *The Communist International*, after dissolution of Comintern.
1947	November 10: *For a Lasting Peace, for a People's Democracy!* published in Belgrade, characterizing itself as "Organ of the Information Bureau of the Communist Parties in Belgrade" (published in Bucharest, Roumania after Cominform attack on Tito).

1956 April: *For a Lasting Peace, for a People's Democracy!*
       ceased publication.

III

Communism in Russia

1883 Group for the Emancipation of Labor, first Russian
       Marxist group, formed in Geneva, Switzerland.
1903 Bolshevik (majority) and Menshevik (minority) factions
       resulted from split in Second Congress of the Russian
       Social Democratic Labor Party, held in Brussels and
       London.
1905 December: Bolshevik Conference in Tammerfors (Tam-
       pere), Finland.
1914 Start of World War I.
1917 March: Provisional government formed in Russia. Czar
       Nicholas II abdicated.
1917 July 20: New revolutionary government formed with
       Kerensky as Prime Minister.
1917 October 23: Bolshevik Central Committee approved
       Lenin's proposal for armed insurrection.
1917 November 7: "Red Guards" and revolutionary troops
       occupied Petrograd (Russian capital) and overthrew
       government (called October Revolution).
1917 December: Soviet government signed armistice with
       Germany and Austria at Brest-Litovsk to end hostilities.
1918 March 3: Russia signed Treaty of Brest-Litovsk, aban-
       doning Poland, Lithuania, the Ukraine, the Baltic
       provinces, Finland, and Transcaucasia.
1918 March: Soviet government and Party headquarters
       moved to Moscow.
1921 March: Kronstadt sailors' unsuccessful revolt against
       Lenin.
1921 March: Tenth Party Congress adopted Lenin's New
       Economic Policy.
1922 March 27-April 2: Eleventh Party Congress elected
       Stalin General Secretary of the Russian Communist
       Party (Bolsheviks).

1925	December: Fourteenth Party Congress changed name to Communist Party of the Soviet Union (Bolsheviks) or CPSU (B).
1927	December: Fifteenth Party Congress of CPSU (B) instructed preparation of first Five-Year Plan.
1929	Trotsky arrived in Turkey as exile from U.S.S.R.
1932-33	The Stalin Famine due, in part, to excesses of agrarian policy. Victims estimated from 4,000,000 to 10,000,000 dead.
1933	November 17: Soviet Russia recognized diplomatically by the United States.
1934	September 18: U.S.S.R. formally became member of League of Nations.
1934-38	Purges of Communist Party members and government and military officials as "counterrevolutionaries."
1936	New constitution approved and adopted by the Eighth Extraordinary Congress of Soviets.
1939	August: Soviet-German Nonaggression Pact ratified.
1939	September 17: Soviet Russia invaded Poland.
1939	November 30: Soviet Russia invaded Finland.
1940	March: Soviet Russia and Finland signed peace terms.
1941	June 22: German armies invaded Russia.
1945	May 9: Stalin announced end of war to Russian people.
1953	March 5: Stalin died.
1953	December 23: Beria executed as "enemy of the people."
1956	February: Twentieth Congress of the Communist Party of the Soviet Union at which Stalin was denounced.
1957	June: Vyacheslav Molotov, Georgi Malenkov, Lazar Kaganovich, and Dmitri Shepilov denounced as "enemies of the Party."
1957	October: Marshal Georgi Zhukov, Red Army hero, ousted as Soviet Defense Minister.

IV

Communism in the United States

1918 November: Communist Propaganda League formed.

1919 June 21: National Conference of the Left-Wing of the Socialist Party in New York at which Left-Wing Manifesto adopted.

1919 August 30: Reed-Gitlow left-wing group expelled from emergency Socialist Party convention.

1919 August 31: Communist Labor Party of America formed from Reed-Gitlow group in Chicago.

1919 September 1: Communist Party of America formed in Chicago.

1920 May: United Communist Party of America formed at Bridgman, Michigan.

1921 May: Communist Party of America, Section of the Communist International, formed from Communist Party and United Communist Party at Woodstock, New York.

1921 December: Workers Party of America formed at New York City.

1923 April: Communist Party and Workers Party consolidated at New York.

1925 August: Workers Party of America changed its name to Workers (Communist) Party.

1928 October: Expulsion from Workers (Communist) Party of Trotskyites led by James Cannon.

1929 March: Sixth Convention of Workers (Communist) Party of America at New York changed Party name to Communist Party of the United States of America.

1929 June: Expulsion of Lovestone group from Communist Party.

1939 September: War broke out in Europe. The Comintern and the Communist Party, USA, called war an "imperialist war."

1941 June: Germany attacked Russia. Communists shifted their "line"—called war a "just war" against fascism.

1944 May: Communist Political Association (CPA) organized

when Communist Party, USA, dissolved at Twelfth National Convention in New York.

1945   July: Communist Party reconstituted and Communist Political Association dissolved at an emergency convention as a result of Jacques Duclos' article in April, 1945, issue of French journal, *Cahiers du Communisme*.

1948   Arrests of top communist leaders by the FBI under the Smith Act; trial began in January, 1949.

1951-55   Period of intensive underground activity by Communist Party, USA.

1956   Communist Party jolted by Khrushchev's denunciation of Stalin.

1957   February: Sixteenth National Convention of Communist Party held in New York City.

INDEX

Index

Duclos, Jacques, 67
Dues, Party, 77, 144. *See also* Funds, how Party collects
Dupe (innocent victim) of communist propaganda, 65, 86-89, 193, 194, 213, 215, 219, 287, 304

Education Department (CP-USA), 131
Educational program, communist, 59, 60, 111, 131, 150-154, 214, 311
Ehrenburg, Ilya, 248
Elections, running of communist candidates, 62, 87, 88, 224, 225
Emergency Civil Liberties Committee, 83
Engels, Friedrich, 23, 24, 28, 39, 126, 153, 158, 318; biographical, 14-17; co-author of *Communist Manifesto*, 21, 286; works of, 329-330
Escape routes, communist, 256, 262. *See also* Underground
Espionage, Soviet, 271-283; make-up of networks, 278, 279; motivation of agents, 280, 281; objectives in United States, 281, 282; relationship of Communist Party, USA, 271, 283
Estates willed to Party, 146, 147
Ethics, communist, 151, 165. *See also* Morality
Exceptionalism, 68

Factionalism (faction), 49-52, 54, 55, 63, 67-71, 170, 321
Family life, communist influence on, 78, 79, 105-107, 114, 118, 140-144, 171, 175, 176, 267-269

Fascism, 65, 101, 280
Fast, Howard, 99, 109, 115-116
The FBI Story, 293
Federal Bureau of Investigation, 103, 109, 113, 142, 164, 256, 259, 263, 266, 274-277; hatred of by Party members, 116-117, 125; informants, 136, 168, 275, 283; investigative jurisdiction, 288-291; Party attacks against, 184, 198; protecting civil rights, 291-294
Feffer, Itzik, 248
Fellow traveler. *See* Sympathizer
Feudalism, 19, 317, 320, 322
Feuerbach, Ludwig, 14
First International, 22
Flynn, Elizabeth Gurley, 87, 136
Folks-Shtimme, 46, 249
Force and violence; definition of, 321; essential for revolution, 21, 22, 26, 32, 33, 72, 126, 181, 184, 286, 319, 321, 325. *See also* Revolution, communist concept of
Ford, James W., 227, 234
Foster, William Z., 3, 50, 56, 57, 61, 68, 69, 130, 225, 237, 285; chairman, Communist Party, USA, 68, 110, 128; factional struggles, 63, 70, 156; presidential candidate, 62, 227; quotations from, 3-8, 38, 93, 177, 189, 199, 211, 225, 299, 300, 302; sees Lenin, 57; writings on religion, 304, 305
Fronts, 83, 84, 106, 159, 208; aid to underground, 214, 262, 263; how to identify, 225, 226; role in mass agitation,